THE CONSCIENCE OF THE COURTS

THE *Conscience of the Courts*

LAW AND MORALS IN AMERICAN LIFE

By Graham Hughes

1975

Anchor Press/Doubleday, Garden City, New York

Portions of the chapter "Preferential Treatment" are adapted from an earlier essay, "Rights to Special Treatment," in The Rights of Americans, *edited by Norman Dorsen and published by Pantheon Books, a division of Random House, 1970. Permission to use this material is hereby gratefully acknowledged.*

Library of Congress Cataloging in Publication Data
Hughes, Graham Beynon John.
The conscience of the courts.
Includes index.
1. Judicial process—United States. 2. Law and ethics. 3. Sociological jurisprudence. I. Title.
KF380.H8 340.1'12
ISBN 0-385-08943-0
Library of Congress Catalog Card Number 73-10807

PRINTED IN THE UNITED STATES OF AMERICA
FIRST EDITION

FOR

Hélène,
Geraint, and Dafydd

PREFACE

This book is not aimed solely at a professional audience of lawyers, philosophers, and sociologists, though I hope that members of those groups will find something of value in it. It is an attempt to write for the general public about moral problems of our society, all of which have a great deal to do with the law and the courts.

In 1972 I covered these topics in lectures on CBS television in the New York University "Sunrise Semester" series. The response to those lectures encouraged me to believe that one can communicate effectively about legal and constitutional doctrine with people who are not lawyers. This may involve the trimming away of some of the refinements of legal argument, but it need not sacrifice recognition of the fundamental difficulties and complexities. With that in mind, I have tried to steer between the dangers of oversimplifying and overloading.

For this reason the wealth of literature and case law on these topics is not reflected in the notes. I have only given citations to cases or works mentioned in the text or those from which I have drawn a particular point or argument. My thanks are especially due to my editor, David Harrop, who labored mightily to excise unnecessary legalisms from this manuscript and generally to make it more readable.

G.H.
New York, 1975

CONTENTS

I *Introduction* 1

1 Victimless Crimes

II *Sexual Conduct* 17

III *Offensiveness* 38

IV *Who Is a Victim?* 58

V *Saving People from Themselves* 77

2 Drug Use and Abuse

VI *Drugs and the Criminal Law* 95

VII *Why Regulate Drug Use?* 115

VIII *Other Approaches to Drug Abuse* 135

3 Disobedience and Disruption

IX *Civil Disobedience* 163

X *Disruption* 182

4 Compensating the Disadvantaged

XI *Collective Responsibility* 205

XII *Equal Educational Opportunity* 225

XIII *Elusive Educational Equality* 241

XIV *Preferential Treatment* 260

5 Conclusion

XV *The Role of the Courts* 283

Notes 303

Index 313

I

Introduction

To live in a human society imbues us all with moral positions. We arrive at these in a variety of ways. To some extent they are assimilated in the process of growing up, by receiving and incorporating into ourselves the judgments that we perceive being made in the family and in larger social groups of which we are members. We may be much influenced by the popular morality of the group to which we belong and, on particular issues, popular morality may differ from group to group. We can hardly escape being influenced, too, by what may be called the Establishment morality, the official positions and pronouncements of community leaders (government officials, teachers, judges, and religious leaders) on what is to be accounted good or bad conduct. Sometimes this Establishment morality may conflict with popular morality, and this may produce confusion or tension.

Some people dissent from or refine the received popular or Establishment morality by exercising their critical faculties. They reason from basic principles and find some received judgments to be faulty or unacceptable. But, for many, long-sanctified moral positions make comfortable burrows in which to snuggle. When these moral fortresses are buttressed by threats of punishment from the criminal law against those who breach their walls, their sense of security is even greater.

There will always be conflict when this majority is confronted by a minority who wish, either from conviction or impulse, to act in a deviant manner. If the minority acts out this deviant behavior or presses hard in argument for law and moral judgments to be changed to permit the prohibited behavior, the majority will become uncomfortable, as any earthed animal does when a stick is poked into his lair. The result will be, at the least, social friction and possibly a good deal of anger, bitterness, and some disorder.

These metaphors should not be taken to mean that the majority, which favors the enforcement of traditional moral positions, is obviously in the wrong and deserves to be rudely torn away from its security blanket. It can always count in its ranks many impressive intellectual figures who can point to a long and honorable tradition of argument in support of its position. These advocates of the majority position may say that the disapproved and prohibited conduct is harmful to individuals and thus deserves to be condemned; or they may urge that in some more general sense the conduct is harmful to society and that any loosening of the reins thrown over us by the law would breed social ferment and, perhaps, even disintegration. At a less persuasive level, dark references may be made to the historical coincidence of a general slipping of moral restraints with the collapse of great civilizations, such as that of ancient Rome. One of the aims of this book is to assess the worth of such arguments.

For these majority positions have of late come more and more under assault. Precepts of traditional morality, particularly with respect to sexual behavior, are challenged. Looking back a few generations, many cannot help but regard the public Victorian anathematizing of all forms of sexual behavior (other than moderate heterosexual intercourse within marriage) as a symptom of a very disturbing communal emotional illness. But if that may be so, is it not also possible that generations to come will look back with the same amused incredulity on many of our moral strictures on sexual conduct? Some already ardently preach that message. Gay liberation movements energetically invite radical revision of long-accepted majority attitudes to homosexuality. The models of marriage and the nuclear family as the best life-styles are openly questioned. Some advocate and practice a wide sampling of varied forms of erotic contact as a most natural and desirable way of life.

The debate ranges far beyond sexual behavior. The spread of drug use (or abuse), coupled with the apparent lack of success of the criminal law in stemming this tide, have led to insistent questions about the moral foundations of our present edifice of prohibition. These questions are put both by those who seek greater freedom to use drugs and by others who doubt the justifications for interfering with freedom of conduct and who are also concerned about the social costs of law enforcement. Much the same kind of argument rages around gambling practices, and here the law in some jurisdictions has yielded significantly in recent years. This is partly due to the lure of substantial state revenues from legalized betting and partly because of a genuine lessening of adherence to the moral position that gambling ought to be condemned.

These debates are about particular prohibitions contained in the law, and they question both the wrongness of the conduct involved and the suitability of the criminal law as a mechanism of prohibition. But other accusatory fingers have been pointed more generally at the entire law-enforcement apparatus. The law has been pictured by some radical political dissenters, both in its substantive content and in its discretionary application, as an engine harnessed to the pursuit of socially unjust aims and goals. Acting from this belief, they have taught and practiced noncooperation with legal agencies and even active disruption of the judicial process. Others, who would not so generally condemn the legal system, have come to accept the propriety of deliberate law-breaking as a means of attempting to change what they take to be unjust social arrangements. Civil disobedience and disruption have become habitual practices as well as central themes of intellectual discussion.

At the same time, there has been great pressure upon lawmakers, particularly the judges (who make law in a very important sense), to charge the law more affirmatively with the pursuit of social justice in the United States. This has been most noticed by the public in the area of race relations, particularly with respect to school desegregation and equal educational opportunity. But it has taken place, too, in such contexts as the law relating to housing, welfare, health care, and employment. Both intellectuals and the general public have been troubled here by profoundly difficult questions of moral and social dimensions. What kind of duty is owed to distinct classes or groups who have, admittedly, suffered from past discrimination, and who may now be in a condition of what we euphemistically call "disadvantage"? Does it include some duty to make reparation or to compensate? How should this be done, if it should be done at all, without seeming to do injustice to others? And, if such steps are appropriate at all, how much power in a democracy should be wielded by judges to bring about change of this kind, especially the judges of the Supreme Court of the United States, who are not elected and, therefore, as one commentator has said, "have no earth to draw strength from"?[1]

Law and Morality

In philosophy, law, and political science, those questions that excite most debate are often, naturally and rightly, the expression at an intellectual level of problems that cause deep concern for many people in society. Today, the areas of concern we have just listed have converged to stimulate the most intense discussion about the proper relationship of laws to ideas in society about what is moral and what is immoral.

Some continuing debate about this connection between law and morality is an inevitable public theme in any society at any time. A legal system tells us what rights we have with respect to other people, what kind of claims we can make against them, what duties we owe them, what conduct is permitted and what is not. But morality is also concerned with outlining for us the nature of our duties and rights, our obligations and privileges, and the kinds of claims others can make on us and we on them. So if morality and law are not concentric circles, they are at least overlapping ones.

But any reflection on the proper relationship between law and morality quickly drives us back to other questions. Doing carpentry requires at the outset an appraisal of the tools and, if necessary, a sharpening job. We cannot stand outside the law and subject it to moral scrutiny without acknowledging the need for a critique of the morality we are to make use of in examining the law. For the very criticism often made of the law in this connection is that it woodenly reflects a popular morality (perhaps with respect to sexual behavior) that itself cannot withstand the test of a more rational, critical morality. Recognizing, then, that the law often mirrors a popular morality, or sometimes an Establishment morality that may differ from the popular one, we shall need at the outset to subject to critical re-evaluation the prohibitions involved in popular morality itself. This cannot, of course, be done by plucking higher standards out of the air. Unless we reject out of hand the very ethical foundations of our society, the task will consist of using the most basic ethical notions about fairness, justice, tolerance, liberty, and so on, to re-examine the particular precepts of popular morality and to determine whether they can survive a testing of this kind. Those that cannot must be discarded like the salt that has lost its savor.

Analysis of this sort does not require any very recondite learning of a technically "philosophical" kind. In everyday life, people are in the habit of drawing certain distinctions that are invaluable as an initial insight here. For example, we often dismiss the accusatory or censorious judgments of other people as being grounded in prejudice or hypocrisy or distorted and inaccurate appraisals of the facts. We do not think a judgment of disapproval or condemnation is worthy of any respect if it has that kind of provenance. If a person's judgment of disapproval springs from an inaccurate appraisal of the facts, we would hope to change that judgment by educating the person as to the true facts.

For example, someone might tell us that prostitution is obviously morally wrong because it leads to grave emotional and physical illness in those who practice it. We have a right to expect that person to revise his opinion if we can produce a comprehensive and scientifically immaculate study that demonstrates beyond all reasonable doubt that prostitutes are by and large as physically and emotionally healthy as the rest of the population. If, without offering any fresh arguments, the person blindly adheres to his condemnation, then we may properly conclude that the judgment is inspired by dark irrationalities that take it out of the field of moral judgments and strip it of any weight. Very often, in practice, disagreement will persist because the facts are not entirely clear. All we can do in such a situation is to delineate as precisely as possible the facts that are reliable, to take into account the significance of the uncertainty of other facts, and to hope that future study will yield a fuller picture.

The concept of prejudice is more elusive. Ronald Dworkin has given us a very helpful insight here by suggesting that we look upon a judgment as prejudiced when the one who makes it cannot support it by any reason that our morality regards as acceptable for supporting such judgments.[2] If X tells me that Y is an unworthy person to run for office, and when I press for a reason, X says, "Why, he's black" (or Jewish, or Hispanic, or Lithuanian, or whatever), I have an immediate warrant to dismiss X's judgment as unworthy of consideration. He has come up with *a* reason, but, since it is a precept of our established morality (if not always of our popular morality) that people are not to be judged on the basis of their color, religion, or national origin, it is not a reason that is admissible. As Professor Dworkin says, being prejudiced is then a matter of not being able to give any reasons, or giving reasons that are ruled out by the general principles of our morality.

But the swift dismissal of certain judgments in this fashion does not take us very far in grappling with the problems in this field. More stubborn difficulties confront us about what claims are legitimate, what interests are worthy of protection, what is the strength of countervailing claims and interests, what moral principles should govern, and which should moderate the decision to make conduct criminal.

The "victimless crimes" controversy is a good example here, for it raises all these questions and has in this regard a double importance. It is clearly a matter of the greatest public concern to come to particular judgments about what criminal prohibitions in this area should be lifted, both for the sake of those people who wish to pursue harmless conduct that is now prohibited and also for the better employment of law-enforcement resources. But the debate may yield a further dividend by compelling thoughtful and continued public discussion of the legitimate principles that should underlie the general social practice of telling people not to do things under threat of punishment.

Such a debate has now gone on in desultory fashion for a considerable time. Its modern origins lie in the liberal utilitarianism of Jeremy Bentham and J. S. Mill and the sharp opposition they encountered in the nineteenth century from James Stephen, the English jurist of the criminal law, who advocated a strict enshrinement of popular morality in the criminal code.[3] The controversy slumbered for a long time until it was hotly revived in the past decade or so by public debate in England about law reform with respect to offenses of homosexuality and prostitution. In a report, known, after its chairman, as the Wolfenden Report, an English government-appointed committee recommended, in 1957, that consensual acts of homosexuality between adults, and private acts of prostitution, be decriminalized. Few quarreled with these particular recommendations, but the general philosophy of the report, which drew a sharp line between private sin and public crimes, brought a vigorous retort from an English judge, Lord Devlin, who echoed his distinguished predecessor, Stephen, in arguing for the retention in the criminal code of serious moral offenses.[4]

Only in America

The same debate has proceeded in the United States, in the literature of criminology and philosophy, and more urgently in the legislatures of those states that have embarked on a revision of their penal codes. But it is of the utmost importance to notice that in America there is a unique aspect to the argument that makes the bridge between law and morality more dramatically apparent than in any other legal system. This is because of those portions of our Constitution, comprising the Bill of Rights and the Fourteenth Amendment, that proclaim a series of entrenched guarantees having to do with principles of liberty, justice, equality, and fairness. Since the earliest times of the Republic, the Bill of Rights has been interpreted as imposing absolute restrictions on federal legislative and executive action. More recently, through the Fourteenth Amendment, state action has also come under these curbs. The courts, particularly the Supreme Court of the United States, sit as the interpreters and guardians of these rights and wield the power to declare an apparent statute of Congress or a state to be quite null and void and no statute at all, if it offends incurably against a constitutional commandment. In this fashion, general moral principles setting up standards of fairness and equality are built solidly into the heart of the legal system, so that in the United States it is often difficult to make any sharp distinction between what is moral argument and what is legal argument.

It is true that a lawyer's argument and a court's decision will take a peculiarly authoritative form since they must rely on legal precedent wherever that is possible. But, in this context, legal precedent does nothing more than embody a history of argument about what it means to be unfair, arbitrary, or discriminatory. In most countries, lawyers cannot argue in this fashion, since there is no recognition of judicial power to strike down legislative and executive acts. A British lawyer would certainly appeal to notions of fairness and equality in trying to persuade a court to interpret a statute in a way favorable to his client, but he could not openly invite the court to say that what looks like a statute on its face is really no statute at all. But this is exactly what American lawyers do when they argue constitutional issues, and at times they persuade the courts to take the same view.

The model with which we began, of standing outside the law and subjecting it to a moral critique, turns out, then, not to be quite suitable for the American experience. Those principles that in other legal systems are thought of as extralegal standards of criticism or evaluation and as having a status deriving solely from ethics and morality, are in the United States the most basic principles of the legal order itself. This adds complexity to the analysis that awaits us, for it means that in the United States there are questions to be asked that are not obviously relevant in other societies. One of these questions will be to what extent ought judges to draw on a developing moral consciousness in shaping and interpreting the constitutional norms and in exercising their tremendous power to strike down the enactments of an elected legislative body.

AN EXAMPLE

The decision of the Supreme Court in the case of *Furman v. Georgia* (1972),[5] declaring the death penalty in its general mode of application to be unconstitutional, is a good illustration of the dilemma. The question of whether or not to modify or abolish capital punishment has occupied the attention of legislators, public officials, criminologists, and philosophers in most Western countries for a considerable time. But the framework of the debate and the authoritative means for its resolution are significantly different in the United States from, say, what they are in Britain. In Britain, discussion of such issues will generally surface in intellectual periodicals, in newspapers, on radio and television, and through scholarly research. If the debate becomes sufficiently serious and heated, we may expect the setting up of a public body of inquiry.

This is exactly what happened in the case of capital punishment with the appointment of a royal commission that produced a scholarly and enormously helpful report in 1948. At this point the argument will inevitably move to the floor of the legislature, and there may be amending legislation. After the report of the royal commission, the British Parliament moved slowly through a statute of 1959, which severely restricted the scope of capital punishment, to a statute of 1965, which finally abolished it altogether.

Being constitutionally subservient to the will of Parliament, the British courts had no technique available for taking an initiative to abolish capital punishment. Though they might indirectly narrow its scope by their interpretations of the boundaries of the law of murder, they had to stand aside on the central issue and await the determination of Parliament. But the Supreme Court of the United States, armed with authority unknown to the British courts, could itself seize the issue and anticipate or override any legislative resolution by deciding that the current scheme of applying the death penalty could not stand against the clause of the Eighth Amendment that prohibits cruel and unusual punishments and that is applicable to the states through the due process and equal protection clauses of the Fourteenth Amendment. This it did in *Furman* v. *Georgia.*

The exercise of such an awesome power rarely escapes criticism, and *Furman* v. *Georgia* was no exception. There were those who argued that when the founding fathers, the Constitution makers, drafted the cruel and unusual punishments clause, they were perfectly familiar with existing death penalty provisions. They saw the death penalty in operation around them, and apparently they accepted it and went on living with it after the passage of the amendment. So they could not have thought the death penalty cruel and unusual, and if they did not think so, what warrant can we have today for saying that it is?

This appeal to history is customarily countered by the argument that a constitution cannot be frozen into the interpretations of a bygone age. We may even put this point itself in terms of an appeal to history, by contending that it was never the intention of the Constitution to lay the dead hand of the past so resoundingly on future generations. Napoleon said that an effective constitution should be short and obscure. Perhaps, by this superficially cynical remark, he meant to point to the dangers of putting a society in chains by specific fundamental laws of an entrenched kind. The United States Constitution is neither short nor terribly obscure, but it is certainly open-textured enough to allow each generation to shape interpretations to fit the needs and the morality of its own time without doing obvious violence to the governing language. In the case of the death penalty, we might make this point by saying that what is thought to be cruel and unusual in the way of punishment may very well be a changing notion (we might hope a progressive one), which takes on different meanings from generation to generation as moral ideas become more refined. This is not to say that we have abandoned the notion of fidelity to the Constitution, for our fidelity should be to the concept of "cruelty," as that is meaningful for us today, and not to some historical search for what cruelty might have meant to an enlightened legislator of the late eighteenth century.[6]

THE SUPREME COURT

Later in this book we must return again, in a more sustained fashion, to the proper role of the courts in shaping the law in areas of great moral sensitivity. Our present concern is only to stress and illustrate the singularity of the American technique for resolving these great social debates. In all the problem areas that we shall examine, the Supreme Court of the United States and lower federal courts must reach authoritative decisions that will be nationally binding, and they must do this by working, as lawyers are supposed to work, but with constitutional clauses that are essentially sweeping propositions of an ethical nature. This does not mean that decisions must be arrived at by intuitive leaps or that we are at the mercy of the political, social, or emotional predilections of the nine nonelected persons who form the Supreme Court. We have a right to expect that the judges who make these decisions should arrive at them by a process of tough debate that pays close attention to all that has been said on these questions in the accumulated wisdom of the past, found in earlier judicial decisions, and all that can be said with respect to relevant moral and social considerations for our society today. It is the duty of the legal profession to urge all possible arguments on the Court and the duty of the Court to be attentive to those arguments and to canvass them and resolve them in the reasoned opinions that it offers to the public to justify its decision.

For the process of judging at any level and especially at the highest, as with the Supreme Court of the United States, is essentially a process of justifying. When the Court delivers its opinions, it is speaking to two audiences. In one aspect, the judgment and opinion are offered to the community at large; in another aspect, they are offered to the legal profession, with an awareness that the standards of criticism to which they will be exposed at this level are different. Insofar as the judicial opinion is addressed to the community at large, its persuasiveness will rest on the case that it makes in terms of public ideas about justice and injustice and of public attitudes to the social policies that the decision seems to foster.

Insofar as the opinion is addressed to the profession, there will, of course, again be interest and attention paid to the aspects of justice and policy, but these will now be seen through a filter of rules and principles and traditional techniques of arguing with those rules and principles. The decision will be subjected to scrutiny in the light of the shared standards of a community of craftsmen. At the highest level of constitutional adjudication, the arguments to do with morality, justice, and policy become so intertwined with technical arguments about the movement from past precedent, that any attempt to draw a line between the two is unprofitable.

One consequence of this is that we cannot make simple judgments about the "rightness" or "wrongness" of Supreme Court decisions in sensitive areas that lie on the frontiers of constitutional doctrine. The recent decisions on abortion and pornography, which we shall be examining later, are excellent examples. A decision is difficult to arrive at exactly because there are persuasive arguments to be made on both sides. We agonize over moral or prudential decisions in private life because it is not easy to see what is best or wisest to do. We sometimes make a choice between two courses of action with full knowledge that, whatever choice we make, we shall probably experience some regret in the future. This cannot relieve us from the necessity to make some choice, and the responsibility is to make the best one. But this does not mean one that could not in any way be questioned, for if it were that kind of a situation, we would have had nothing to worry about in the first place. It does, however, mean a choice based on careful and subtle evaluation and weighing of all the considerations and arguments that can reasonably be raised, and it is a display of these qualities that we look for in a good judicial decision.

It is outside the theme of this book to investigate at any length the question of whether the American way of affording protection to individual rights and liberties, by proclaiming standards of fairness and equality that the courts can use to veto public laws and acts, is a better way than the British one. But it is not difficult to make a few observations of a historical and cultural kind that make the need for judicial review seem more pressing in the United States. Unlike Britain, America is an infinitely diverse society, not only populated with peoples still conscious of very different origins, background, and interests, but also with a distribution of authority between federal and state governments that often sharply diverge from each other in general political outlook. In such a complex organization, with such disparate components, there is obvious merit in the unifying role of a supreme national tribunal that can impress minimum standards of propriety upon all units of the federated governments in their dealings with citizens. If one of the miracles of America is that it has stayed together and preserved its Union, then the Supreme Court is in no small way responsible for this.

Then, again, the recent history of the United States is characterized by bitter divisions and divisiveness, by appeals to violence for the settlement of disputes, and by a readiness to pursue disagreements into a punitive harassment of opponents. In such a climate there can often be no safe reliance on tradition and lifestyle to moderate and soften the ways in which people deal with each other, and, in particular, the ways in which government deals with citizens. It may be necessary to express standards of minimal fairness and justice in a public document and to ensure compliance with them through the orders of a court.

In the rest of this book we shall be trying to unravel some of the arguments that surround points of collision between the law and areas of present moral controversy. We shall ask what crimes are truly victimless and which ones may, after all, be found to have a victim, whether individual or social, who deserves protection. In Part 1 of the book, these questions will be asked in a general, principled fashion and also with reference to particular areas of sexual behavior, abortion, gambling, and so on. In Part 2, this general discussion will be given an extended application to the topic of drug use and abuse, not because the issues there are different in principle from those deployed in Part 1, but because of the tremendous public preoccupation with and concern over drugs. Part 3 will move us into the rather different topic of civil disobedience and disruption, and social responses to them. Part 4 will deal with claims for equality and compensation, especially in the field of education. In each case the range of moral and social arguments will be compared with actual and possible legal responses.

There is no single thread of principle binding these topics together. What does connect them and justifies their treatment within the covers of one book is that they all involve peculiarly insistent claims, either for changes in the law and the legal system or in the discretionary responses of officials acting within the system. A hundred years ago the answers to the questions raised here might have seemed obvious, or the questions themselves uninteresting. A hundred years from now, or perhaps in a very much shorter time, these questions may, again, fade from public consciousness. But for us in America today, they are lively and fascinating topics for debate, involving, as they do, deep questions of moral and legal principle, with implications of great practical significance for the lives of many people.

PART 1

Victimless Crimes

II

Sexual Conduct

Many people are moved by nothing in life so profoundly as by erotic experience, or the imagining of it. Here the deepest and most hidden layers of the human psyche are involved, and we have come to realize that erotic energy may work itself out in our lives in ways that we cannot always overtly connect with a sexual impulse. While the huge new dimension of awareness awakened by the work of Freud and his followers may have left us in some bewilderment about the circumference of the sexual ripples in our own lives, it has at the least produced greater understanding of the social neuroses of earlier times.

In the English-speaking world, the Victorian age was the high-water mark of sexual repression and prudery, and it is significant that many of the sexual prohibitions on our statute books date back to that period. The Victorians displayed enormous social energy, which amassed impressive technical and intellectual achievements, but it may be that in part they were able to do this by imposing on themselves a set of terrifyingly harsh sexual restraints. In an "enlightened" book published about the turn of the century, which is by and large an eminently modern and sensible manual of female health care, the author, a doctor, has a passage on the dangers of masturbation. Having lectured her readers on how masturbation leads to general debility, a host of nervous diseases, epilepsy, and possibly brain damage, she tells the story of a mother whose young son was exhibiting symptoms of debility and listlessness. On the doctor's advice the mother began to observe him closely:

> On going to his bed, after he had gone to sleep, she found his hands still upon the organ, just as they were when he fell asleep. She watched this carefully for a few days, then took him into her confidence and told him of the dreadful evil ef-

> fects. Finding the habit so firmly fixed, she feared that telling him, at his age, what effect it would have upon his future would not eradicate the evil as soon as she had hoped so, after studying the case for a time, she hit upon the following remedy . . . She said, "Did you know, Charlie, that if you keep up this habit of 'self abuse' that a brown spot will come on your abdomen, light brown at first and grow darker each week, until it eats a sore right into your system, and if it keeps on, will eventually kill you?"
>
> After Charlie had gone to sleep, and finding his hands again on the sexual organs, to prove to him the truth of her argument, she took a bottle of Iodine and, with the cork, put on the abdomen a quantity sufficient to give it a light-brown color and about the size of a pea. Next night, in bathing him, she discovered the spot, and said, "Look! already it has come." The boy cried out in very fear and promised not to repeat it again.
>
> The next night the mother put on a second application, which made the spot still darker and a trifle sore. Charlie watched the spot as he would a reptile that was lurking, about to do his deadly work—and the mother was never again obliged to use the Iodine.[1]

If we quail at the horrors inflicted on young children in this way, we must at the same time concede that, given the factual premises that they accepted, the Victorians were behaving quite commendably. If masturbation really did lead to a hideous package of physical and nervous diseases, we would have the strongest moral warrant on a utilitarian basis to go to great lengths to prevent our children from indulging in the habit. We may, though, wonder at the genesis of Victorian medical opinion about the connections here. Were their doctors unconsciously tailoring the evidence to fit conclusions that they intuitively accepted as part of the moral climate of the times? Was their medicine in this regard any more scientific than the long-held belief of the Australian aborigines that conception has nothing to do with sexual intercourse? (The aborigines may have been a good deal more reasonable for, as they patiently pointed out to Western teachers, they knew of countless cases of intercourse that did not lead to pregnancy.)

But before we become too superior about the attitudes of the Victorians, we should remember that only in the past few years have we done serious research about the medical and social implications of the use of narcotic and hallucinogenic drugs. Resounding affirmations by public-health officials of the gravely damaging effects of using marihuana (now largely discredited), are very recent. We can never ignore the scientific teaching of our time, for though it may be a poor thing, it is the best we have. But the Victorian medical learning about the devastating effects of comparatively modest sexual activity ought at least to inculcate an attitude of reasonable skepticism and demands for further inquiry, when prohibitions involving established moral beliefs are under scrutiny.

With this in mind, we may examine two areas of sexual conduct that still generally inspire disapproval and moral condemnation: homosexuality and incest. One of these, incest, is legally prohibited everywhere in the United States, while homosexual activity remains prohibited in the great majority of jurisdictions. Even where private consensual acts of homosexuality are no longer criminal offenses, as in England and Illinois, other legal disabilities may be retained.

Homosexual Conduct

Why should homosexual behavior be thought to be morally wrong and a proper object of criminal prohibition? Perhaps the ordinary person's readiest answer would be that it is unnatural. But "unnatural" points to a sprawling notion that must be unpacked into several possible meanings in order to do justice to the positions that it telescopes. One meaning could be that there is only one divinely ordained right and proper way to achieve erotic satisfaction and that God's game plan does not include homosexual relations. A person who honestly believes this to be God's will, as revealed to humanity, is certainly taking a moral stance when he condemns homosexual conduct. If we do not share his kind of religion, then it will be difficult to find a common ground on which we may join with him in dispute. But, at least, we could point out that we live in a society which, by the fundamental terms of its Constitution, rejects the establishment of any religion. It is therefore impermissible to contend that any conduct should be criminally prohibited simply because the religion of some people in our society condemns it.

Another meaning of unnatural might be that, quite apart from theocratic predetermination, sexual intercourse is wrong when it does not have at least the possibility of conception as a consequence. This view is put forward in a passage from a curious biography of Oscar Wilde by the Irish writer St. John Ervine:

"We must take into account the fact that all men discriminate between natural and unnatural sin. Fornication is natural sin, sodomy is not. The mind of the average sensual man is not outraged by the thought of unlawful copulation with women, no matter how much he may profess to disapprove it; but it *is* outraged by the thought of pederastic relations. Nor is his sense of outrage without reason. Sodomy is a denial of life, a cult of sterility. Life would end, or be disastrously reduced, if it were common. Their sense of dangerous sterility, of barren relations, forces average sensual men to condemn and denounce sodomites, even although they may think the seduction of women is no great matter, since it is part of the process of fertility. . . ."[2]

If this argument turns on a threat to the survival of the species, it now seems patently absurd. In the first place, homosexual acts do not preclude a more or less concurrent practice of heterosexual acts, which may lead to procreation, as the life of the subject of St. John Ervine's book demonstrates. Second, there is no evidence in any society at any time that heterosexual relations have dropped to a dangerous level of unpopularity when homosexuality was tolerated. And even if a threat to the species were a ground for morally disapproving of homosexual acts, it would hardly be a ground for prohibition by the criminal law, unless one believes that people are likely to be driven into making babies by threats of criminal sanctions against other kinds of sexual pleasure. Now that contraceptive practices are so refined and so widely employed, babies will more and more be made by people who have a desire for children and make a fairly conscious choice to beget them. Given this state of affairs and a general climate of fear about overpopulation rather than underpopulation, this aspect of the "unnatural" argument has nothing to commend it.

It is also hard to see why the elements of pleasure and relief from tension that people pursue and often find in sexual relations should not be regarded as in themselves sufficient and natural aims of erotic activity. An analogy with eating might be helpful here. Suppose we invented a small pill that would provide us with all the nutriment we needed for a day, so that the lengthy and laborious business of preparing and eating food would become unnecessary. A great number of people would no doubt still want to go on eating steaks or bouillabaisse or whatever they happen to like, just because they enjoy the taste of the food and the social atmosphere of the meals. A school of thought might develop at that time that would say that this activity was unnatural and sinful, since one could get all the necessary nutrition by taking a second to swallow a little pill. The unreconstructed eaters might surely retort with good sense that they are not neglecting to take nourishment, and if they choose to do it in a way that is pleasurable to them, it is not at all clear what is wrong with that.

The person who practices homosexual relations exclusively could not of course make quite the same response, since he is not "taking nourishment"; in this context he (or she) is not procreating or doing an act that has a tendency to procreate. The critic who condemns homosexuality might argue that pleasure is perfectly acceptable if it is joined with a possibility of perpetuating the race through making babies, but it is not acceptable (and becomes unnatural) when that possibility does not exist. But if pressed, that argument would catch our critic in the curious position of condemning heterosexual relations where one of the parties is sterile or barren, and all sexual relations where the parties consistently use contraception.

The most sensible way out of this debate may be simply to assert that we do not have a moral problem here until circumstances confront us with a real threat of human extinction or serious underpopulation. If most people were exclusively homosexual (or if most people continuously practiced contraception) we might get to a point where there would be cause for worry, always assuming that we are willing to recognize a moral duty to continue the existence of humanity. But until such a point is reached, or a perceptible risk of reaching it appears, the facts simply do not present a moral issue. Talk of "unnaturalness" simply confuses the contours of the utilitarian nature of the problem.

Perhaps the best that can be made out of the "unnaturalness" point is that those who engage exclusively in homosexual activity are missing an important dimension of human experience, since they presumably do not enjoy deep relationships with the opposite sex and are thus closed out of knowledge of or intimacy with members of one half of the human race. This of course ignores what enriching dimensions of experience may be missed by those who know only heterosexual relationships, and, if pressed, can perhaps best be seen as an argument in favor of bisexuality. Even at its strongest, it does not justify moral condemnation, still less criminal prohibition. For a person is surely not to be condemned because his or her erotic desires lead to a life less enriching than we suppose another's to be.

Behind talk of unnaturalness there usually lurks the simple abdominal response of aversion or disgust at the thought of a deeply repugnant act. Imagining homosexual activity is no doubt deeply offensive to many people, just as bad smells, nose picking, or long hair may deeply offend the aesthetic sensibilities of others. Whether conduct that deeply offends or even disgusts others ought to be prohibited by the criminal law is a very important question, which will be taken up centrally in the next chapter, with particular reference to obscenity and pornography. With respect to homosexual behavior, it may be enough to say now that even if the offensiveness principle has any validity, it is hard to see how this could extend to acts done in private. We can all understand how a person may be shocked by something that is obtruded before him, which he cannot escape seeing or hearing. This is, in a sense, an invasion of his privacy. But when X complains that he is bothered by what he thinks other people may be doing behind closed doors, then (always provided that what they are alleged to be doing is not in some other sense to be condemned) we are inclined to think that X is invading *their* privacy.

Yet another traditional objection to homosexual conduct is that such acts threaten the security of the family. We could argue here about how necessary the family is as a social institution, but, making the concession to the advocate of prohibition that the family is important, we are at least entitled to demand that he be more specific about how the family is threatened by homosexual behavior. Does this mean that there are many people who now marry and raise families but who would not do so if the criminal prohibition on homosexual relations were removed? Even if this is true in some cases, it is doubtful whether it could be quantitatively of substantial importance. We may ask, too, how much such marriages are worth if people are driven into them to purchase some façade of respectability in defiance of the natural drives of their erotic propensities.

Arguments have also been raised that lifting criminal bans on homosexual conduct would lead to an increase in such conduct; homosexuals, it is contended, will proselytize fiercely for the pleasures and rewards of their way of life if the law would allow them to do it. Several points may be made in rejoinder here. In the first place, it is not clear from this argument why an increase in homosexual conduct would be undesirable. Some other reason would have to be given for that. Then, it is empirically doubtful if such a result would occur. No doubt some number of people who have strong homosexual urges, which they currently suppress because of a fear of legal consequences, would release them and practice homosexual acts if the law were changed. Others who now behave in this way only occasionally and very discreetly might do so more often and somewhat more openly. But the countries of Western Europe, which have for the most part generally abolished criminal offenses of homosexual behavior between consenting adults, have not reported any very apparent or significant increase in such conduct. Certainly, marriage continues, and heterosexual relations do not seem to have wilted under the competition. There is indeed something of a contradiction in the position of those who regard homosexuality as revolting and disgusting but yet are so afraid of a great increase in its practice if legal bans were removed. Any substantial increase in its incidence would at the least mean that a significant number of people had ceased to view such behavior as disgusting, and might mean that we were mistaken all along about the intensity of popular disgust.

One may conjecture that the point about a notable increase in such conduct begins, on analysis, to merge or slide into another point to the effect that, if homosexual conduct were legalized, this would inevitably have a slow but sure effect on life-styles, public taste, and entertainment, so that many things that now seem shocking and impermissible would with the passage of time be accepted or even commonplace. This is an interesting argument, which ranges far beyond homosexuality, for it has to do with the general question of the justification of striving to continue present tastes and aesthetic standards into the future through the agency of the criminal law. As such, it will be discussed fully in the next chapter.

Perhaps the last argument that can be raised here is the contention, often made, that homosexuality is an illness; that homosexuals are likely to suffer, perhaps physically but certainly emotionally, from their life-style; and that therefore we must prohibit what homosexuals do in order to save them from themselves. But there is an ambiguity about the notion of illness here. In the weak sense it could mean that homosexual behavior is in the eyes of the majority so distasteful, so aberrant, and so incomprehensible that we can only comfortably explain it by regarding it as a symptom of pathology and those who practice it as emotionally disturbed. This was until recently a generally held point of view in the profession of psychiatry, but one that is now strongly challenged as representing nothing more than the translation of popular disapproval into a medical label, devoid of any more specific content. In 1973 the American Psychiatric Association ruled that homosexuality should no longer be considered a "psychiatric disorder" but should be defined instead as a "sexual orientation disturbance."

In a stronger sense the assertion could be that the practice of homosexuality, or a propensity toward such conduct, leads to anxiety, guilt, emotional disturbance, and, in short, unhappiness, and therefore ought to be regarded as an illness that we should cure if we can. This would be very difficult to measure, though it must be true that some homosexuals are unhappy in this way and would be rid of their inclinations if they could. For others it is surely not true, and we may also be hard put to decide how much of such unhappiness is due to some inherent "unnaturalness" in the conduct and how much to immemorial social disapproval. Whatever the answer to these hard questions, it is very difficult to see how this argument could seriously be presented as one justifying criminal prohibition. Homosexuals are quite free to seek counseling and medical help if their way of life makes them so unhappy that they feel they must seek change. Sometimes they may be helped to accommodate to different sources of erotic pleasure; at other times, the best outcome may be a better adjustment to their homosexuality. Life presents all of us with a legion of possibilities for making ourselves unhappy by indulging neurotic promptings or yielding to temptations, and it is perhaps unnecessary to spin out the obvious reasons why the criminal law is not a helpful intervener in such areas.

So far we have reviewed a parade of arguments, all of which try to assert that homosexual conduct is immoral and some of which might be used also to support criminal prohibition. It may be thought that, in both lights, the arguments are extremely tenuous and fragile. When the countervailing arguments against criminalization are produced, the scales tilt decisively in their favor. For here we may point first to the extreme deprivation inflicted on those who, out of fear or a strongly law-abiding temperament, give up the pursuit of the only erotic pleasure to which they are inclined. Countless others who cannot or will not stifle their desires may be subjected to the anguish of surreptitious liaisons and the possibility of threats and blackmail. To enforce the law in this area, the police will have to indulge in distasteful snooping (often including long vigils observing activities in public lavatories) and other procedures that skirt the borders of entrapment. It is very difficult to assess what percentage of law-enforcement time and money goes into such procedures, but, even if it be small, it could surely be better employed. While it remains to be argued whether some degree of prohibition should be retained on more or less public displays of homosexual propensity or affection, the time is overdue for the abolition of criminal prohibitions on such conduct when it is done between consenting adults in reasonably private circumstances.

Incest

Incest is one of the most invariant taboos of human history. Fragmentary exceptions may be recorded, but there appears to be no general exception to the prohibition on marriage or sexual intercourse between father and daughter, mother and son, or brother and sister. Modern incest statutes in the United States have gone much farther, generally adding grandparent and grandchild (presumably for greater caution) and often first cousins. In some jurisdictions the crime may also cover sexual relations between stepfather and stepdaughter or stepmother and stepson.

Widely differing explanations have been offered as to the social origins of the incest taboo. A nineteenth-century historian of ethics, Westermarck, suggested that propinquity breeds a natural absence of erotic feelings and a positive aversion at the contemplation of sexual contact.[3] Family members thus experience what appears to them to be an intuitive disgust at the thought of intrafamily erotic relationships. But if Westermarck's analysis were correct, it is hard to see why rigid prohibitions on incest should be necessary at all, since presumably nobody would have any inclination to commit it. In fact, it is very doubtful if propinquity does generally kill sexual desire.

A more exotic approach was initiated by Freud in his work *Totem and Taboo.* In his story of the primal horde, Freud depicted the father or male leader of the group as driving out the other male members so that he might have unrivaled possession of the women. The other males rebelled and slew the father figure but were then overcome by guilt and constructed the incest taboo as an assuagement. This may have as little historical foundation as the social contract theory, but, like the social contract theory, it is a powerful allegory of human relationships and has contributed much to the development of psychoanalysis and also to popular beliefs. In the form of the Oedipus complex, the Freudian approach depicts the instinctual urge to possess the parent of the opposite sex, coupled with instinctual rivalry with the parent of the same sex. Freud thus seems to have regarded the incest drive as a part of human biology, and the incest taboo as having the very deepest roots in human nature.

Following upon Freud, a school of psychoanalysis has accorded the greatest importance to incestuous desires and has traced back to them a whole complex of sexual aberrations. Homosexual behavior has been explained as a flight from the opposite sex undertaken to escape the incest urge. The fetishist or sadomasochist, it is said, may be renouncing more usual modes of sexual gratification for the same hidden reasons.

But the Freudian view is by no means held with unanimity. Some psychoanalysts advance alternative explanations. It has been suggested that the incest motive is not so much explicable as showing genital love for one parent and rivalry for the other, but rather as a defense mechanism in an anxiety state caused by rejection by the mother. Other writers minimize the biological aspects of the incest taboo and advance instead explanations based on cultural and environmental factors. Incest is considered harmful because it ties the individual too tightly to the nuclear family and thus is inimical to general social relationships. White suggests that the growth of incest taboos is explicable as a device to ensure economic development and security. By marrying out of the family unit, wider bonds of kinship and mutual relationship developed, so that larger and more viable co-operative units could be formed.[4] Inbreeding would tend to contract the circle of relationships and to lead to economically weak and physically indefensible units. So White quotes the remark of a nineteenth-century anthropologist, Tylor:

"Again and again in the world's history, savage tribes must have had plainly before their minds the simple practical alternative of marrying-out or being killed out."[5]

Whatever the genesis of the incest taboo, it is not difficult to list the harmful effects of certain kinds of incestuous behavior. The one most often advanced is no doubt the eugenic one. Births resulting from closely incestuous intercourse are likely to produce children who accentuate the recessive traits of the parents. This does not mean that the children born would of necessity be inferior or retarded. If the recessive traits of the parents are healthy, the tendency may, indeed, be to produce extremely fine and talented children. But it is certainly true that a general practice of incestuous intercourse would create a risk of a number of inferior children being born. This point, whatever its weight, hardly goes to justify the scope of the present crime of incest in most jurisdictions, for the crime covers steprelationships, where no consanguinity is involved and no risk of inferior births. And, if the eugenic risk were the decisive reason for criminalization, then it ought to be a defense to show that one of the parties was sterile or barren or that efficient contraceptive measures were used. But no such defense is recognized.

Harmful consequences to members of the family from incestuous behavior are easy to see. There may be a general disorganization of family relationships through confusion of roles. The suffering caused to the wife who discovers an incestuous relationship between her husband and her daughter will be immediately obvious. The nature of the harm caused to the daughter will depend on the precise relationship between her and her father or stepfather. Sometimes there may be a love relationship with erotic expression between two close relatives. Even so there is always the possibility of psychic harm to a young girl involved in such a situation. More usual may be the relationship in which the daughter is a passive and coerced participant. It is here that the real horror of incest lies, in the case histories of miserable physical and mental pressures exerted by fathers on daughters and stepdaughters to secure their compliance.

Sister-brother relationships are less productive of harmful effects. The literature suggests that such relationships usually grow out of sexual curiosity at puberty and that they generally come to an end when other sexual partners are found. Mother-son incest appears to be a very rare phenomenon, though, if occurring, it could no doubt hold traumatic psychic legacies for a young son.

A review of the incest relationship does, then, demonstrate clearer possibilities of harm to others than can be seen when discussing homosexuality. But it is equally clear that the really grave threat here is to young female members of the family from older male members. Now, all legal systems have on their statute books general offenses of having sexual relations with young females, even if the girl consents. Is there, then, any point in perpetuating a second offense of incest to cover the same conduct, and, usually, with a far more severe maximum punishment? In response, it might reasonably be contended that because of the peculiar opportunities for coercion and pressure within the family, the age of consent needs to be somewhat higher than when we are dealing with sexual relationships outside the family. So if, for example, the general age of consent in a jurisdiction is sixteen, we might agree that when the man is the father or older brother of the young woman, then the age of consent for the girl should be eighteen. In view of the abuse of what might be thought of as a kind of fiduciary relationship, we might also agree to a somewhat more severe punishment than in other cases.

But a rational and secular morality appears to offer no justification for the savage punishment that the law generally applies to incest offenses (sometimes a maximum of life imprisonment) or for the sweeping range of the offense. It is hard to see what reason there is to declare it a heinous crime for a thirty-five-year-old man and his thirty-year-old sister to decide to go to bed together. As we saw in discussing homosexuality, possibilities of emotional distress that people may bring upon themselves when they enter into certain relationships pervade all life. The heavy institutional hand of law enforcement has no qualifications to do therapy either through restraint or punishment. A rational criminal-law system might very well abolish the crime of incest altogether and absorb its necessary, vestigial parts into a general offense of obtaining sexual relations through coercion and into offenses of having sexual relations with young people.

Law Reform

Our discussion of homosexuality and incest was intended to serve as a model for a type of analysis and a range of arguments that might be paraded with respect to many kinds of sexual conduct that the law now prohibits. It is important to notice that the discussion has to proceed in two stages. In the first place, quite apart from the presence or absence of legal prohibition, we must ask in what sense the conduct in question can be thought to be wrong or immoral. With respect to homosexuality, there appears to be little or no purchase for climbing over this first hurdle. In the face of such an absence of any reasonably persuasive arguments that conduct is wrong or immoral, it is of course unnecessary to advance further arguments as to why it should not be the subject of criminal prohibition.

In the case of incest, the arguments tending to show immorality and wrongfulness were in some aspects stronger. This compelled us to pass on to the second stage of the inquiry, whether conduct that is in some respects harmful and wrong ought to receive the attention of the criminal law. Here the considerations ought to be many and would include: (1) the gravity of the harm that may be done by the conduct in question: (2) the likely efficacy of the criminal law in preventing the conduct in question: (3) the restrictions on liberty and other deprivations that criminal prohibitions will impose; and (4) the harmful side effects of criminal law enforcement, such as distasteful police practices and diversion of law-enforcement resources from the pursuit of dangerous offenders.

Decisions about criminalization are primarily for the legislature. In discharging his or her duties in this regard, the ideal legislator would do well to cultivate the posture recommended by Bentham in a memorable passage:

"I suppose myself a stranger to all the common appellations of vice and virtue. I am called upon to consider human actions only with relation to their good or bad effects. I open two accounts; I pass to the account of pure profit all the pleasures, I pass to the account of loss all the pains. I faithfully weigh the interests of all parties. The man whom prejudice brands as vicious, and he whom it extols as virtuous, are, for the moment, equal in my eyes. I wish to judge prejudice itself; to weigh all actions in a new balance, in order to form a catalogue of those which ought to be forbidden."[6]

The legislator who ignores this duty runs the risk that critics will "pity the pretended criminals and reserve their indignation for their persecutors."[7] But, in spite of much talk of a sexual revolution and an undeniable thawing in public attitudes toward multiforms of sexual behavior, legislatures have not shown much zeal for law reform in this field. The repeal of the crime of incest is not exactly a catching slogan for the hustings, and changes in the law on homosexuality will appeal directly to a minority constituency who are still only discreetly vocal. Aside from cynical calculation of political advantage or discredit, there is another practical reason why law reform in some of these instances may not seem urgent. This is because law enforcement is usually restricted to that aspect of the statutory prohibition that is properly directed against truly harmful conduct and thus can command rational support. So, in the case of incest, it is virtually unknown for prosecutions to occur except in cases of a man having sexual relations with a young female member of the family. But we cannot rely on prosecutorial discretion always being exercised in a sensible manner. Principle and prudence require continuing efforts for rational law reform.

We must remember that in the great majority of states, persons convicted of sodomy are guilty of a felony, even though they are adults and the act was both consensual and done in private. And the definition of sodomy in most jurisdictions encompasses a variety of heterosexual acts as well as homosexual ones. In spite of the recommendation of the American Law Institute in its Model Penal Code that consensual acts of sodomy between adults should be decriminalized, little response has been shown by state legislatures. While in some parts of the country, police and prosecutors may follow a policy of benign neglect toward consensual adult activities, this is by no means universally so, and homosexuals, and even heterosexuals who pursue gratification in any but the most orthodox fashion, are beset by a not unreal threat of legal penalties in many jurisdictions.

Faced with legislative inertia, we must examine the possibility of intervention by the courts. But what constitutional doctrines and concepts could provide an avenue for judicial access to the criminal law of sexual offenses?

In the first place, any penal statute is open to constitutional attack if it fails to define the prohibited conduct with sufficient precision. A citizen is entitled to know with a high degree of exactness what behavior may render him or her liable to prosecution and punishment. And if a statute does not sufficiently meet this standard, it is said to be "void for vagueness," which is an application of the due process clause of the Fourteenth Amendment.

Some statutes to do with sodomy are couched in the old language of the common law and make the most general reference to "buggery" or "sodomy" or, even more mysteriously, to the "crime against nature," without descending into any detail on what particular acts are prohibited. In 1973 the United States

Court of Appeals for the Ninth Circuit held in *Jellum* v. *Cupp*[8] that the phrases "unnatural conduct contrary to the course of nature" and "abnormal sexual satisfaction" were without commonly accepted, definite meaning, and that the Oregon statute prohibiting such conduct was unconstitutionally vague. The defendant in that case had accosted a woman in a shopping center parking lot, knocked her down in a scuffle, and then urinated on her. There can of course be no doubt that such conduct amounts to numerous crimes of assault and public indecency and certainly calls for punishment, or at least treatment, for the defendant. The federal court of appeals was not challenging such propositions but was dealing only with the question whether the conviction could be maintained under the "unnatural conduct" statute. Its holding was that concepts of "unnaturalness" and "abnormality" do not furnish a jury with generally intelligible standards for determining guilt and thus put the statute in breach of the due process clause.

Judicial weapons of this kind, however, will not be lastingly effective against a determined legislature, for the vagueness can be remedied simply by recasting the statute in more precise language. Several states have done just this with their sodomy legislation. An example is the Iowa statute of 1962, which provides:

"Whoever shall have carnal copulation in any opening of the body except the sexual parts, with another human being, or shall have carnal copulation with a beast, shall be deemed guilty of sodomy."

Such statutes will presumably weather attacks under the vagueness doctrine, but there may be equally powerful constitutional guns to be brought up against them. Though the Constitution contains no express mention of a right to privacy, the Supreme Court has gone a considerable way in spinning such a right out of a concatenation of clauses in the Bill of Rights. The Fourth Amendment, with its prohibition on unreasonable searches and seizures, has a central concern with the protection of privacy, which has become even more apparent in its modern application to eavesdropping and wiretapping. Relevant here, too, is the Ninth Amendment, which instructs us that the express reference to particular rights in the Constitution should not be taken "to deny or disparage others retained by the people." The general Fourteenth Amendment guarantee against deprivation of liberty without due process contributes another strand to the argument. In *Griswold* v. *Connecticut*[9] in 1965, the Supreme Court put these threads together in holding that a state criminal statute forbidding the use of contraceptives was unconstitutional insofar as it infringed on marital privacy.

The Court observed that:

> . . . specific guarantees in the Bill of Rights have penumbras, formed by emanations from those guarantees that help give them life and substance . . . the right of privacy which presses for recognition here is a legitimate one. The present case, then, concerns a relationship lying within the zone of privacy created by several constitutional guarantees. . . . We deal with a right of privacy older than the Bill of Rights.[10]

It is important to note that the Court's ruling does not expressly extend to the privacy of adults in general but is limited to the protection of married couples. Indeed, the opinion of Justice Goldberg notes that the decision "in no way interferes with a State's proper regulation of sexual promiscuity or misconduct."[11] However, a prohibition on the distribution of contraceptives to unmarried persons was struck down by the Supreme Court in *Eisenstadt* v. *Baird* (1972),[12] through an extension of *Griswold* under the equal protection clause of the Fourteenth Amendment. Suspect as the technical reasoning of *Eisenstadt* may be (for it is not clear why equal protection should carry a marital privacy principle over to unmarried people), the case is the first clear extension of constitutional protection by the Supreme Court to practices connected with the sexual activity of the unmarried.

The Court's abortion decision in *Roe* v. *Wade* (1973),[13] which we shall examine in more detail in a later chapter, holds the potentiality for carrying the constitutional protection of sexual conduct much farther. *Roe* held that a woman has a constitutionally protected right to dispose of a nonviable fetus that she carried in her body. Though *Roe* built on *Griswold,* it clearly goes beyond privacy concepts and enters the realm of a right to autonomy or a right to do as one pleases with one's own body. Abortion is the disposal of the product of a sexual act; if such disposition of the fruits is constitutionally protected, then why not the planting of the seed?

These Supreme Court decisions provide lower courts with the materials for further limits on state power to criminalize conduct, for in each of these instances the Supreme Court has declared, in accordance with a line of established doctrine, that once a fundamental right is identified in constitutional terms, then no state encroachment is permissible unless the state can show that its legislation is necessary to pursue an overriding or compelling state interest. The forward march of the boundaries of what are regarded as fundamental rights is thus an effective barrier to state legislation.

So a consensus now appears to be developing that no legislation is constitutionally acceptable if it imposes limitations on the sexual activities of a married couple in privacy. The Seventh Circuit Court of Appeals in *Cotner* v. *Henry* (1968)[14] granted a habeas corpus petition to quash the conviction of a man who had pleaded guilty to sodomy on the complaint of his wife. The federal court held that the state could not constitutionally interpret its sodomy statute to make private consensual relations between married persons a crime in the absence of some compelling state interest that outweighed the constitutional claim to privacy.

Most lower courts have been unwilling to use *Griswold* or *Roe* to open the constitutional umbrella wider to shelter sexual conduct between the unmarried. This seems unduly cautious. Sexual relations between consenting adults in private constitute a peculiarly important, intimate, and harmless activity. They are often the expression of deep physical and emotional needs, the stifling of which can bring deprivation and suffering. As the Supreme Court did with abortion, the time has surely come for courts to acknowledge in adults a fundamental right to sexual freedom in the absence of force, coercion, or offensive public display. A few courts have already shown a readiness to do so.

In the District of Columbia in 1972, a group of adult male homosexuals brought a civil rights action against the chief of the Metropolitan Police Department. The plaintiffs claimed that they desired to engage in consensual sexual conduct in the privacy of their homes, including acts of oral and anal intercourse, which appeared to be prohibited by the District's sodomy statute. The action was settled when the government agreed to a stipulation that conceded that, in the light of the *Griswold* case, the local statute could not constitutionally be applied to private acts between consenting adults. In effect this amounted to a promise by the prosecuting authorities that such acts would not (and should not) be prosecuted in the future and represents a very significant movement in this area.[15]

A decision of much broader scope was handed down early in 1973 by Judge Hallek of the District of Columbia Superior Court. While not of high precedential authority, this case, *United States v. Doe*,[16] is a strong pointer to the direction in which a vigorously inclined judiciary could move if it wished to curtail the scope of criminal offenses relating to homosexuality. Judge Hallek first held that a sodomy statute is unconstitutional insofar as it applies to private acts between consenting adults. But the decision goes much farther and holds, too, that even public acts of homosexual conduct cannot be constitutionally characterized as felonies, with a ten-year maximum penalty, as the local statute did. The court pointed to the fact that public displays of heterosexual intercourse between a man and a woman were punished only as disorderly conduct or public nuisances, with much less severe penalties. To single out public homosexual acts as felonies with a much graver penalty thus raised serious constitutional questions of equal protection and cruel and unusual punishments. While the public has a quite legitimate interest to be protected from grossly offensive public displays, this interest can be effectively guarded by general statutes relating to disorderly conduct. Accordingly, the court held that the sodomy statute could be regarded as constitutional only insofar as it applied to forcible assaults or activities with young persons below the age of consent.

It would be rash to imagine that Judge Hallek's opinion, with respect to public acts, will soon be followed in many jurisdictions.

But, although there is as yet no controlling Supreme Court decision, it does now appear that there is a growing body of argument and rulings by courts that powerfully challenge the constitutionality of prohibitions on private consensual sexual conduct, whether homosexual or heterosexual. There are, as yet, no decisions raising these arguments with respect to incestuous behavior, nor are there likely to be. The kind of incest that is prosecuted tends, as we have seen, to be that involving a man and a young female relative, under the age of consent. No constitutional arguments would be relevant here, except conceivably the Eighth Amendment's barring of cruel and unusual punishments. Consensual adult incest is likely to be conducted in circumstances of such privacy and discretion that prosecutions are a remote possibility. We do not have "incest bars" in the way that we have "gay bars," and the adult brother and sister who offer themselves up as a test case to challenge the constitutionality of a statute would have to be quite ferociously principled.

Homosexuals rightly contend that the legal and social slings and arrows that are pointed at them extend far beyond simple criminal prohibition. They may suffer from discrimination in public employment, which historically has stemmed from the notion that, once identified or confessed as practicing homosexuals, they must logically be habitual criminals. The present erosion of the criminal prohibition will inexorably lead to a concurrent dismantling of these accompanying barriers of discrimination. Decisions to this effect are already appearing in the law reports. In *Norton* v. *Macy* (1969),[17] the Court of Appeals for the District of Columbia was confronted with a case where the appellant had been discharged from a civil service position for alleged immoral conduct involving homosexual acts. The court held that the dismissal was unjustified since the appellant, being a protected civil servant, could only be dismissed for a cause relevant to the efficiency of the service. The court could find no rational basis under due process standards for a determination that the appellant's conduct had an adverse effect on efficiency.

In 1971 the United States District Court for the Southern District of New York was called upon to decide questions relating to a petition for naturalization that the Immigration and Naturalization service opposed on the ground that the petitioner, as a homosexual, was not a person of good character. The court held, in *In re Labady*,[18] that the validity of the government's action must turn on whether the conduct was of a public or private nature. Here it could only be shown that the petitioner had engaged in private acts of homosexuality with consenting adults. Following *Griswold*, the court held that the petition should be granted.

Cases of this nature are beginning to accumulate and will no doubt rapidly coalesce into a distinctive unit of constitutional jurisprudence as litigation will be more aggressively pressed in this field in the years to come. The arguments with which the courts must deal when they decide these cases most obviously swirl around the language of the Constitution, but the constitutional concepts here are of a marvelously general nature, having to do with "equal protection," "due process," "privacy," "liberty," and "cruel and unusual punishments." All the moral and social arguments that we have reviewed in this chapter are just the ones, among others, that courts listen to and on which they base their decisions in this field.

There is here one difference of the greatest significance between the roles played in our system by the courts when compared with the legislature. Courts cannot escape deciding cases when they are brought before them. Once citizens, backed by able lawyers, are ready to thrust questions about the constitutionality of laws governing sexual behavior before them, the courts must in the discharge of their public duty take up the debate. Legislatures may be indifferent, consumed with political calculations, or even neolithic in their perceptions, but the court remains as a forum in which the issue must be seized and can be disposed of only after that kind of subtle moral debate that the Constitution forces upon us. It is surely one of the splendors of the American system that a citizen can always compel authoritative adjudication of such issues in the light of a reasoned body of moral exchange. This is not to say, of course, that we shall always like the outcome; but we ought to be thankful for the process.

III

Offensiveness

A concept of harm confined to the most obvious case of the visibly suffering individual would be too narrow to serve the aims of the criminal law. Conduct may also be justifiably prohibited when it has a general tendency or potential to inflict injury on some members of a group, even though it may be difficult to arrive at a final identification of the individuals who suffer it. The area of obscenity and pornography is a good model for sorting and scrutinizing arguments of this kind.

In current usage there is no sharp distinction between the concepts of obscenity and pornography. Perhaps obscenity is the broader notion, referring to what generally shocks or disgusts, while pornography refers more narrowly to writing, pictures, or displays that have the sole and unmistakable purpose of arousing sexual excitement in the reader or viewer. Such displays are of course very offensive to some people.

To experience revulsion and disgust is, after all, a painful business. It may not be directly compared with the pain from a broken ankle, but it may not be any the less distressing. There may be immediate aesthetic and psychic discomfort, which can express itself in physical symptoms of nausea, and there may well be lingering feelings of emotional distress.[1] If we are entitled to be protected from noxious smells and inordinately loud noises, it would seem reasonable to claim protection also from displays that have a tendency to cause revulsion in most people.

As Joel Feinberg has pointed out, this does not mean that those who are offended would deny that a pornographic spectacle can give erotic stimulation.[2] Indeed, it may be precisely the awareness of this that produces the revulsion, for many people are comfortable with sexual stimulation only in privacy and are beset by storms of confusion and shame when confronted with public exhibitions of an erotic kind. The same may be true about nonerotic obscene displays of excretory functions. It is not that excretion ought to be thought of as disgusting, but that we are accustomed or accultured into regarding it as properly a very private activity, so that an unexpected public act of that kind is psychically distressing. In other societies or at other times, public excretion may give no offense at all.

Those who complain of deep offense of this kind are clearly asserting an interest worthy of protection within the utilitarian calculus. There will be qualifications that we shall want to interject (such as that the person complaining is not just eccentrically oversensitive), and there are other interests that have to do with freedom of speech and the rights of minorities, to which we must, as we proceed, be attentive, but in terms of harm, the indictment has at least been properly returned. But important questions remain about the degree of regulation thought to be necessary, for this will vary sharply, according to the type and range of harm that we apprehend and seek to fend off.

We might have a total scheme of prohibition that would make it a criminal offense to possess pornographic materials even in the privacy of one's home. A less draconian position would permit private possession but would prohibit any commercial dealings in pornography or any displays in places to which the public might resort, even though discreet and nonpornographic warnings were given of the nature of the display, so that those who entered could fairly be deemed consenting adults. A more permissive position would permit pornographic displays even in places to which the public might resort, as long as young people were not allowed entry and as long as the display did not publicly obtrude itself. This would require regulations with respect to the nature of the warnings and barriers necessary to protect those who wished to avoid such displays. In the last fifteen years or so, the interpretation of the law and the Constitution started out from the first position, appeared to be heading strongly in the direction of the third, and then recoiled and tacked back to the middle ground. Canvassing the merits of the different positions leads us into a deeper analysis of the interests and values involved.

Is Pornography Harmful?

A simple (perhaps simple-minded) condemnation of pornography, which would justify the most sweeping prohibition, would be that exposure to it incites the reader or viewer to the commission of crimes. Sexual crimes might appear the most obvious candidates here, but there is no evidence to support such a connection. The Commission on Obscenity and Pornography, which reported in 1970, examined this issue thoroughly and concluded that no case had been made out on either side. Neither is common sense of much help here. Perhaps the occasional person is so inflamed by looking at or reading pornography that he goes out and commits a sexual assault, but he may be outnumbered by those who are cooled down by the masturbation, which is the usual culmination of such viewing, and so are relieved from the impulse to launch the sexual assaults they otherwise might have. Those countries, such as Denmark, that have been the most ready to lift regulation of pornography, have seen no consequent rise in the number of sexual offenses. If the burden of proof is on those who wish to prohibit conduct to come up with a convincing demonstration of resulting harm, they have not done the job here.

There are other versions of this first position, which could be advanced to justify a total prohibition on even private possession. The least believable assertion would be that a person who gets into the habit of poring over pornography will suffer a general moral degeneration, which will cause him or her to commit crimes in general, not just sexual offenses. This is quite unsupported by any empirical evidence and seems to defy an intuitive perception of the reality of the connections. More forthrightly, the argument could be made that, quite independent of any causal link with the commission of crimes, the state has a proper concern for the moral welfare of its citizens and has a right (perhaps a duty) to throw up legal fences between them and indulgences that will corrupt them.

If this means only that the individual would be, within himself, a better and more moral person if he were prevented from ever viewing pornography, it scarcely goes to justify the intervention of the criminal law. We all agree that it is the business of the law to make people better by preventing them from hurting others (and, in extreme situations, from hurting themselves), but if the quality of goodness involved relates only to some inner state, then most of us might think that such matters are better left to churches or individual consciences than to the police. The argument also suffers fatally from the lack of any demonstration of exactly what it is about viewing pornography that damages a person's goodness. Many people, when they indulge themselves by looking at pornography, will realize very well that the material is unreal, fantastic, and even sometimes degrading in its representations, but they may well think that it is better to look than to burn. In this way they may relieve their sexual tension and anxiety and so become kinder and gentler in their dealings with other people. A system of prohibitions that is strongly paternalistic in its desire to save people from themselves should always be scrutinized with suspicion. One that acts on this premise without any evidence that the forbidden practice is harmful is simply stupidly repressive. But this question raises the whole topic of paternalistic regulation, which will be more fully discussed later.

OFFENSE TO THE PUBLIC

So far, offensiveness has emerged as the strongest justification for the prohibition of public displays of obscenity or pornography. But offensiveness is a dangerous beast that must be handled carefully, for an overly zealous reliance on it can threaten other moral values of basic importance. An example, frequently cited in the literature, reveals one of the dangers. Suppose that a black man and a white woman are walking hand in hand down the main street of a town where racial prejudice is rife. The great majority of the local population feels a deep sense of shock and outrage at this display of interracial affection. The injury to their feelings is as real and hurtful as the reaction experienced by people in unprejudiced towns if they were to see an act of sexual intercourse in the middle of the road. Can this be taken to justify a local ordinance prohibiting contacts of this kind between different races? We have an intuitive perception that such a regulation cannot be tolerated, but there is a difficulty in stating the governing principle here, once we have conceded that offensiveness may be a good justification for prohibition. How do we resolve this dilemma?

One escape is simply to say that the standards we ought to look to must be national ones. Eccentricity or local idiosyncrasy in taking offense cannot be accepted as good grounds, especially when the conduct in question can make strong claims to constitutional protection. The protestation of shock and offense at the sight of interracial affection is in itself a frontal attack on established moral standards. The morality that we profess nationally asserts the equality of all people and their right to free choice of association. It cannot countenance and must condemn cries of offense and distress at the sight of citizens peacefully exercising their constitutional privileges and their human rights. It may, indeed, be the case that many individuals, and the majority in some communities, would either expressly repudiate this established moral position or simply do not live up to it. But this only shows that the immorality resides, not in the conduct of the couple of different races, but in the response of those who object to their behavior.

The offensiveness principle must, then, be limited by a qualifying principle to the effect that offensiveness is not to count as a justification for criminal prohibition when the conduct arousing offense is the expression of a morally or constitutionally guaranteed right or privilege. It is not enough that the conduct be harmless, apart from its tendency to shock, for this might be said about most obscene, sexual displays. What is necessary to defeat the offensiveness justification is a demonstration that a prohibition on such conduct is itself a trepass on constitutionally guaranteed moral rights. The Supreme Court has held that statutes that prohibit miscegenation or intermarriage between members of different races are unconstitutional.[3] In the face of these holdings, those who are offended by interracial relations must learn to live with their displeasure.

After accepting this qualification, we may still imagine delicate and difficult marginal cases. Suppose that in a heavily Jewish section of one of our larger cities, people who proclaim themselves to be Nazis demonstrate in the streets and peddle anti-

Semitic propaganda. Here, to be offended is very much in accord with our established morality, and we would expect and approve such a reaction on the part of both Jewish and non-Jewish spectators. Is this a good ground for passing laws that prohibit this kind of behavior? What gives us pause is that, however discredited and abhorrent, the message being touted by the Nazis may be in a sense the dissemination of a political idea, and we have come to venerate the notion that political ideas should not be suppressed simply because we violently disagree with them. This concept is at the same time built into the First Amendment's guarantee of freedom of speech. Even if we regard some political platforms as beyond the pale because they devalue and degrade the human status of groups of people, we know how very difficult it is to draft statutory prohibitions that neatly and precisely excise this kind of political preaching without impinging on political activity that is simply unpopular.

Struggling with this dilemma, many Western nations, such as Britain and Canada, have passed statutes that prohibit incitement to racial hatred. These laws are difficult to apply, risking, as they do, the possibility that cracking the Polish, Scottish, or Italian joke may run one into the arms of the police. No such general statutes are in force in the United States, no doubt because of the barrier of the First Amendment. But political speech that is violently abusive of any group of citizens may amount to a breach of the peace or disorderly conduct under the "fighting words" doctrine that the Supreme Court has carved out as a small territory unprotected by the First Amendment.[4]

This borderline between the protected dissemination of ideas and offensive insult or obscenity exercised the courts in the case of *Cohen* v. *California*.[5] The defendant in that case had strolled around a courthouse in Los Angeles, wearing a T-shirt emblazoned with the slogan, "Fuck the Draft." He was arrested and charged with an offense of "disturbing the peace . . . by engaging in tumultuous and offensive conduct." The theory of the prosecution was that, although the defendant was not physically assaulting people, he was, as it were, assaulting their sensibilities. The obtrusion of such an offensive slogan, they argued, was eminently likely to cause people to react in a violent manner and could thus fairly be called a disturbance of the peace by offensive conduct. The offensiveness resided, presumably, not in the social or political content of the defendant's frankly virulent opposition to the system, but rather in his choice of a socially shocking epithet to express it.

The California courts agreed with the arguments of the prosecution and convicted the defendant, but in 1971 the conviction was vacated by the Supreme Court of the United States, which found a First Amendment shelter for the defendant's behavior. It is clear, as the Supreme Court pointed out, that the defendant's message was addressed to a most important subject of moral and political controversy on which people were eminently entitled to speak out. Certainly, the tone of the message was deliberately provocative and would give offense to many people, some of whom might react violently. But the prospect of violent retaliation is not a sufficient reason to suppress freedom of speech in an area of such social importance. The Court did not deny the offensiveness of the verb employed (whether it be understood in the indicative, hortatory, or imperative mood), but added that people could, after all, avert their eyes if they wished.

This last point is a little difficult to follow, since nobody would have any reason to avert his eyes until he had seen the slogan, by which time the offense would have already been communicated. The decision might plausibly have gone the other way, since the Court could have persuasively reasoned that, while great freedom must be accorded to the expression of political opinion, this does not have to be stretched into a license to use words that are in themselves obscenely offensive to a majority of people. After all, the defendant might have expressed an equal depth of feeling in acceptable language, as by holding up a sign that read, "Let us abominate, excoriate, and spit upon the draft." While less pithy, this does not seem much less virulent. Perhaps the decision is best understood (though this was not the reasoning of the Court) as a recognition of a lessening in the obscene connotations and shock effect of the operative verb used. Would the Court have decided differently if the defendant had used a string of popular verbs inviting his audience to perform all their waste-disposal human functions on the draft?

Why did the Court not use the "fighting words" doctrine here to uphold Cohen's conviction? Perhaps the best explanation is that the "fighting words" exception can only be used when the words spoken are directly insulting *of* people as people. Now, the draft is not a group of people, but a set of social arrangements and regulations. Of course, there are (or used to be) people who are called "draftees," but it would not make sense to say that they are the members who make up the group called "the draft." By contrast, use of the words, "Fuck the Catholic Church," might possibly be punishable as inciting a breach of the peace, since the Church can much more plausibly be regarded as an institution made up of members. In this way the statement could be understood as a direct insult to each and every one of its members. What about wearing a T-shirt with the slogan, "Fuck the Army," while walking through a group of soldiers? A court might well distinguish such a case from *Cohen* and reach a different result.

The Cohen case does not in any way shake the validity of the offensiveness principle. It simply illustrates the eternal difficulty of resolving borderline cases where arguments are nicely balanced. But if the offensiveness principle, as it has so far been expounded, is the only justification for prohibiting obscene and pornographic displays, then, as we have already argued, it would only support the prohibition of public exhibitions. Private possession, for example, would not be touched, and the Supreme Court has acknowledged this, when it held in the case of *Stanley* v. *Georgia* (1969)[6] that the *Griswold* principle precluded the punishment of an individual for the possession of pornographic materials in his own home for his own use.

But where lies the dividing line between public and private? Should we tolerate bookstores that avowedly sell hard-core pornography and theaters that put on pornographic shows or films, as long as they firmly but discreetly warn patrons of the contents in notices and advertising that are themselves impeccably not obscene? Or does "private" mean only the license to huddle over pornography in one's own house? Those who wish to defend the narrower meaning of privacy and to outlaw displays in places to which the public may resort are pushed into an extended notion of offensiveness to justify their position, or into arguments that rest on grounds essentially remote from the core concept of offensiveness.

CULTURAL EROSION

One of these arguments invokes the pervasive deterioration of moral standards and aesthetic ideals to which the display of pornography in places of public resort would lead. President Nixon, in rejecting the recommendations of the Commission on Obscenity and Pornography, expressed this point of view:

> Pornography can corrupt a society and a civilization. . . . The warped and brutal portrayal of sex in books, plays, magazines, and movies, if not halted and reversed, could poison the wellsprings of American and Western culture and civilization. . . . Moreover, if an attitude of permissiveness were to be adopted regarding pornography, this would contribute to an atmosphere condoning anarchy in every other field—and would increase the threat to our social order as well as to our moral principles. Alexis de Tocqueville, observing America more than a century ago, wrote: "America is great because she is good—and, if America ceases to be good, America will cease to be great." We all hold the responsibility for keeping America a good country. American morality is not to be trifled with.[7]

Two different ideas are embedded in this onslaught. The first is one we have already noticed, that a decline in sexual morality may be attended by an increase in the commission of crimes, or at least a dilution of all the social virtues that make communal life at all possible. H. L. A. Hart has called this the "disintegration" thesis and has justly pointed out that there is simply no empirical evidence to support it.[8] But it is a belief that those in positions of authority are traditionally much attached to. The contention, in one form, is that established morality is important, not so much for its content, but simply because it is there. It is seen as a kind of cement holding the social walls together, so that any chipping or flaking is much to be feared. This has perhaps never been more pungently expressed than in the answer given by Lord Thurlow, an English Lord Chancellor of the early nineteenth century, to a group of religious dissenters who came to ask his help in getting certain legal disabilities removed. "I'm against you, by God, sir," he said, "I'm in favor of the established church; and, if you'll get your damn religion established, I'll be in favor of that too."[9]

This viewpoint was echoed in the statement by Lord Devlin, the present leading advocate in England of the retention of morals offenses in the law, when he said that "the suppression of vice is as much the law's business as the suppression of subversive activities."[10] But it is hard to believe that the growing toleration of pornographic spectacles for those who wish to view them will lead to more muggings or thefts or even more corruption in government. The deterioration or disintegration of society in this sense is just not a likely result.

The thesis is not, for that reason alone, to be summarily dismissed for there may be another sense in which a deterioration of some aspects of social living, cherished by many, could come about. This argument has been very well put by Alexander Bickel, in a passage much quoted by the courts in recent obscenity decisions:

> A man may be entitled to read an obscene book in his room, or expose himself indecently there, or masturbate or flog himself, if that is possible, or what have you. We should protect his privacy. But if he demands a right to obtain books and pictures he wants in the market, and to foregather in public places—discreet, if you will, but accessible to all—with others who share his tastes, then to grant him his right is to affect the world about the rest of us, and to impinge on other privacies. Even supposing that each of us can, if he wishes, effectively avert the eye and stop the ear (which, in truth, we cannot), what is commonly read and seen and heard and done intrudes upon us all, want it or not.[11]

Professor Bickel's presentation is superficially appealing, but on a cool appraisal, the argument is less convincing. Why, after all, is it not possible for those who might be offended to "avert the eye and stop the ear"? We cannot fail to see an ugly building or to hear a grating noise or to smell a hideous stench if we are in the vicinity, but regulation that prohibits offensive advertising while permitting pornographic displays inside premises accessible to the public would seem to have a fair chance of success in protecting our eyes and ears, if we do not wish to sample the offerings. How then would the displays "intrude upon us"? Is Professor Bickel referring only to the shudder of distaste that some might experience at the thought that a number of fellow citizens are resorting to public places to look at books or spectacles that many find repulsive? But surely, the inability to stop thinking about what other people might be doing, however painful, is not in itself a sufficient reason for denying the others freedom of action.

Perhaps the case can be put more strongly in the following way. With a discreet licensing of pornography, neighborhoods would spring up in cities and towns where pornographic offerings would tend to be clustered and where people seeking them would therefore tend to gather. Such neighborhoods could in theory be aesthetically quite pleasing, if there were strict regulation of the form of advertising. But they would exist, and everybody would know they were there. This sensational type of entertainment might gather such a large following and be so profitable that other forms of entertainment (novels, plays, films) would more and more edge toward the borderline of pornography in order to capture some of that audience. In this way a deterioration in forms of art and culture might come about. This pressure, together with a simple consciousness of licensed pornography living its discreet existence would perhaps, with the passage of time, subtly erode general public standards of decency so that what was once permitted only discreetly for those who wish to encounter it would become fully public and eventually be thrust on those who deplore it and are shocked by it.

We are today very rightly concerned about the physical and aesthetic quality of the environment in which we live, so it would be unwise to dismiss these anxieties in a cavalier fashion. But there are empirical and morally principled counterquestions to be put. The dangers are, after all, speculative and perhaps remote. The few countries, such as Denmark, that have allowed pornography in places accessible to the public, have not reported any such developments in the way of environmental decay or decline in cultural standards. Indeed, the experience seems to be that, after an initial rush to view the formerly forbidden exhibitions, the first feverish interest declines. Public demand settles down to a steady and tolerable level, and the purveying of pornography may actually become less profitable than before, as often happens when sought-after but forbidden commodities are made legally available.

There is indeed something puzzling about the position that Professor Bickel represents, for it seems to rest on the assumption that the demand for prurient entertainment is so overwhelming that it will simply engulf us all if it is not kept strictly under leash. Now, it is certainly very important to most people that they be free to pursue sexual stimulation at times. But people's desires in this regard differ very much, and many would under no circumstances be interested in watching pornographic displays in public places. Those who like that sort of thing would for the most part want to indulge this taste occasionally and not continuously or for great lengths of time. Someone may quite enjoy going to a pornographic movie once a week without wanting to turn his or her back on the doing of law, philosophy, or medicine, which might occupy most of his or her time. If this picture approximates to reality, then no catastrophic environmental or aesthetic changes are to be expected from allowing pornography in public places, provided there are strict and strictly enforced regulations about advertising and the exclusion of young people. But if this picture is wrong, then we are surrounded by legions of fellow citizens, constantly obsessed with sex, who wait only for legal permission to choke all the channels of communication with the pornography for which they would insatiably clamor. This portrait and this prospect simply seem untrue to human nature. If a demand of such ferocity existed, legal prohibitions could never have held it in check.

After making all these qualifications, it would be wise to concede that some change in public ambience and taste would probably slowly come about with a liberal attitude to the regulation of pornography. Here we reach moral and prudential arguments about the propriety of attempting to hold back changes of such a kind of legislation. As H. L. A. Hart has pointed out, the "disintegration" thesis that we have been examining often tends to slide (or collapse) into what he calls the "conservative" position.[12] This would be a simple claim on the part of the majority to keep things as they are, to legislate against the possibility of change that they dislike. But if we cannot call back yesterday, neither can we hold back tomorrow. Human history has witnessed the most radical shifts in what is deemed decent and acceptable for public appearance or performance. Our Victorian forebears, who discreetly shrouded the legs of furniture, would have climbed to an apogee of shock and fulmination at the sight of a woman in a bikini or a mini-skirt, but these fashions have come, and people have not stopped writing good books and doing good thinking. We cannot now experience the aesthetics of the future, so there is good sense in saying that the public deserves to be protected from what is deeply shocking. But the argument becomes much thinner when it is contended that people should not be allowed to pursue their tastes for stimulating sexual spectacles in discreet places of public accessibility, simply because, in a subtle and not clearly articulated fashion, this might bring about changes in cultural and aesthetic standards.

This is not to say that the aesthetic quality of the environment cannot be regulated and that we should abandon efforts to control pollution or to preserve historic buildings or to remove unsightly billboards. These are all matters either of total visibility or of direct impact on the physical health of people. They thus meet without difficulty the proof of harm that needs to be shown to justify regulation or criminal prohibition. To make available pornographic entertainment in a discreet fashion for those who seek it is altogether distinguishable.

The Law on Pornography

We have set out some of the interests and values that courts must weigh and evaluate in determining what degree of prohibition is constitutionally permissible with respect to pornographic material. Constitutional values of free speech and privacy have to be balanced against the concept of offensiveness and the more elusive notion of deterioration of the quality of social life. To make matters more difficult, the concept of privacy is a double-edged sword here. In one sense, it points to the right of the general public to be protected from shock to their sensibilities; but, in the other direction, it can be invoked to support the rights of individuals to choose modes of sexual behavior or stimulation that do not demonstrably harm others. This second sense is an extended notion of privacy that could perhaps better be styled a right to "autonomy," but the decision in *Griswold*, with respect to the rights of married couples to use contraceptives, and some of the cases following *Griswold*, indicate that this extended sense now has a good constitutional lineage. At the threshold, and cutting through every question of balancing these values, is the inherent difficulty of providing a satisfactory definition for purposes of regulation of what material is pornographic.

In a group of decisions in the 1950s and 1960s, of which the most notable were *Roth* v. *United States*[13] and *Memoirs* v. *Massachusetts*,[14] the Supreme Court laid down a set of propositions that (while leaving room for much disputation) did provide a framework of articulated standards. These were that (1) obscenity is not protected by the First Amendment from the intervention of the criminal law; (2) material is obscene when (a) the dominant theme of the material, when taken as a whole, appeals to a prurient interest in sex, (b) the material is patently offensive because it affronts contemporary community standards relating to the description or representation of sexual matters, and (c) the material is utterly without redeeming social importance. *Stanley* v. *Georgia* (1969) held that, even in its permissible regulation of pornography, the criminal law could not reach into the privacy of the home, so that private possession for personal gratification could not constitutionally be a crime. This in turn was qualified in *United States* v. *Reidel* (1972),[15] which made it clear that the commercial purveyor of pornography was not protected, even if the matter was being distributed through the mails for the private use of individuals.

At this point the law appeared to be poised to move to a position that would accord with the principal thesis of this chapter—that there are no sufficiently convincing arguments to justify prohibiting the discreet enjoyment of pornography by adults, even in places of public accessibility. Certainly some of our larger cities had already seen a proliferation of erotic films, bookstores, nude dancing, and so forth, which proved exceedingly difficult for prosecutors to move against successfully. But early in 1973, a Supreme

Court of changed composition handed down the decisions in *Miller* v. *California*[16] and *Paris Adult Theatre I* v. *Slaton*[17] that are now controlling.

In the *Paris Adult Theatre* case, the movie house in question had used no erotic advertising to lure the public into its showings. Instead, it displayed signs that read, "Adult Theatre—You must be 21 and able to prove it. If viewing the nude body offends you, Please Do Not Enter." The film shown inside was of a kind that the state court had characterized as "hard-core pornography." Speaking directly to the issue raised by these facts, the Supreme Court said:

> We categorically disapprove the theory, apparently adopted by the trial judge, that obscene, pornographic films acquire constitutional immunity from state regulation simply because they are exhibited for consenting adults only.[18]

The Court found that a state has legitimate interests in prohibiting the showing of pornography even to such consenting adults, though its analysis of these interests is somewhat cloudy and relies heavily on the quotation from Professor Bickel, which we have already noticed, with respect to the proper and laudable aim of preserving the "quality of life."

The rejection of a constitutional freedom to view pornography in places accessible to the public was joined with other tightening of the judicial clamps. No longer must the state prove that the material is utterly without redeeming social importance. It is now enough if the work "taken as a whole, lacks serious literary, artistic, political or scientific value,"[19] a much lower hurdle for the prosecution to vault and a standard that can surely be dangerously puritanical, for we can well imagine a novel, play, or film which, while containing very explicit sexual descriptions or exhibitions, is at the same time somewhat amusing, occasionally witty, or photographically innovative. Would this give it sufficiently serious literary or artistic value to save it from the condemnation of a local jury?

The Court was at the same time anxious to give more precision to the notion of what material may properly be deemed pornographic. While not assuming expressly the mantle of state legislatures, the Court gave the following examples of what a state may legitimately classify as obscene:

> (a) Patently offensive representations or descriptions of ultimate sexual acts, normal or perverted, actual or simulated.
> (b) Patently offensive representations or descriptions of masturbation, excretory functions, and lewd exhibitions of the genitals.[20]

These formulations lead one to conclude that *some* representations or descriptions of sexual acts, etc., may *not* be patently offensive. Two interpretations of this are possible. Either some representations, even if inartistic, are inherently not offensive; or some representations that, taken alone, would be offensive, are rendered inoffensive by being embodied in a work that, taken as a whole, has serious artistic merit. Either way, it is a jury who must decide (unless the parties agree to have the case tried before a judge alone), and a burning question is whether the jurors are to be instructed to apply their own responses, their sense of the local standards of acceptability, or some broader national standard, which might differ substantially from local feeling. No matter what instructions are given to a jury, they may naturally be inclined to lean toward an application of local standards, but the state of the law on the point is not for that reason unimportant. For the instruction to look to a national standard will presumably have some influence on some juries and on prosecutional discretion, so that with the passage of time it will tend to bring about more uniform prosecutorial practices. More important, abuse of their function by the jury in blatantly ignoring the parameters of a national standard can lead to the reversal of a decision by higher state courts or in the federal courts.

Before *Miller* and *Paris Adult Theatre,* a national standard was the one employed. This was blown away in *Miller,* where the Supreme Court said:

> It is neither realistic nor constitutionally sound to read the First Amendment as requiring that the people of Maine or Mississippi accept public depiction of conduct found tolerable in Las Vegas or New York City.[21]

This, the Court explained, was not to say that the Constitution guarantees less in Maine than in Las Vegas, but only that the concept of offensiveness (which the Constitution accommodates as a ground for prohibition) may differ from place to place.

While this explanation is not invalid as a formal distinction, it does gloss over the practical conclusion that one may rely on the Constitution to reach a certain result in Las Vegas that one cannot obtain in Maine. If the Court's reasoning were advanced as a ground for regulating displays that are in themselves public and so force themselves on the eyes and ears of local citizens, it would have something to commend it, though it would still result in a crazy-quilt pattern across the country of permission and prohibition with respect to the same book, magazine, or film. But since the issue with which the Court was dealing was that of displays *accessible* to the public but not thrust upon them, the logic is much less persuasive. Standards for what people are permitted to view or read discreetly without impinging on their fellow citizens, if they are to be imposed at all, ought to be national. A local threshold of sensibility, more easily touched than blunter natures in other regions, appears eminently relevant to the question of prohibiting what shall be thrust upon the public. But why are local sensitivities relevant at all, provided that the display is only made available, as in the *Paris Adult Theatre* case, to those who choose to view it with a prior general knowledge of its nature?

If *Paris Adult Theatre* was ever intended to settle the dust over the pornography issue, the Court was soon disappointed. The gloomiest predictions of critics quickly came true when, in *Jenkins* v. *Georgia* (1974),[22] the Supreme Court was called to pass on a state conviction of a theater owner for showing the film *Carnal Knowledge*, which had drawn much praise from critics as having substantial artistic merit and social significance. Impelled, one hopes, by a desire to save itself and the Constitution from ridicule, the Court reversed the conviction. It contrived to do this by patiently pointing out that the consignment of decision making in this area to the mercies of local standards was not meant to withdraw all constitutional protection from literary and artistic productions. However shocked to the core a Georgia jury may be, the presence of "serious literary, artistic, political or scientific value" in a work still brings it under the protection of the First Amendment. But *Jenkins* shows that, while prohibitions on the discreet exhibition of pornography remain, the Supreme Court will never be able to escape the somewhat comic task of reviewing individually from time to time the entangled strands of artistic merit and prurient appeal in books and films.

A proper appraisal of the *Miller* and *Paris Adult Theatre* cases can only be made in the setting of other Supreme Court decisions touching on sexual conduct, some of which were considered briefly in our discussion of sexual offenses. *Griswold* v. *Connecticut* (1965) decided that a statute that barred the use of contraceptives by married couples was unconstitutional. Married couples, *Griswold* decided, have a fundamental right of privacy, either because this is implicit in the Fourteenth Amendment's concept of "liberty," or because it can be located somewhere among the "emanations" that various portions of the Bill of Rights give off. If *Griswold* itself can be narrowly restricted to the rights of married couples, the Supreme Court itself soon flung off this restraint with respect to contraception. In *Eisenstadt* v. *Baird* (1972), the Court reviewed a Massachusetts statute that prohibited the sale of contraceptives to single persons. With little analysis and considerable brevity, the Court came to the swift conclusion that if the sale of contraceptives to married persons could not be constitutionally prohibited, then neither could such sales to unmarried persons. A distinction of this kind would be an invidious discrimination that would offend against the equal protection clause of the Fourteenth Amendment. *Eisenstadt* seems to rest on the proposition that the regulation of sexual pleasure so as to control the birth of children is a fundamental right of all people, whether married or not, and thus cannot be checked by the state, unless perhaps some overbearing and compelling state interest could be demonstrated. So from *Griswold* to *Eisenstadt*, with little fanfare and not much reasoning, the Court made a great leap from finding constitutional protection for the privacy of the marital bed to a more general recognition of freedom from certain kinds of state interference with sexual pleasure.

The use of contraceptives is, admittedly, not quite the same as viewing pornography. But the privilege to look at pornography in one's own home has also been proclaimed by the Court in *Stanley* v. *Georgia*. All these decisions, considered collectively, can only be understood as announcing that there is a special quality to an individual's sexual life that imposes limitations on the state's power to regulate. It is not after all that the individual may choose to do anything he pleases in his own home; we know very well that there are many things that are serious crimes whether done in public or at home. It must be that there is something special about erotic activity that entitles a person to protection from the law, unless the activity is being offensively thrust before members of the public. *Stanley* v. *Georgia*, properly understood, surely demonstrates that it is not the viewing of pornography in the *home* as such that is constitutionally protected but the viewing of it in circumstances that are not offensive to the public. Can one doubt that *Stanley* would extend to bar a conviction of a person who kept pornographic photographs locked up in his office desk, or carried them in his wallet while he walked on the street? Nor is the solitary nature of the enjoyment the explanation for the *Stanley* decision, for surely it would apply equally well to a man who invited three friends to his home to look at a pornographic film.

What we were entitled to expect from the Supreme Court in the *Miller* and *Paris Adult Theatre* cases was a careful and reflective analysis of the implications of *Griswold*, *Eisenstadt*, and *Stanley* for the dimensions of constitutionally protected freedom of sexual action and pleasure taking. Why exactly should five people be permitted to view a pornographic film in the home of one of them, but not two hundred in a theater accessible to the public, even though careful measures are taken to shield members of the public whose sensibilities would be shocked? Does it have anything to do with deploring commerce in sex? Is it the element of arrangement and offering that is objected to, perhaps because it is feared that this may seduce inquisitive innocents into corruption? Is it because there is felt to be some special indecency in a host of strangers gathering for the express purpose of each pursuing solitary stimulation? Can any of these reasons be seen as sufficiently compelling to halt the maturing constitutional freedom to engage in discreet sexual stimulation or gratification?

Miller and *Paris Adult Theatre* rest too easily on the traditional platform that the First Amendment does not protect obscenity. *Griswold* and *Stanley* have opened up another line of constitutional argument to do with concepts of privacy, discretion, accessibility, and their relations with the concept of liberty. The latest Supreme Court law on pornography is unpersuasive because of the Court's failure to wrestle these concepts and these cases into the shape of a continuing constitutional theory.

IV

Who Is a Victim?

It is fashionable these days to talk of "victimless crimes," but the phrase can be dangerous, for it may lead us with deceptive simplicity around problems that deserve to be squarely faced. If everyone agreed that an offense was truly without any discernible victim, then arguments for its retention would be hard to imagine. But, as we saw already in the discussion of sexual conduct and pornography, the disagreement is really about whether in particular cases we can convincingly identify victims who may legitimately claim protection. The primitive model of the victim is the individual human being who is knocked on the head or whose goods are stolen. Other candidates for the role of victim also claim attention and invite us to consider what social interests may legitimately be protected by the criminal law other than the person and property of the individual. The discussion of pornography was a first exploration of this theme. We shall now pursue it further by looking at two test cases: cruelty to animals and abortion.

Cruelty to Animals

Many people (most, we may hope) find it extremely repugnant to witness or imagine the infliction of torture or other kinds of cruelty upon animals. And yet our relationships with animals and our moral views about what it is permissible to do with them are very ambivalent and difficult to harmonize. We think it perfectly proper to kill animals for food, and the law does not generally prohibit killing animals at all, as long as they do not belong to somebody else. I may kill my pet dog any time I like, always provided that I do not do it in a cruel manner. We also find it quite acceptable to exploit animal labor and to control the lives of animals so that they are useful for human purposes. For the most part, we still view animals as nonhuman pieces of property with which we can deal as we please. The one exception is the prohibition on treating them cruelly, and this is of comparatively recent origin. In England and America, such laws got on the statute books in the mid- or late nineteenth century, through active lobbying and pressure from a minority of enthusiasts. It does not appear that there was at the time any great majority sentiment backing such legislation.

Today there is broadly based support for such laws, and this may be an interesting example of how legislation and law enforcement can, with the passage of time, make an important contribution to elevating the morals of the community. But we are still left with the task of explaining exactly why it is wrong to be cruel to animals. One explanation has been offered by Professor Louis Schwartz, one of the architects of the Model Penal Code:

"It is not the mistreated dog who is the ultimate object of concern; his owner is entirely free to kill him, though not cruelly, without interference from other dog owners. Our concern is for the feelings of other human beings, a large proportion of whom, although accustomed to the slaughter of animals for food, readily identify themselves with a tortured dog or horse and respond with great sensitivity to its suffering."[1]

But this explanation, stressing as it does the element of shock or offense to human sensibilities as the justification for prohibiting cruelty to animals, is surely not acceptable. Suppose I get great pleasure out of torturing my dog, but, realizing that my neighbors would be upset by the howls of the tormented animal, I insulate and soundproof my attic and take the dog up there to torture him at leisure, leaving my neighbors quite undisturbed.[2] It is true that, if I were detected by the authorities and my conduct made public, my neighbors would then suffer indignation and shock at contemplating what I had done. Their reaction would be the same, and to an even greater degree, had I been killing or torturing a human being. But this would hardly justify the conclusion that the law of murder is designed to protect the sensibilities of the public rather than the murderer's potential victim. The shock to sensibilities is a result of knowing that a murder has been committed, but it is not the prime evil aimed at in the law of homicide.

In the same way, the rules about cruelty to animals are surely primarily designed to protect animals, and not the sensibilities of people. Bentham made this point very well when he said that it might one day come to be recognized that,

> The number of legs or the villosity of the skin or the termination of the os sacrum are reasons equally insufficient for abandoning a sensitive being to the caprice of a tormentor. What else is it that should trace the insuperable line? Is it the faculty of reason or perhaps the faculty of discourse? But, the full grown horse or dog is beyond comparison a more rational as well as a more conversable animal than an infant of a day, a week or even a month old. But suppose the case were otherwise, what would it avail? The question is not, "Can they reason?," nor, "Can they talk?," but, "Can they suffer?"[3]

The justification rests, then, on the proposition or axiom that it is wrong to inflict suffering on sensate creatures. This leaves great uneasiness about where we presently draw lines. You may uproot plants, but you cannot tear limbs off dogs. And, although you may not tear limbs off dogs, you may kill them in a noncruel manner if they belong to you. We are left with a patchwork sort of morality about animals, where we are, it seems, willing to embrace them with ourselves in the circle of sensate creatures for limited purposes only. In the theme of our discussion, we could say that animals are sometimes recognized as victims and sometimes not.

A further useful lesson flows from the animal example. The discussion reveals that it would be a mistake to elevate privacy to a pre-eminent position in this debate. The criminal law has the strongest warrant for invading our privacy when the activity we choose to pursue privately involves inflicting suffering on a nonconsenting sensate creature. Privacy assumes importance only when it negates the only potential for inflicting harm that we can perceive in the conduct in question. This will be the case with consensual sexual conduct between adults but not with torturing dogs.

Abortion

The difficulties of deciding who is a victim worthy of protection crystallize in the most agonizing fashion in the debate about abortion. Here the past few years have seen a dramatic shift in public opinion and also in the state of the law. Ten years ago we might have thought it absurd if someone had forecast that in such a short space of time the legislatures of some states would be permitting abortions on demand. The decision of the Supreme Court in *Roe v. Wade* (1973),[4] requiring such permissive procedures and nullifying the laws against abortion, was a surprise even to many of those who most welcomed it. But the swift change in the law cannot dissipate the moral argument, for the debate here is quite unlike the one surrounding homosexuality or other sexual behavior. Those who condemn abortion do not rest their case on principles of offensiveness or unnaturalness. They assert quite simply that to abort a fetus is to take a human life. This is unquestionably a moral position of the strongest kind and must be dissolved by analysis or else accepted.

It is perhaps easiest to begin by looking at the empirical argument, often made by advocates of abortion on demand, to the effect that women always have sought and always will seek abortions. This impulse and apparent need are so strong for many women that the law will not deter them and, in the absence of legalized safe facilities, they will often end by getting themselves killed through unsafe procedures. A major consequence of providing a legal method of abortion will thus be to save the lives of many women.

While this assertion is incontestable, it does not in itself provide an overwhelming argument for the legalizing of abortion and even less for regarding abortion as morally unobjectionable. For, if those who look upon abortion as the taking of a human life without justification are correct, then they could reasonably argue that many women will be deterred from having abortions by the existence of a criminal prohibition, and in this way more lives might be saved than lost. In any case, they might add, a quantitative analysis is not appropriate when we are discussing a species of murder. Murder should not be legalized because, when prohibited, it is a risky business for the murderers, some of whom will lose their lives in trying to kill others. The anti-abortion proponents are at the least right in forcing us to face the central moral question of what we are doing when we practice abortion and how it may be different from murder.

The law itself has always refused to equate abortion with murder. The old common law made distinctions for the purposes of the law of homicide among children born alive, those capable of being born alive, and a mere fetus. The crime of murder (or manslaughter) could only be committed when the child had been born alive, which the old cases defined as requiring total extrusion from the body of the mother, though it was not necessary that the umbilical cord should be cut. Before such time, but after the twenty-eighth week of pregnancy, English statutes designated causing the death of a fetus as the felony of "child destruction": before the twenty-eighth week of pregnancy, the crime was known as abortion. Why should such distinctions be drawn at all and, if they are to be drawn, why should they not be distinctions between criminal and noncriminal conduct rather than among degrees of crime?

The initial difficulty here has to do with the problem of defining what quality it is that we seek to protect through our general moral condemnation of killing and the laws that support it. Are we concerned with protecting "life" or "human life" or the "human personality," and how can we distinguish meaningfully among these notions? The newly born baby is remarkably little different from the baby a week or a month before normal birth, except for the obvious circumstance of its new visibility. The recent conjugation of the spermatozoon and the egg may look very different indeed but, as the anti-abortion advocates always point out, it represents a separate genetic package and, apart from intervention of disease or human act, will inevitably and rapidly develop all the physical properties of a human being, which are even now inexorably programmed into its structure. This is the old "acorn to oak" analogy, and those who condemn abortion launch a powerful offensive when they challenge its defenders to come up with a meaningful principle to justify excluding the fetus from the category of human life.

Even if the debate shifts to the question of the starting point of human personality, the defenders of abortion are in a difficulty. Bentham pointed out, in a passage quoted earlier in this chapter, that a grown dog or horse is infinitely more "conversable" than a day-old baby. In the same vein, there seems little to support the contention that a baby a few days after birth is more of an individual human personality than a baby a little time before birth. The fetus in the womb is admittedly invisible, unlike the baby after birth. But it is not obvious that our inability to see the fetus is a sufficient reason to disqualify it from enjoying human personality. For many people it is no doubt much easier to kill a fetus than a baby, just because we cannot generally see it move or hear it cry. But many of us would also find it easier to drop a bomb on a city far below than to stick a bayonet into someone's body. As one writer has pointed out, it is after all a mere contingency of nature that we cannot see babies in the womb.[5] Science may very soon invent a device to enable us to make movies of babies before they are born. Assertions that babies before birth are quite different creatures from babies after birth would then appear as fatuous to everybody as they already do to those with medical and biological knowledge.

In recent years the abortion debate has swung into new territory with a package of arguments drawn from an emerging consciousness and assertion of the rights of women. The one remarkable feature of the unborn baby that does dramatically distinguish it from other forms of human life is, after all, that it occupies another's body. We certainly believe that we have important rights with respect to our bodies—to take care of them or neglect them as we wish, to place them in proximity to others, if they will permit it, or to withdraw them. How then can a woman reasonably be told that she has no right to expel an unwanted intruder who nestles in the very depths of her body? Nobody would want to claim a right for a woman to kill her born baby because she finds it annoying or inconvenient, but many strenuously assert that the situation is morally quite different when the question is one of disposing of a fetus for which the woman's body is a receptacle.

But fetuses are surely not quite the same as tapeworms—parasites that we may cheerfully decide to expel from our systems. A parasite is an uninvited guest, but whether a fetus is uninvited depends on the degree of the woman's responsibility for its implantation.[6] If a woman is raped and becomes pregnant, then she clearly has no responsibility for the conception, and many moralists and some legal systems have for a long time recognized her right to have an abortion in these circumstances, though religious doctrine has generally denied the right even here. If a woman uses careful contraceptive techniques when having sexual relations, but nevertheless becomes pregnant through some unavoidable failure in the device used, then again we could not say that she has intentionally or even negligently brought about her pregnancy. But if a woman neglects to use any contraceptive precautions, it could reasonably be claimed that she is responsible for her pregnancy, at least in the sense of being negligent as to whether she became pregnant or not.

We might try to set up a moral frontier along these lines, viewing abortion as permissible when the woman is not in this sense responsible for the pregnancy, and as forbidden when she has been negligent. Such a position would not satisfy most advocates of legal abortion, nor would it match the present state of the law. Whatever its moral merits, such a line of demarcation would also be quite impossible to apply as a standard of legality. To entrust a public body with the task of deciding whether a woman did or did not take reasonable contraceptive steps in the act of intercourse that led to her pregnancy would be impractical and ludicrous.

Those who defend the present availability of abortion on demand are not without moral arguments. They can point out that, both under the present state of the law and under their own demands, there remain certain restrictions on abortion. Under the recent Supreme Court decisions, states may still prohibit abortions after the second trimester of pregnancy. This allows prohibition at an earlier date than the time that the old common law recognized as the one where a fetus becomes "capable of being born alive." It thus could be thought to serve as a reasonable, although rough dividing line between a mere fetus and a baby capable of surviving as a human being after detachment from the mother. Certainly before this date, even from the very moment of conception, an entity exists that is a potential human being. But, so the argument might run, the potentiality of becoming a human being is an interest that must yield to the personal right of the woman to determine whether she wishes to carry something in her body to the terminus of birth. Though nobody else has any right to destroy a potential human being, the person who carries such a potentiality in her own body, and who will have to pay a certain price to bring it to fruition, has such a right.

The moral foundation of this right is the extraordinary and in some ways inhuman nature of the burden that its denial would entail. If abortion involves the snuffing out of a potential human life, then to deny a woman an abortion involves the suppression of her human right to make decisions about the fate of her body and the course of her life. We would immediately reject as barbarically unjust any scheme that sought to compel selected women to become pregnant and bear children, when they did not wish to do so. To compel a woman to carry a fetus to term is a similar encroachment on her human dignity, on her right to make a choice for herself whether to have children or not.

Here we must take into account the nature of the burden that pregnancy imposes on a woman in our society. The carrying of the child involves discomfort and perhaps danger to health. The process of birth may be painful and again possibly attended by danger to health and life. Once the child is born, the pressures of tradition and established sentiment combine to persuade the woman that it is her duty to bring up the child to maturity. Though this may impose great hardship on her and radically change the shape of her life, few women are able to resist the weight of the transmitted notion that duty requires such a price once the child is born. The fact that the conception may be in part due to the woman's own negligence does not alter the situation significantly. A mandatory obligation to carry a fetus to birth and then rear a child is a cruel and unusual punishment for a moment's carelessness, often the result of influences, temptations, and pressures that make cool calculation difficult.

Even those who use these arguments to advocate a woman's right to abortion agree that the right is extinguished once the child is born and takes on a full, extruded existence. It is presumably, then, the satellite or incubus character of the fetus in the body of the woman that is decisive in entitling her to determine its disposition. Here we would do well to remember that morality is not a manual of saintliness nor a doctrine of reverence for all forms of life. Our discussion of moral attitudes toward animals has already made that clear. Morality may be regarded as a system of enlightened self-interest, consisting of rules and principles that make social life possible. The system requires that we extend to others the protections and considerations that we would claim for ourselves. This inevitably thrusts forward questions about whom we will regard as members of the group. Primitive moralities may have included within this circle only members of the family or the clan or the tribe or the nation, relegating others to the status of nonpersons who might quite properly be attacked and enslaved or killed. An extension of our moral horizon has brought us to the perception that there are, *prima facie,* no significant differences among human beings with respect to the basic duties that we owe them. While we remain very ambivalent about the status of animals, many have concluded that there are sufficiently significant differences between a human person and a fetus to take the latter outside the sweep of the protective system.

The opponents of abortion are unmoved by such arguments and will catechistically respond that the right to life cannot be displaced by any interests having to do with another's freedom of choice. They will also challenge their opponents with a thin-end-of-the-wedge argument. If the fetus is a nonperson to be disposed of at the will of the mother, why, they will ask, is the same not true of the gravely ill or the mentally retarded or even of young babies? They do well to raise that point, for there can of course be no guarantee that at some time in the future someone will not point to the law on abortion as an analogy justifying the killing of such people. In reply it could be said that those who advocate a free choice for the mother as to abortion are not asking for such choice with respect to live babies or mentally retarded people and that significant differences can be shown among these classes. To hold the line rigidly to ensure the protection of all persons born alive at least provides a workable criterion for division.

But even if the arguments of the proponents of abortion have an initial appeal, we are still left with an unresolved question about the significance of the capability of the fetus to be born alive. Presumably not even the most committed advocate of abortion would want to legalize the killing by a mother of a partially extruded baby in the process of birth. How far back, then, should the line be drawn? One problem here is that advancing medical techniques may eventually force us into responses that would come close to denying the right to abortion altogether. Suppose that doctors may at some time in the future be able to remove a three-month-old fetus from the womb and nurse it to the same development as a normally born baby. Would the advocates of abortion then find it necessary to retreat to a position of permitting abortions only during the first twelve weeks of pregnancy?

The dilemma is more apparent than real. If medical science progresses to the point where most fetuses after removal from the womb could be brought to maturity, the case for abortion would be strengthened rather than weakened. It might be better to say that the demand for *abortion* would disappear and be replaced by a demand for an early termination of pregnancy and relief from the obligation to raise the child. For the mother could then be relieved of her unwanted baby at her request without the necessary loss of a potential human life. If there is felt to be a legitimate state interest in bringing the potential life to fruition, then the detached fetus could be brought to maturity and thereafter cared for at the expense of the state and in facilities provided by the state. The mother requesting the premature termination of pregnancy would forfeit all parental rights with respect to the child, a price she would presumably be willing to pay.

The hypothetical does, however, sharpen the outlines of two issues that recent debate over abortion has not fully brought out. The first is the need to clarify whether the case for abortion involves the assertion of a right to extinguish the life of a fetus or only the demand for the early termination of a pregnancy. At the moment the two possibilities generally merge into one, but this is only a contingency of the present state of medical science. If medicine were able to bring an early detached fetus to maturity outside the mother, and the state assumed the duty to care for the child, the advocates of abortion would have to clarify whether they would be satisfied with such an arrangement or whether they were asserting a right to terminate the life of the fetus. The second demand would be much harder to justify.

Second, the hypothetical shows that the case for abortion

weakens in proportion to the lessening of the burden pregnancy imposes on the mother. If the state regularized good arrangements by which unwanted children were raised in a manner generally accepted as being as healthy, happy, and promising for the future as the average upbringing a child receives in a middle-class home, then the only case a woman could make for abortion would be to be spared the period of pregnancy and the process of birth. These burdens are certainly not inconsiderable, but if it became possible to detach a fetus at an early stage from the mother, the burden would become slight indeed. Let us say that such detachment became safe for the fetus five months into pregnancy. Would a woman three months pregnant then have a right to demand abortion at that time, on the ground that she could not be subjected to the imposition of carrying the child for two more months? This example reveals that the moral arguments for and against abortion on demand are to a considerable extent dependent on the present state of medicine and social arrangements for the care of children.

The Law on Abortion

At the behest of litigants, the courts have been forced to plunge into these thickets of arguments, charged with the task of weighing them against the language of the Constitution and emerging with authoritative determinations. As the old uniformity of state prohibition of abortion began to crumble and some states (notably New York) enacted very permissive abortion legislation, attacks were mounted from both camps.

The New York statute, which permits abortion by qualified medical practitioners in proper facilities on the request of the pregnant woman up to the twenty-fifth week of pregnancy, was challenged in the case of *Byrn* v. *New York City Health & Hospitals Corp.* (1972).[7] The plaintiff contended that an unborn child is a "person" who is entitled to the protection of the Fourteenth Amendment to the United States Constitution, as well as of the similar clause in the New York State Constitution. The Fourteenth Amendment guarantees that no state "shall . . . deprive any person of life, liberty, or property, without due process of law; nor deny to any person within its jurisdiction the equal protection of the laws." The New York State Court of Appeals denied the claim and upheld the New York statute in a somewhat laconic opinion, ruling simply that there was no authoritative constitutional interpretation of the meaning of "person," which was therefore a proper matter for legislative determination.

In the *Byrn* case the plaintiff was asking the courts to strike down a state legislative determination that abortion was permissible. Their refusal to do so is in no way a precedent for the conclusion that a state statute prohibiting abortion is unconstitutional. Both statutes could be allowed to stand, in different jurisdictions, under the theory of the *Byrn* case itself that the matter is one for legislative judgment. But carefully orchestrated attacks were being planned that would compel the federal courts to decide squarely whether it was constitutionally permissible to prohibit abortion. The issue was finally seized and determined by judgments of the Supreme Court of the United States, early in 1973, in the companion cases of *Roe* v. *Wade* and *Doe* v. *Bolton.*[8]

The *Roe* case challenged a Texas statute that made procuring an abortion a criminal offense unless it was done "by medical advice for the purpose of saving the life of the mother." A synopsis of the reasoning of the Supreme Court in this vitally important opinion serves both as an example of the Court's working at this highest level of constitutional decision making and as a basis for an evaluation of the decision itself.

ROE V. WADE

The Court began the substantive part of its opinion with a review of attitudes to abortion through the ages and in different cultures, pointing out that, even in common-law countries, the rigorous prohibition of abortion as a serious felony at all stages of the fetal life is a comparatively recent creation of nineteenth-century statutes. Part of the historical explanation for the passage of these statutes seems to have been a concern for the protection of the mother. But if this was the original legitimate state concern, then its foundation has disappeared with the advance of medicine, which has developed simple and safe techniques for abortion —at any rate, during the early stages of pregnancy.

Other state interests of a legitimate kind are identifiable. The Court recognized that as pregnancy progresses, the abortive procedure becomes more complicated and somewhat more hazardous, so that the state may legitimately require that the operation only be performed in adequate facilities and by qualified persons. Then, in the later stages of pregnancy, as the fetus becomes viable (that is, capable of existence outside the womb, though perhaps only with artificial support), the state may properly assert an interest in protecting prenatal life and thus prohibit abortions altogether. Those who condemn abortion argue, the Court acknowledged, that life begins at conception, and the state interest is therefore apparent from that moment. This position insists that there is a duty on the part of the state (rather than a mere interest) to protect human life. But the Court was not persuaded by this argument. It pointed out, as the New York court had done in *Byrn*, that there is no constitutional guidance on the meaning of "person," which is the entity protected in the language of the Fourteenth Amendment. But *Byrn* had used this point only to reach the conclusion that the state had a right or privilege to *permit* abortion. In *Roe* the Supreme Court put the reasoning to much more devastating use in reaching the conclusion that the state has no right to prohibit abortion.

Taken alone, this premise simply does not support the conclusion. A judgment that a fetus is not constitutionally protected is not dispositive of the state's power to protect if it chooses to do so. Legislation is not to be confined to the four corners of what is mandated by the Constitution. There is nothing in the Constitution that imposes a duty on states to protect gray squirrels, but, if there is any reasonable basis at all for wishing to preserve the species, a state clearly may do so by penal legislation. We need to be instructed why states have a sufficient interest in protecting the fetus capable of being born alive but no such sufficient interest in protecting a fetus before the time it becomes viable.

RIGHTS OF THE MOTHER

The Court attempted to supply this link by dwelling on the woman's rights as having a constitutional dimension. But what constitutional grounding can be found for a woman's right to dispose of a fetus? Our discussion of offenses connected with sexual activity showed that in *Griswold* v. *Connecticut* (1965), the Court had already developed a doctrine of a "fundamental right" to privacy, which was violated in that case by a statute prohibiting the use of contraceptives by married couples. The Court derived this right of privacy from "emanations" or the "penumbra" of several provisions of the Bill of Rights, though at least one Justice invoked more forthrightly the protection of liberty afforded by the Fourteenth Amendment.

In *Eisenstadt* v. *Baird* (1972), the access to contraceptives for married persons was extended to the unmarried by a curious and unconvincing application of the equal-protection doctrine. In this way, when *Roe* came to be decided, the Court had to hand two emerging lines of constitutional theory, one rooted in the doctrine of privacy, and another, arrived at by considering the combined impact of *Griswold* and *Eisenstadt*, seeming to adumbrate a constitutional right having to do with autonomous decisions about the regulation of one's sexual life and the procreation of children.

Now, privacy concepts seem peculiarly unsuited to claims to abortion. The demand to have an abortion has almost nothing to do with the core concept of privacy. It is not a claim that others should not intrude upon an activity that one reasonably expects to keep hidden. Instead it is a claim that others publicly co-operate in providing facilities and services to reach a desired change in the body of the woman and that the state should not interfere. As such it is much more natural to speak of it as a claim to autonomy, to a right to control the contents of one's body and to make personal decisions about whether to have a baby. Linguistically there is no difficulty at all about fitting this under the "liberty" concept of the Fourteenth Amendment.

But tying a right of personal autonomy openly to the hitching post of the liberty and due process concept of the Fourteenth Amendment was not easy for the Court. The explanation involves a little history. In the late nineteenth and early twentieth centuries, the Court had played rather expansively with the notion of what has come to be called "substantive due process," the idea that the legislature is controlled by the Fourteenth Amendment's protection of liberty, not only in the procedures that can be set up for trial and punishment of a person, but also substantively with respect to the degree of control it may impose on people. Unhappily, substantive due process was used a good deal by the Court to strike down reforming social and economic legislation, in defense of the workman's "liberty" to contract with an employer to work enormously long hours for hardly any money at all. In *Lochner* v. *New York* (1908),[9] the Court struck down on substantive due process grounds a New York statute that sought to regulate hours of work in bakeries, and was excoriated in a famous dissent by Mr. Justice Holmes, who said that the case was "decided upon an economic theory which a large part of the country does not entertain."

This kind of decision could not stand long in the path of a President and legislature determined to move away from the economics and social theory of the nineteenth century, and the Court was compelled to back down. Ever since this most unhappy of the Court's adventures, "substantive due process" has become a term of abuse and a specter to be dangled before Justices with a crusading turn of spirit. There can be no doubt that this accounts for the circuitous reasoning of *Griswold*. Terrified by history to talk openly in terms of substantive liberty rights under the Fourteenth Amendment, the Justices talked instead in fragile and convoluted reasoning of privacy rights swirling around in ectoplasmic emanations.

But privacy concepts simply would no longer serve to cope with *Roe*. In *Roe* the Court begins to talk openly of the woman's right as deriving from the liberty-due process clause of the Fourteenth Amendment. In a sense this is a revival of substantive due process, but the Court was careful to point out that it continued to reject that doctine in the area of legislation of a business or economic regulation type. Substantive due process has, then, undergone a metamorphosis and reappeared as the protector of autonomy in areas that have to do with the function and regulation of one's own body, either in isolation or in conjunction with others.

But how exactly does substantive due process work? It is easy enough to see what is meant by procedural due process. In effect, it asserts that nobody shall be punished or significantly deprived of something by a public agency without a fair hearing. Substantive due process does not adapt readily to the same pattern. If a claim is recognized as a fundamental right and so as being encompassed within the constitutional meaning of liberty, how can the due process concept be accommodated? The state cannot deprive one of liberty without due process of law. The state cannot intrude on a fundamental right (liberty) without—what? To stretch fundamental rights out on the due process bed, the Court was forced into borrowings from a different Fourteenth Amendment body of law, equal protection doctrine.

Modern equal protection law has come to say that once a classification imposed by the state is constitutionally suspect, then it may only be upheld if the state can show a "compelling" interest, which is something a good deal stronger than a mere legitimate interest. Transposing this doctrine over to due process, the Court now holds that once a fundamental right is shown, the state may only impede its exercise if it can show such a compelling interest. In *Roe* the ultimate holding is that the state does show a compelling interest once the fetus has become viable, but not before.

This analysis enabled the Court to devise a neat trimester division of adjustment between the competing interests of the state and the woman. For the first three months, the abortion decision must be left to the choice of the woman and the medical judgment of her physician. In practice, this means abortion by untrammeled choice. The situation is substantially the same for the second trimester, except that the state, in promoting its interest in the health of the mother, may "regulate the abortion procedure to the extent that the regulation reasonably relates to the preservation and protection of maternal health."[10] This clearly would not countenance prohibition, but is meant to permit regulations about the medical facilities in which the operation may be performed and the qualifications of the person who performs the abortion. For the last trimester, which is the stage where the fetus has become viable, the state may regulate and, if it chooses, prohibit abortion, except where good medical judgment holds it to be necessary to preserve the life or health of the mother. Presumably the state may permit abortion by choice if it so desires even in the last trimester.

The crucial decision that the state cannot show a compelling interest to displace the woman's fundamental right seems to rest on very shaky foundations. Presumably the protection of human life is beyond argument a compelling interest. It is conceded that there is sharp disagreement about when we should count human life or personality as beginning. Texas made a legislative judgment that the fetus is to be counted as a form of human life worthy of legal protection. In response to this, the only directly relevant passage in the Court's opinion seems curiously lame and feeble:

> It should be sufficient to note briefly the wide divergence of thinking on this most sensitive and difficult question. There has always been strong support for the view that life does not begin until live birth. . . . Physicians and their scientific colleagues . . . have tended to focus . . . upon the interim point when the fetus becomes "viable." . . . In view of all this we do not agree that, by adopting one theory of life, Texas may override the rights of the pregnant woman that are at stake.[11]

But, surely, if it is not unreasonable to take the view that the fetus is a form of human life, and if the protection of human life is clearly a compelling interest, then the abortion question looks eminently like a proper one for legislative determination. To put this another way, a legislature would seem to have amply shown a compelling interest when it points to a very respectable body of opinion to the effect that a fetus is a form of human life worthy of protection. One may disagree with the wisdom of a state's decision to make abortion criminal, but it is much harder to see why it does not have the right in this case to make decisions that one thinks are unwise.

In effect *Roe* silently uses the concept of the woman's fundamental right to do a double service. In the first place, it is the identification of her claim as a fundamental right that places the burden on the state of showing a compelling interest. But, then, the concept of the fundamental right comes back into the picture to cause the scales to tilt in the woman's favor, when the interest asserted by the state is concededly compelling (the protection of life), but there is a sharp division of opinion in society about whether the facts are properly seen as falling within the ambit of the interest. Equal-protection ideas have certainly succeeded here in giving a strange aspect to due-process arguments.

IMPLICATIONS OF ROE

Roe has, at least for the foreseeable future, pretty well settled the abortion question. In so doing it fixed the "fundamental right" approach in the due-process firmament and so opened up a host of intriguing speculations about the future. What enables us to regard a claim as a "fundamental right"? Looking at the cases since *Griswold*, we can see that several factors may be relevant. They include the importance of the activity to the claimant, the deprivation or disadvantage that he or she would suffer if the claim were denied, the privacy of the activity, the extent to which it may be regarded as intimate, its connections with marriage or sexual expression, and its harmlessness. Once a sufficient showing of some of these factors is made to persuade a court to regard the plaintiff's claim as stemming from a fundamental right, the battle is virtually won, for, as *Roe* shows, the state will find it very difficult, if not impossible, to overturn a fundamental right by a showing of a compelling interest.

The all-or-nothing nature of the fundamental-right approach is demonstrated by contrasting *Roe* with the pornography decisions discussed earlier. Since the woman's right in *Roe* was classified as fundamental, even the strongest state showing could not prevail against her. But, in cases like *Miller* and *Paris Adult Theatre*, since the Court was not willing to regard the right to view pornography discreetly in a public place as fundamental, then even the feeblest showing of a state interest, resting controversially on vague allegations of aesthetic decay, was enough to support the legislation and the prohibition. So the law now tells us that the state may prevent freedom of action, where no great harm is involved, on the rather tenuous ground that some cultural deterioration may ensue; but to prohibit the snuffing out of a living organism, which is a well-advanced form of a potential human being, is not permissible. One may believe that a new and vigorous approach to the constitutional protection of personal autonomy was needed and yet be puzzled by such poorly reasoned decisions.

V

Saving People from Themselves

Side by side with a perceived threat of harm to others, another strand of justification for criminal prohibitions sometimes runs. This is the idea that there are some actions that we should not be permitted to perform, quite apart from whether they harm others or not, simply because they are self-destructive or self-mutilating or self-degrading. Sometimes this paternalistic justification of saving people from themselves appears as the only or principal reason for criminal prohibition. More often it is intertwined with other justifications, which look to assertions of harm inflicted on others. Crimes of gambling and prostitution make good examples here.

Gambling

While most forms of gambling remain prohibited in most of the states, a substantial shift of opinion has recently occurred. Some states now run officially sponsored lotteries, and New York City also conducts an off-track betting operation on horse racing. Several factors have evidently contributed to this development:

1. The depletion of state budgets and the sharp need for extra revenue for useful social purposes have turned attention to the substantial sums that could be diverted into public coffers by harnessing the desire to gamble.

2. We have become more and more aware that the criminalization of gambling breeds a huge crime industry. For many people the urge to gamble is, if not irresistible, at least difficult to resist. Perhaps if we made it a serious crime to place a bet, many more people would be deterred. We shrink from such a step, no doubt because of an intuitive recognition that betting cannot sensibly be thought of as a crime of any gravity and because public sentiment would not stand for such legislation. But, while we confine

criminal penalties to those who "privately" provide an organized service of gambling, we shall certainly not deter the ordinary citizen from making use of the service. The paradoxical result may be that we do little to reduce the volume of gambling but do ensure that it is exclusively carried out in a framework of criminality. This spawns a criminal apparatus and has an inevitable tendency at the edges to corrupt some police officers and other public officials.

3. The enforcement of antigambling laws, if it is to be at all effective, requires the allocation of a great deal of law-enforcement time and resources. With rising apprehension in urban areas about the threat to personal safety from crimes of violence, we have come to scrutinize with some jealousy the amount of police time expended in detecting and pursuing those who provide gambling services.

4. Finally, there is growing doubt about the question of closest concern to us in this discussion: Why should gambling be thought of as wrong at all?

Some might argue that it is morally wrong to get something for nothing, or to seek to do so, and particularly wrong for whole institutions to be set up or permitted with the one objective of persuading people to enter into such efforts. Given certain social conditions, we could see a plausible utilitarian case for that kind of ethic. If we lived in a frontier society, a pioneer community, where it was vitally necessary for everyone who was able to work productively and continuously, then the practice of gambling might pose a threat by luring numbers of people into idleness. In the United States we no longer live in that kind of society, and many think that our problems are of a quite contrary nature. It becomes more and more difficult to provide worthwhile jobs for the number of people who are able to work. It is probably the case that we already create, somewhat artificially, thousands of job categories that are not particularly useful but that are symbolically helpful to persuade many of us that we are working. Gambling may in one sense be a boon in such a society, since it operates to create many jobs. It may also have the occasional side benefit of removing a few people from the number of those who need to be employed or supported by the state by sufficiently enriching them when they have a big win.

If this utilitarian argument is not appropriate to the nature of our society, the opponent of gambling could take up instead a stance of a purer and more principled condemnation of the pursuit of chance gains, by contending that it offends against general principles of reward depending on merit and effort. There is something wrong, he could argue, in people getting something for nothing and in the existence of institutions to foster that hope. The wrongness consists partly in the unfairness that is perceived by those who work for modest rewards when they see undeserved chance windfalls descend on others. Such a critic might concede that we cannot altogether expel the element of chance from the distribution of rewards in society, but he might argue that we should look upon the merit and desert principles as the properly governing ones and seek to minimize the intervention of chance as much as possible. Institutionalized gambling cannot be tolerated because it is a direct, organized attack on the merit principle and a standing temptation to everyone to forsake the pursuit of gain and advancement through effort.

But our society has endured for a very long time a system that seems far removed in many ways from a thoroughgoing allegiance to the principle of no reward without desert. We accept the institution of inheritance, so that very many people are rich because their grandparents were rich. Others become rich because they marry a rich person or because they fall into jobs that they do not really deserve through the influence of friends. The desert principle has thus never been a rigorous one but has accommodated itself to a host of exceptions. We might also point out that many in our society, perhaps through the accident of birth and the circumstances of their early life, are just never in a position where they are able to receive reasonable rewards for hard work. So the person who wants to disapprove of gambling, on the grounds of the desert principle, would have to argue for a rather extensive social revolution if he is going to be consistently principled and escape a charge of hypocrisy. Most critics of gambling are not in fact pressing for such a revolution.

A more principled reply would be that the moral claim of the desert principle for absolute sovereignty in the field of rewards is not readily apparent. We may admit that in a social setting where survival and the refinements of living depend on productivity and physical and intellectual effort, at least by some of the people some of the time, it would be hard to imagine the total abandonment of some correlation between the quality of such efforts and the distribution of rewards. But there is no compelling reason in ethics or utility why such a connection should not be leavened and interspersed with the play of chance. The human personality has qualities of imagination and emotion to which chance makes great appeal; there are human needs for social drama and diversion that are satisfied by viewing and taking part in the lottery side of life. An arrangement under which the basic operation of the merit system is shot through with the occasional intervention of luck will not necessarily inject such a sense of unfairness that people will give up working. Experience teaches that it is more likely to supply a complementary level of excitement, hope, and diversion that most people can incorporate with the general merit principle as a qualifying principle that affords welcome relief.

When we get through with these arguments that look to the general ethical significance of gambling or its general social impact, we are still left with the most favored traditional ground of attack, that gambling must be prohibited to protect the gambler. We should notice in passing that this does not necessarily involve making it criminal for him to gamble. We may achieve the same goal (and may think there are good reasons to prefer this path) by simply prohibiting the activity of those who provide gambling services. But whatever the technique chosen, the rationale of protecting the gambler from himself will be the same. Gambling, it has been often said, affords opportunities to people to lead themselves into penury in a peculiarly sterile and unproductive way. They may beggar themselves and their families and become charges upon the state. Even if they avoid such an extreme outcome, they may consistently diminish their income and so cause distress and deprivation to themselves and their families.

This is no doubt always a possibility and must be the case with some gamblers. But there is a host of ways in life in which people can behave foolishly with their money and so make themselves and their families suffer. We may buy cars or take vacations that we can't afford, or be foolish with our investments in a hundred ways. Though it might be desirable for everyone to be prudent and thrifty, no one would suggest that the criminal law should enter fully into this field and enforce thrift and husbandry generally by penal legislation. The criminal law is not a good teacher of that kind of wisdom, and any such attempts would involve vast and intolerably intrusive schemes of regulation. Those who want to retain the criminalization of gambling have a burden to point to any special features that could justifiably single out this one way of being improvident with one's money as suitable for penal intervention. On the other hand, once we concede that gambling may indeed cause some deprivation and distress for some gamblers and an acute amount for a small number, we have a corresponding duty to give principled reasons why a paternalistic imposition of restraints is not permissible.

This must involve us in a general discussion of the justification of paternalistic intervention through the agency of the criminal law. We shall look first at some particular issues to do with the crime of prostitution and then consider arguments surrounding paternalism that we can connect with both gambling and prostitution.

Prostitution

We know from experience that there are several aspects of active prostitution that can be socially objectionable. Blatant solicitation on the streets can be a public nuisance, and the keeping of a brothel may be offensive to those neighbors who cannot help but be aware of what is going on. But the need to regulate abuses of this kind does not amount to a justification of criminalizing the act of prostitution itself. In Britain the act of selling one's body for sexual purposes is no longer any crime at all, but prohibitions on soliciting and maintaining a brothel remain.

Looking for utilitarian justifications for the prohibition on prostitution itself, we meet the traditional argument that it tends to spread venereal disease. No doubt it does, but so of course does all sexual promiscuity, and there is no convincing evidence that prostitution has a very significant role in this distressing and unpleasant epidemic. Lack of hygiene and of social responsibility on the part of those who are sexually promiscuous are more important contributors. In addition, since it is generally conceded that no amount of law enforcement can drastically reduce the incidence of prostitution, it may be that legalization could bring a better opportunity to control its impact on the disease factor.

But the primary justification for making prostitution criminal is not a utilitarian one at all; rather it is the contention that it is degrading and dehumanizing to sell one's body to another for sexual use. We have traditionally thought of this as primarily a question of the degradation of women, but we should remember that it may apply to men, and that some jurisdictions, such as New York, now make prostitution a crime applicable to both men and women. And if prostitution is dehumanizing to the person who sells herself or himself, the responsibility for the degradation is presumably as much that of the buyer as of the seller. Those who patronize prostitutes, on this approach, should at least be equally guilty of participating in the process of abusing a human being. With a recognition of this principle, some jurisdictions, among them again New York, now make it an offense to patronize a prostitute, though prosecutions for this are rare, and it is still generally the prostitute who bears the weight of the law's attack.

But the notion of being degraded or dehumanized is a complex one. It is very likely true that most people would say that they would feel degraded if they had to sell their bodies for sexual use, and it is also true that some people who have been driven to this step by acute economic need have felt degraded in this way. But it is no doubt also the case that some prostitutes would sharply retort that they don't feel in the least degraded, and that they have made a voluntary decision to pursue a profession that they find quite agreeable, not too demanding and moderately rewarding. Is degradation then simply a concept of individualized reactions, on the same footing with personal distastes for certain kinds of food or scents that other people may enjoy?

One explanation would be to view the social stigma attached to prostitution as the artifact of a male-dominated society, which feels a need to purvey and reinforce its own image of the nature and function of woman and to use social and criminal sanctions to keep women in that role and place. Some students of human sexuality have suggested that the male's relationship to women has been dominated by a consciousness of woman's constant sexual availability, as contrasted with the physiological facts, which render a man only occasionally sexually available. Starting with this observation, the practice of prostitution could be seen by men as a constant threat, through its open and flaunting proclamation of the continuing sexual readiness of women. For that reason, it shelters and comforts a male-centered view of the world to regard prostitution as a manifestation of womanhood at its worst. Since women have been accultured by a male-dominated society, they have often of course absorbed this view of themselves.

We have traditionally admired the ability of some people to offer us entertainment and diversion through their perfected physical skills. Athletes and dancers are nowadays much respected and even honored. The articulate prostitute could make a case for herself in similar terms as one who fulfills a great social need, for which there has been an unwavering demand; one who gives great pleasure and may practice her art with skill and a sense of accomplished endeavor. She might add that the social sense of degradation attached to prostitution may have a great deal to do with a historical connection between its practice and poverty and poor working conditions. The majority of prostitutes at most times have been poor and have worked in harsh and sordid conditions. The drug-addicted street walker is not likely to stimulate respect for the trade that she pursues. But actors were also at one time generally poor and socially despised. Significantly the social attitude, at least in some places at some times, to those in the highest ranks of prostitution has been very different. The fashionable courtesan of nineteenth-century France or the expensive Manhattan call girl has rarely received the contempt given to her sisters on the streets.

The notion of being degraded may thus be an amalgam of projections of male sexual fears with consequent socioeconomic manifestations. A vigorous assertion of independence by women, coupled with generally better working conditions for prostitutes, might do much to dissipate such emanations. But it is by no means safe to assume comfortably that the question can be so easily resolved.

After all, if the prostitute contends that she does not in the least feel degraded or dehumanized by what she does, the reply can always be made that she should have these feelings whether in fact she does or not. She fails to have a sense of degradation, it could be said, because her sensibilities were always blunt or crude or have become blunted by the business of engaging in prostitution. In one light such a point of view may appear simply pontifically arrogant, but it may be rooted in more defensible conceptions of human nature. The sexual act is one of peculiar human intimacy, often associated with deep emotions of love and always profoundly affective of one's view of oneself and others. It is not necessary to say, as was once often said, that for these reasons the unique sexual union of one man and one woman through life is the only desirable state. But it may still be valid to point out that a constant trivialization of the sexual act, by indiscriminate promiscuity, may deprive one of the capacity to relate to anybody through sexual union in the most enriching way we believe to be possible. This is not offered as a proposition of unimpeachable psychosexual validity, but it at least deserves the status of a prudent caveat. And if this is so, the constant dealing in the commerce of sex with one's own body is presumably the highest form of danger in this direction. The concepts of degradation and dehumanization could in this way be given that much objective content.

But it may be that this is a risk that a person should be allowed to run. There are many occupations or activities in life that could be thought to carry with them the possibility of collateral consequences of psychic harm. Among them could be counted being a hog slaughterer, a funeral undertaker, an army officer, and so on. Since all of these occupations are thought eminently necessary for the orderly flow of social life, we should perhaps feel admiration for the nobility and self-sacrifice of those who for our sake engage in such activities, which many find very distasteful. In a similar light, the prostitute could be seen as doing a useful if sometimes unpleasant job, which carries some risk for her erotic stability. Only an extreme view of paternalism, which we now come to examine, could justify criminalization.

Paternalism Generally

Nineteenth-century English liberalism, which found a warm echo in the United States, was hotly opposed to the principle of paternalistic intervention by the state. John Stuart Mill wrote in his celebrated essay "On Liberty":

> Neither one person nor any number of persons is warranted in saying to another human creature of ripe years that he shall not do with his life for his own benefit what he chooses to do with it.

And later,

> The only purpose for which power can rightfully be exercised over any member of a civilized community against his will is to prevent harm to others. . . . He cannot rightfully be compelled to do or forbear because it would be better for him to do so, because it would make him happier, or because in the opinion of others to do so would be wise or even right.[1]

Pressed as flatly as Mill does in this excerpt, the thesis appears, as many critics have pointed out, exaggerated. Should we not intervene to prevent suicides, or at least some suicides? Is there no justification for enforced savings schemes such as mandatory contributions to Social Security? Mill did of course say that power could not be exercised against a person for his own good *against his will*. Some of the difficult counterexamples can be disposed of by maneuvering within the concept of "will." We could say that the potential suicide must be so disturbed that his decision to take his own life cannot be regarded as an expression of free will. With respect to Social Security, we could argue that the majority approves of such a scheme, and the minority must be compelled to participate, since the scheme could not operate efficiently unless it were applied to all.

This style of reconciliation becomes more difficult when we deal with compulsory measures designed for the self-protection of individuals. What about a law requiring motorcyclists to wear crash helmets? The safety of others has little to do with such a provision, which is clearly primarily aimed at the protection of the rider himself. Courts have had difficulty with just this regulation, some at times holding that it contravened the requirements of the due process clause on the ground that the protection of a person himself was not, taken alone, a sufficient state interest to justify interfering with his liberty. In terms of Mill's own analysis, it would not be persuasive here to rely on the suicide analogy. We do not generally think that people who refuse to wear helmets while riding a motorcycle, or who refuse to fasten belts while driving a car, are not in possession of their senses in the way that a suicide might be. We may think that they are foolish, imprudent, even reckless, but not that they have lost the capacity to make rational decisions. Reflection on whether compulsory regulation in this area is justifiable drives us back into a further consideration of the policy or ethical basis of Mill's opposition to paternalism.

Here a valuable analysis is to be found in an essay by Gerald Dworkin.[2] Professor Dworkin points out that Mill's position cannot be defended on the utilitarian ground that it is always better in practice for a person to make his own decisions about his own safety. The motorcyclist who has sustained a fractured skull while not wearing a helmet would probably ruefully agree that he would have been better off if the law had compelled him to wear one. The chief principled strength of Mill's position, Dworkin suggests, is rather in a notion of human dignity. This involves the idea that part of the concept of being a person is the independence to make decisions for oneself when such decisions cannot harm others. As we often put it simply, people must make their own mistakes in life. But if we grant the force of this position, we have also seen that there are extreme cases where we might think it right to draw the line, as with some suicide attempts. To chart the path of this dividing line is very difficult.

Mill himself thought that since the purpose of his maxim was to preserve freedom of choice, it ought to be abandoned when the action contemplated would involve imposing irrevocable fetters on such freedom for the future. So he himself suggested that it would be proper to restrain a person from selling himself into slavery. Professor Dworkin suggests that a similar argument could be used to justify restraints that are aimed at saving people from the risk of death or terrible injury, as with the crash helmet and seat belt examples. If slavery deprives a person of freedom of action, then so of course does death or maiming. The only freedom people cannot be granted is the freedom to choose not to be free.

This is an appealing position that nevertheless still leaves us with difficulties. Many activities in life involve risk of serious injury or death. They include mountain climbing, car racing, cigarette smoking, and so on. There may be an arguable case for prohibiting some of these activities, but certainly not all. This is because we recognize that there are many admirable aspects of the human story that could never have unfolded without such risks. We recognize risks as legitimate when they further discovery, exploration, the rescue of others, or even, to a substantial extent, the entertainment of others or oneself. Mountain climbing is not a spectator sport, and it does put the climber into great danger, but no one seriously argues for its total prohibition. The matching of physique, skill, and technique against the challenges of nature makes an appeal to a side of human nature that we do not regard as ignoble. We believe it may nurture qualities of steadfastness and heroism that contribute greatly to human welfare. If the crash helmet example is different, it is because it lacks these features. The person who wants to ride a motorcycle without a crash helmet is not pitting his physique and skill against the forces of nature. He is simply stupid, thoughtless, or reckless, and engaged in running barren risks for a purpose devoid of any nobility.

This brief discussion of the general principles underlying the opposition to paternalism gives us some additional vantage points to look back at the arguments to do with gambling and prostitution. Neither gambling nor prostitution can be fairly equated with suicide or selling oneself into slavery. The slavery analogy may have some compelling aspects when we turn later to a discussion of the use of heroin and other drugs, but it seems inappropriate here. Clearly prostitution may have some harmful physical or psychic effects on the person engaging in it (though this is not a necessary result), but it would be unacceptable to say that prostitutes have abdicated all freedom of choice. People can be prostitutes by way of occupation in the same way that people can be plumbers or lawyers. We know that many people have been prostitutes for a time and then made a decision to cease. When we add to this the circumstance that prostitutes undoubtedly supply a much-needed social service, we would seem to have as little paternalistic warrant to forbid the practice as we would to prohibit people from becoming morticians.

It is true that, in connection with gambling, we do speak of obsession or addiction. Some people are described as compulsive gamblers, and their condition is for some meaningful psychological purposes regarded as a sickness. Such people usually do inflict great harm on themselves and on their dependents. But this is not a high-risk factor for everyone who indulges in gambling. The instructive comparison here is with the use of heroin. The prevailing opinion, though one that is questioned by some experts, is that a single experiment with heroin or at least the frequent use of it over even a short period exposes the user to the greatest peril of profound addiction. But we know that millions of people gamble occasionally, or even perhaps regularly, without falling into such a condition of helplessness and certainly without involving themselves in deep psychological trauma. If the best defense of paternalism is that it is a justifiable policy when it saves us from the destruction of our freedom of choice and thereby our human dignity, then a case along these lines is not made out with respect to gambling or prostitution, and even less so in connection with homosexual behavior or viewing pornography. Social duty is sufficiently discharged here by making therapeutic services available to anyone who feels that he or she has fallen into a pattern of obsessive behavior in one of these directions, or whose activity appears to be a cause of deep emotional distress to that person.

Constitutionality

The notion that courts might declare criminal laws prohibiting gambling or prostitution to be unconstitutional may seem to be far-fetched, and, indeed, there is little prospect of such judicial action in the near future. But arguments of some plausibility could be put up, at least with respect to prostitution.

As the earlier discussion of sexual conduct showed, the Supreme Court decided in *Griswold* v. *Connecticut* that there is a constitutionally protected zone of privacy that includes marital regulation of procreation through a decision to use contraceptives. Later cases in lower courts have extended this principle with some readiness to give constitutional protection to all sexual activity by married couples in the home. The abortion decision of *Roe* v. *Wade* taught us that the Griswold doctrine of privacy has now acquired an extended application in the direction of autonomy with respect to control of one's body and its contents, at least in the context of the abortion decision itself.

From these Supreme Court cases it is possible to argue for a "fundamental right" of constitutional dimension to engage in any variety of sexual act one pleases as long as the act is done between consenting adults in circumstances of privacy. We saw earlier that a few courts have been pushing out in this direction, though the majority remains cautious and relies on the Supreme Court's reservation in *Griswold* that the decision should not be read as striking down laws that prohibit sexual promiscuity. But if the position should gain ground that freedom of choice as to sexual expression or fulfillment is constitutionally protected, we should then have to ask whether the commercial element involved in an act of prostitution would be enough to take it outside the constitutional shelter.

If courts come to view sexual conduct as a constitutionally protected fundamental right, it will presumably be because of elements of intimacy, autonomy over the use of one's own body, privacy, and fulfillment of deep human need that inhere in the activity. The patron of a prostitute could certainly make all these claims, though the prostitute would be less well placed to advance them, since her prime motivation is presumably financial. But if there is a fundamental right to use one's body as one pleases sexually, should it cease to be fundamental because a financial condition is annexed to the transaction? *Roe* v. *Wade* is based on the doctrine that once an individual's fundamental right has been identified, the state may prohibit the conduct only if it can show a "compelling interest." If sexual freedom is a fundamental right, then, in the prostitution context, the state would have to rely on the parade of arguments examined earlier in this chapter to show its compelling interest in intervening. They scarcely seem to rise to a compelling level.

The content or enforcement of prostitution laws may also be subject to attack on the ground that they are sexually discriminatory, in violation of the equal-protection clause of the Fourteenth Amendment. If the statute (as many do) makes the act an offense only for women, the tacit license to men to engage in sexual commerce could be viewed as a denial of equal protection to women.

This argument was accepted by an Alaskan court in *State* v. *Fields* (1973).[3] The local statute defined the crime so as to apply it to a female prostitute or client but not to a male prostitute or client. The court took the view that statutory classifications based on sex were generally suspect, in the light of the Supreme Court decision in *Frontiero* v. *Richardson* (1973),[4] which held that female officers in the armed forces must be allowed to claim husbands as a dependent, since male officers were permitted to make such a claim for wives. Under equal-protection doctrine, once a suspect classification is involved, then the state must show the necessity of such a discrimination in order to further a compelling state interest. The court could find no compelling interest that would justify exempting men from laws against prostitution and therefore struck down the statute as unconstitutional.

If, on the other hand, the statute on its face applies to sales by persons of both sexes, then evidence that the statute is never or very rarely applied to male prostitutes or male patrons could be taken to amount to discriminatory enforcement of the law and so, again, to a denial of equal protection.

In 1974 one court in the District of Columbia was persuaded to take this view in the case of *United States* v. *Wilson*.[5] The District of Columbia statute made it criminal for "any person" to invite, entice, persuade, or address another for the purpose of prostitution. The police evidence freely conceded that males who patronized prostitutes or who might approach women with offers of money for sex were never prosecuted, and that law-enforcement efforts were directed exclusively at women who sold themselves. The court took the view that this amounted to an admission of discriminatory enforcement and dismissed the prosecution before it. But a minimal showing by the state of some efforts to pursue male prostitutes or male patrons would be enough to escape such a result.

Gambling laws are probably safe from constitutional attack, however much they may be thought to lack a sound foundation of good reason. The concept of "fundamental right" as part of the "liberty" guarantee of the Fourteenth Amendment may in time be stretched to include a number of intimate and personal acts, such as the range of sexual behavior. Conduct of this kind has a continuing connection with the original privacy concept and, for most people, sexual fulfillment is a value of such importance that it does not seem exaggerated to think of choice in this area as a fundamental right. But the claim to stake money on the outcome of a contest or a lottery, stimulating and diverting as it may be for many, is both remote from the starting point of privacy and difficult to view as essential to the quality of an individual's life. For this reason it seems very improbable that constitutional interposition could take place with respect to gambling laws.

Conclusion

Before leaving the themes of the first part of this book, we must sound a qualifying note to which we shall have to return in the discussion of drug use that follows. To say that there is no good case made out for a flat criminal prohibition on certain modes of behavior does not mean that no good arguments can be made for some degree of regulation in that area. Our social arrangements are full of examples of activities that we think are either positively good or at the least not worthy of condemnation but that we perceive a need to regulate in a host of ways. So most jurisdictions have no general ban on the sale or consumption of alcohol, but we impose numerous conditions and restrictions, among which may be listed the prohibition on sale to or use by minors, the requirement that those who sell liquor be licensed, the ban on sale to those who appear intoxicated, and so on. In the course of our discussion, we have already noticed numerous restrictions of a similar kind that we might very reasonably want to impose if decriminalization of some of the kinds of conduct we have been discussing should occur. In the case of pornography, we would want to forbid access by young people, to restrict advertising so that it is inoffensive and not unduly obtrusive, and perhaps to license wholesalers and retailers. With respect to prostitution, we should probably want to retain bans on street solicitation, on offensive advertising, and on maintaining nuisance-type brothels.

In connection with gambling, interesting collateral issues arise that would have to be thoroughly canvassed and debated before we should embark on general decriminalization. These would include whether there should be a state monopoly in providing gambling services, or whether the service should be largely handed over to licensed private bookmakers (as in Britain), or whether some sharing between the state and private enterprise is desirable. We should want to discuss the age limit at which gambling becomes permissible for a young person. Most sensitive of all is the degree to which advertising should be permitted, and possible restrictions on the nature of the advertising; for it is quite a tenable position to say that, while we have no warrant to forbid an activity, there are dangerous aspects to it that make it at the same time undesirable to permit strenuous and seductive appeals to people to engage in it. This is, after all, the position that we have already reached with respect to cigarette smoking. Decriminalization, then, does not have to mean a total lifting of any claims to regulatory intervention. Its essential assertion is only that no good ground can be perceived for a primary and general prohibition of the conduct in question.

PART 2

Drug Use and Abuse

VI

Drugs and the Criminal Law

Few issues have more vexed public opinion in the United States in recent years than the spread of drug abuse. There may be sectors of the country that have scarcely been touched by the problem, but in large urban centers the prohibited use of drugs has become a pervasive cause of anxiety, a constant preoccupation of law-enforcement authorities, and a great breeder of misery and crime.

The one feature that drugs of abuse have in common is that they are mood altering in their effect. If they were not, there would be little reason to take them. People in Western society, and probably in most human societies, have always indulged in taking such psychoactive drugs. The report of the Task Force on Narcotics and Drug Abuse, published in 1967, contains the provocative but surely accurate comment that the really abnormal behavior in our society would be to take no mood-altering drugs at all. At the same time we have come to a series of public judgments that certain drugs should not be taken under any circumstances (cannabis, heroin), while others should only be taken under medical prescription (barbiturates, amphetamines). But side by side with these restrictions we manage to be very permissive about the use of that very powerful mood-altering drug, alcohol.

This ambivalence in our approach surely stems from the connection between drugs and our notion of what it is to be happy, or to lead a happy life. Happiness is an inner state, but we traditionally connect it with certain valued social arrangements and capacities. So we think it includes having good and loving relationships with other people, in one's family and outside the family. Again, the notion of the good life, the happy life, has encompassed, particularly in the Western world, the idea of doing good work. Good work may be a number of different kinds of work. It may be artistic or intellectual; but many people are not gifted with the talent for performing creative works of this kind. They may still do good work in the sense that what they do is useful, that it helps others either in an immediate individual way or by making a contribution to the well-being of society in some collective sense. It may be a lack of conviction in many people that they are doing "good work" in any of these senses that contributes significantly to personal feelings of unhappiness.

The idea of the happy life includes, too, the appreciation of beautiful things and the pursuit of pleasure. This could embrace the enjoyment of nature, of works of art, the pleasures of eating and drinking and conversation, and of course erotic activity. Simply to list these elements is no doubt not a definitive analysis of happiness, but it may serve as a rough signpost to the aspirations that many of us do include in our concept of what it is to live well. Historically there has been an important link between the pursuit of happiness and the ingestion of mind- or mood-altering drugs. The explanation is not hard to find. The difficulties and strains that ordinary life imposes on most of us often make the components of happiness frustratingly elusive. Certain drugs have remarkable capacities for relieving tensions, for liberating us so that we can achieve joy and peace, at least fleetingly. Some of these drugs are said to be "psychedelic," which means that they sharpen sensual and aesthetic awareness and appreciation and bring the user to a state of tranquil enjoyment and peace.

Traditionally in Western society the great mood-altering drug of fashion has been alcohol, which is so socially accepted in most places at most times, and also so respected and feared for its power, that it plays a central part in the most solemn sacrament of the Christian religion. The established place of alcohol in our social life is a recognition that the sensible and moderate use of a drug can, by relieving us of tension and anxiety, liberate us better to pursue happiness. But there is a conflict and a dualism here, for we have also always known, as far back as history goes, that mood-altering drugs may at times work in a quite contrary way—for, when taken excessively on one occasion, or when taken consistently over a long period, they may dehumanize us. We may become besotted or enslaved to them so that they cripple us in the attempt to lead a good and happy life.

One traditional but essentially crude and misleading way of expressing this conflict has been to view it as a struggle between the work ethic, on the one hand, and the pleasure ethic, on the other. We might think here of the archetypes, in Shakespeare's *Antony and Cleopatra,* of Octavius and Antony. Octavius is the cold, dedicated executive, whose abstemious work habits bring him to the top of the corporate ladder, while Antony abandons himself to the pleasures of life, as exemplified in the symbols of Cleopatra and Egypt, leading to his ruin. But this would be a vulgarization of the conflict. The antithesis is not simply between regarding productive work as the only proper aim of life as opposed to the pursuit of some euphoric concept of pleasure in a gross sense. What makes the dilemma about drugs acute is precisely the awareness that both Octavius and Antony represent abstractions, and that for most people a harmonious integration of these aspects of human life is desirable. Drugs can both help and hinder this quest, and this is why their use at once so attracts and disturbs us.

Our dilemma is sharpened by the grip that fashion and tradition have on us and the difficulty this interposes in the way of rational distinctions and classifications. For example, in our society, alcohol is still the drug of addiction par excellence. The number of alcoholics enormously exceeds the number of heroin addicts, and the total damage done by alcohol in society is incalculably greater than that done by heroin. In the simplest terms of lives cut short, lives that are crippled, work hours lost, the infliction of accidental death and injury on others, and the unhappiness caused to family members, alcohol wins the race from heroin by a vast distance. Though this would be impossible to calculate with any precision, it must also be the case that alcohol generates much more violent crime than heroin; for it is in the nature of alcohol that it often disposes its user to violence, while this is not at all in the nature of heroin. But, although we maintain a polite level of lip service to the dangers of alcohol, we are not frenziedly preoccupied with it in the way that many of our public spokesmen have been about heroin. The *prima facie* strangeness of this constrast in attitudes must impel us into an examination of the relevant characteristics of drugs, the use of which is either wholly prohibited, or permitted only in a medical context, in order to identify what singular features might justify this patchwork of prohibition.

Classification of Drugs of Abuse

Drugs may be classified in a number of ways: according to their derivation from plants, as opposed to their synthetic fabrication; according to their physiological operation in the body; according to their psychic impact; according to the significance that the law attributes to their use, and so forth. The classification that follows cuts across the frontiers of a conceptual strictness and rests partly on pharmacological and partly on social criteria. The comments made are of the briefest kind necessary to illuminate the discussion.

THE HALLUCINOGENICS

Literally, these are drugs that can produce hallucinations, though this should not always be understood in the strongest sense of conjuring up to the eye or ear images or sounds that are not objectively present. Certainly such results are possible from heavy use of these drugs (as they are from alcohol), but the more usual expectation from moderate use is an altered state of consciousness, which may be experienced as a pleasurable enhancement of visual, auditory, and tactile perceptions, accompanied by a mood of tranquility and mild euphoria. In this sense these drugs are often described as psychedelic. The reactions of the inexperienced user are as unpredictable as with alcohol, and unpleasant experiences can result.

While a broad range of drugs could fairly be counted in this group, the ones in most popular use and uppermost in popular awareness are marihuana, hashish, and LSD (lysergic acid diethylamide). Marihuana and hashish are both products of the cannabis or hemp plant. Their ingestion in moderation may produce a psychoactive effect, which is likely to be stronger in the case of hashish than with marihuana. Indeed, the hallucinogenic effect of marihuana is so slight that the most recent literature tends to classify it rather as a tranquilizer or mild depressant. There is no evidence that death or serious illness can ever be expected from a single ingestion of even a large quantity of marihuana or hashish. Long and consistent use may carry with it a risk of a damage to health, as is true of tobacco or fatty foods.

LSD, a synthetically manufactured substance, is a more powerful psychedelic or hallucinogenic drug than the cannabis group. Though evidence is scanty, it is probably sometimes psychotomimetic, which means that it may produce symptoms resembling those found in certain conditions of serious mental illness. Such reactions are exceptional, but LSD would appear to be a substance that should be treated with considerable caution.

None of the drugs in this group are said to be addictive. Since the concept of addiction is always featured centrally in discussion of drug regulation, it becomes crucial at this point to spell out exactly what is indicated by the term. In saying here that the hallucinogenics are not addictive, we mean principally that using them does not with time produce a sharp craving for the repetition of the experience, with acute discomfort at its absence. When a drug is addictive, as with tobacco (nicotine) or heroin, we are often not sure exactly why this is so. It may well have something to do with cellular changes that the repeated ingestion of the drug may produce in the body. Whatever its genesis, the experience of addiction (as all confirmed cigarette smokers will know) is a powerfully distressing one, if a keen desire to cease using the drug comes into conflict with the brute demand of the body for repeating the sensations of use. Such a problem does not exist with the drugs we are now discussing.

It also appears that marihuana and hashish do not carry a tolerance factor. Tolerance refers to a phenomenon by which repeated use of the same drug fails after a time to produce the desired effect without increase in the dose. The sedation, tranquility, euphoria, or whatever may be the desired goal, is only to be achieved by a graduated escalation in the amount taken, though the level may be reduced by abstention for a time. Such a tolerance factor plainly adds a dimension of risk when the drug is one that poses danger to life or health through overdose. Both from their comparatively innocuous nature and the absence of a tolerance factor, the cannabis drugs pose no danger of this kind. Indeed, in the case of marihuana, some users may experience a curious reverse tolerance factor, by which the desired result can after a time be reached by smaller doses than at the outset of use.

Unlike the cannabis group, LSD, in the view of most experts, does have a strong tolerance factor. It would be a mistake, however, to conclude from this that it is a drug of addiction. LSD is not noted for producing a craving for repeated use, and, conversely, neither does abstention after repeated use produce those withdrawal symptoms, familiar to users of barbiturates or heroin, that constitute the other great mark of addiction. To say that these drugs are not physically addictive is not to say that they cannot lead to what is often called "psychic dependency." But the notion of psychic dependency may be of less significance than its high-sounding designation would imply. On reflection it means no more than that one has a strong emotional or psychic drive to repeat an experience. So most of us are in this way psychically dependent on being in the company of a certain person, or watching baseball games, or eating candy, or whatever it may be. The business of living brings with it ineluctable dependencies, and it is not surprising that those who have found the use of psychoactive drugs to be pleasant or enriching should be strongly drawn to repeat the experience. Psychic dependency only becomes a matter of concern if it can be shown that the relationship is such that some demonstrable harm is done to the life or health of the user. With some people who use almost any drug, this may be the case.

THE DEPRESSANTS

A drug is said to be a depressant in the technical sense that it depresses the central nervous system, and not in the more popular meaning of causing one to feel depressed, though this may sometimes be a result.

After alcohol, the barbiturates are the most fashionable depressants. These drugs are refinements of a synthetic chemical derived from barbituric acid. The long-acting barbiturates (such as phenobarbital) are mild drugs, of the greatest use for a variety of medical purposes and can safely be taken in moderate doses for long periods of time. The short-acting barbiturates, so called because they take effect and wear off quickly, are more powerful drugs, with great danger attending their abuse. It is these short-acting barbiturates that are the chosen drugs of use by many people, either under medical prescription or when obtained illegally.

These drugs may be useful in achieving sleep when beset by insomnia, if taken under careful medical supervision. But they are strongly addictive and have a high tolerance factor. Anyone using them consistently thus runs a risk of having to increase the dose to produce the desired effect, coupled with a craving to repeat the experience and the possibility of very unpleasant and even acutely dangerous withdrawal symptoms on abrupt discontinuance.

Barbiturates are not hallucinogenic, but are used, outside medical prescription, because they produce a reaction very similar to that gained from taking alcohol. Thus, depending on the amount taken, they may induce sedation, tranquility, or a drunken euphoria. Since they are central nervous system depressants, overdose may result in death. They are particularly dangerous when taken in combination with alcohol. They are certainly more dangerous in a short-term and long-term sense than heroin, and yet they remain comparatively easily available on prescription, while heroin is in the United States not a drug of legal use under any circumstances.

THE STIMULANTS

The most popular drugs of abuse in this category are cocaine and the amphetamines. These drugs, in a fashion quite contrary to the barbiturates, are stimulants of the central nervous system. They are sought after because they allegedly produce a high level of euphoria and are able to sustain people over long and exhausting periods of work or through long bouts of any kind of activity. The addicting qualities of the stimulants and the tolerance factor associated with them are not definitely established. It is clear that they do not impose the strongly addicting grip that heroin may clamp on those who experiment with it for any length of time, nor do they share the high tolerance factor found both with heroin and the barbiturates. But it appears that for some people a tolerance factor does develop with use of stimulants, and in some, a psychic dependency arises so strong as to be virtually indistinguishable from physiological addiction.

Continued use or occasional use of high doses of cocaine or the amphetamines poses substantial danger to health. All these drugs have some legitimate medical uses, though it is probable that amphetamines in the recent past have been prescribed too freely, with some serious consequences.

THE OPIATES

When we speak of drug addiction, as opposed to drug abuse, it is no doubt the opiates that spring to mind most readily. These drugs take their name from the opium poppy from which they are all ultimately derived, whether in the form of opium itself, morphine, or heroin. We must also include here the synthetic companions or substitutes, such as methadone.

These drugs are sought after because of the sedative, tranquilizing effect they produce, with a liberation from concern and tension, and often an accompanying more affirmative condition of cheerfulness and mild euphoria. When injected intravenously it is said that the initial response also includes a joyous experience often referred to as the "buzz" or the "rush." Heavy overdoses of opiates can kill, though death is not swift but is reached after a prolonged coma when the patient may easily be rescued by available antidotes if medical attention is at hand. There is much controversy about the alleged high number of deaths of street addicts from overdoses, since the symptoms and manner of death in these cases do not appear to conform to what we know of opiate coma. One theory is that these deaths are not properly attributable at all to simple overdose but are the result of a violent reaction found in some people to a combination of opiates and alcohol or barbiturates.[1]

Apart from the danger from a very substantial overdose, the deleterious effects of opiate use are not necessarily grave. Professor Lindesmith writes:

> The relative normality of the heroin or morphine addict contrasts sharply with the state of the alcoholic, the barbiturate addict, or persons under the influence of marihuana. While the opiate addict suffers more than his share of physical disease and minor troubles, such as constipation, lack of sex-

> ual desire, and tooth decay, there is no known major tissue pathology associated with heroin and morphine addiction as there is with the abuse of alcohol. There are many examples of drug addicts who have continued to engage in productive work and who have even had positions of eminence while they were using drugs.[2]

Constipation, lack of sexual desire, and tooth decay are not exactly desirable conditions, but they are a far cry from the catastrophic images of physical breakdown often associated with heroin addiction. One explanation for this is that the addict's pathology has more to do with the social attitudes and regulations that cluster around heroin use than with the pharmacology of the drug. What is distinctively dangerous about the opiates is their potent combination of a high tolerance factor with a strong addictive grasp. But even this long-entrenched dogma, while not basically challenged, is now being subjected to some qualification. Research on addiction is of recent origin, and some of the latest studies conjecture that large numbers of people have used opiates frequently without becoming addicted. It is also believed now that some people are able to achieve voluntarily a comfortable state of maintenance on regular doses of the drug without feeling a sharp need to escalate the intake. Even the pangs of withdrawal, so often dramatically portrayed in fiction and in the Establishment literature on addiction, may not be as hideous as we had been led to believe. Some students of the subject think that breaking heroin addiction may not be any harder than the task of the confirmed smoker in giving up tobacco (though this may be agonizingly difficult), and that the attendant discomforts, though very real, are of a dimension much less than we had supposed. It is undoubtedly true that the propensity to addiction and its strength once it attaches vary a great deal among people and that until recently we had generalized much too broadly.[3]

Penal Legislation

At least in comparison with the barbiturates, the opiates appear as comparatively mild and even beneficent drugs. We are again led back to the question of why heroin use has attracted so much of the organized energies of the state, so much Establishment fury, and so much concern from ordinary people. A partial explanation must lie in the simple misconceptions about the properties of the drug. This has led in turn to a campaign of criminalization, a street life associated with crime, and a rootless departure from the ordinary norms of settled life, which have forced heroin upon the popular consciousness. The more deadly barbiturates have been used and pursued more quietly, away from the spotlight, and cloaked with the respectability of their easy availability by medical prescription.

It was not always so. Opium smoking became known in the United States in the early nineteenth century, through the arrival of addicted oriental immigrants. Later, morphine base was isolated from opium, and German chemists developed the even more powerful derivative, heroin. Until late in the nineteenth century, not much was known about the addictive properties of opiates, and many people became addicted (including thousands of Civil War wounded) as a result of continuing medical prescription. Others turned to cheap and easily available morphine as an escape from brutish living conditions or to relieve anxieties and inadequacies. One study suggests that there existed in the late nineteenth century a large group of poor white, rural addicts in the South and that, all over the country, there was a significant number of middle-class addicts, many of them professional people and with many housewives among them. It is quite impossible to estimate the number of addicts in the United States at that time, but some recent studies have made informed guesses that the addicted proportion of the population was considerably higher then than now.[4]

While apprehension increased with a growing awareness of the powerful addictive properties of opiates, no public connection was made in the nineteenth century between these substances and the commission of crime or danger to persons other than the user. Since opiates are in themselves tranquilizing and mildly euphoric in their effect, the legal and untrammeled use of them had no natural tendency to lead to crime. And since morphine is very cheaply manufactured, so that the largest habit could be satisfied for a few pennies a day under conditions of legal sale, no collateral incentive existed to commit crimes to raise money for the purchase of the drug. If the legislators of the early twentieth century could have foreseen the cocoon of criminality that would in time surround the continuing use of these drugs, they might well have shrunk back from the criminalizing legislation that they introduced. But of course they could not foresee this, and they were quite rightly much troubled by the easy availability of a potently addictive substance. They chose the path of enacting penal legislation.

On the federal level the basic statute that set the pattern for all regulation until very recently was the Harrison Act of 1914.[5] This statute, aimed primarily at opium and its derivatives and cocaine, was in form a tax measure, prohibiting all transactions in the drugs without obtaining appropriate licenses. Since such licenses are unavailable except for medical and legitimate manufacturing purposes, the effect was to criminalize the use and possession and sale of these drugs except within narrow medical boundaries.

Many states had introduced their own criminal legislation even before the Harrison Act. Then in 1932 a Uniform Drug Act was drawn up as a model by the National Conference of Commissioners on Uniform State Laws. This model statute, soon adopted by most states, harmonized state laws with the federal pattern and threw a tightly woven blanket of criminalization over the use of opiates, cocaine, and marihuana. Federal law was revised in a consolidating and rationalizing statute of 1970, known as the Comprehensive Drug Abuse Prevention and Control Act.[6] This statute welds the welter of federal prohibitions into a more elegant and harmonious structure and makes sensible reductions of penalties for the mere possession of small quantities of certain drugs. At the same time, it can only be seen as a continuation of a general policy of criminalization. Changes in state laws in recent years tend to reduce penalties for the use of marihuana but are also often marked by a steep escalation of penalties for sale or possession of opiates or cocaine.

Judicial Response

In the courts the approaches to drug legislation have kept step with the level of popular sentiment. The language of the original Harrison Act did not explicitly rule out the possibility of legal prescription of morphine by private doctors to addict patients. But a series of court decisions following that statute restricted the range of legal prescription so tightly that private doctors were in effect scared out of the business of treating addicts and simply ceased to do so.[7] More recently, a growing body of studies that reveal the medical and social realities of addiction and drug abuse has contributed to a more inquiring and critical examination of penal drug statutes by the courts.

"HARD" DRUGS

In 1961, in the case of *Robinson* v. *California*,[8] the Supreme Court of the United States had to pass on a challenge to a California statute that made it a crime for a person to be addicted to the use of narcotics. Under the statute it was not necessary for a person to be caught in the act of using a drug, nor even with the drug in his possession. It was sufficient simply to prove that the person was in fact addicted to the use of the drug. Presumably this could be shown by evidence of frequent recent use and by such physical marks as needle tracks.

The common law has always frowned on criminal liability in the absence of proof that the defendant has done some prohibited "overt" act. In England, where there is no Bill of Rights giving judges a power of veto, the courts will nevertheless go to great lengths, in interpreting a statute, to avoid a finding of guilt in the absence of an overt act, or prohibited omission. The California statute clearly appeared to offend against this traditional common-law abhorrence of guilt without action, but only a doctrine of constitutional dimension could permit the Supreme Court of the United States to strike down a state enactment. Armed with its constitutional weapons, the Supreme Court took a radical route and held that the statute violated the "cruel and unusual punishments" clause of the Eighth Amendment, which is applicable to the states through its incorporation in the due process clause of the Fourteenth Amendment. The statute was thus unconstitutional on its face.

Before *Robinson* the "cruel and unusual punishments" clause had been applied sparingly and only in cases where some feature of the punishment itself or its mode of application was barbaric, bizarre, or capricious. *Robinson* rests on the wider proposition that any punishment will be cruel and unusual unless it meets the moral test of being imposed as a response to the doing of a prohibited act. Being an addict, said the Court, is in itself a status or condition or sickness. This condition does not logically entail doing any voluntary acts, even in the past, since addiction could conceivably have been implanted by medical negligence. Even if the addiction, as is more likely, came about as a result of the defendant's voluntary experimenting with heroin at some time in the past, the prosecution need offer no proof of this under the California statute. The basis of the statutory liability was simply that the defendant presently was in the condition of being an addict. To punish a person for being in such a condition is no more constitutionally defensible than to punish a person for having a cold.

Robinson is a splendid demonstration of the overlapping nature of legal and moral argument in the constitutional area. Its implications for several areas of criminal liability are large, for it raises, among others, the following question: If a condition is not a proper reason for punishment, how can an irrepressible symptom of the condition be a proper reason? If we cannot punish a person for having a cold, can we with justice punish the person for sneezing? If we cannot punish an addict for being addicted, how can we with justice punish him for using the drug or for possession of such a quantity as is necessary to maintain his habit?

The Supreme Court retreated from some of these implications in *Powell* v. *Texas* (1968).[9] In *Powell* the petitioner had been convicted for being drunk in a public place. He argued that he was an alcoholic and that his drunkenness was an irrepressible symptom of that condition, thus in effect invoking the *Robinson* decision to urge the Supreme Court to reverse his conviction. But the Court was able to distinguish *Robinson* and leave Powell's conviction undisturbed. Though different reasons for this holding are distributed among the Court's majority opinions, the principal theme is that we cannot be clear that alcoholism deprives a person of choice and control to such an extent that he cannot help being drunk in a public place. The conduct of the defendant could be construed as a voluntary act and not as the irrepressible symptom of a condition.

This argument may not be very convincing, particularly if applied to vagrant alcoholics who have no home in which to be drunk privately. It may seem even less persuasive when applied to the heroin addict. If the received wisdom about addiction is reliable then, at least for many addicts if not all, the craving and urge to take regular doses of the drug are overwhelming, perhaps irresistible. A federal statute of 1970 speaks of an addict as "one who is so addicted to the use of narcotic drugs as to have lost the power of self-control with reference to his addiction."[10] When the government itself, in its own legislation, makes an express judgment that the power of self-control is gone, it would seem to have abdicated its right to punish.

One legal concept that could be applied to relieve the addict of criminal liability for possession of the drug would be the traditional common-law defense of duress, recognized in all jurisdictions. The chemically controlled craving to possess the drug has been called a kind of pharmacological duress. But it could be said in reply that duress is not applicable since the addict initially exposed himself to the dangers of addiction by voluntary experimentation with the drug. Here we could fall back on the stronger *Robinson* constitutional position. The status of addiction logically entails the regular use of heroin and consequently the regular possession of the drug. Surely a person should not be punished because he happens to be detected in the course of conduct that is an ineluctable incident of a condition for which he constitutionally cannot be punished. The force of this moral theorem appeared to be impressing itself on some courts, who suggested that there would be such a barrier to conviction. But the jurisdiction in which the matter has been most fully aired, the District of Columbia, rejected the defense by a majority of a full court in *United States* v. *Moore* (1973).[11] The Supreme Court refused to review this decision by the United States Court of Appeals for the District.

It is true that an acceptance of the radical potentiality of *Robinson* would bring us to a position that at first sight might appear strange. Under this reasoning a person who could show himself to be an addict could not constitutionally be convicted of use or possession of a small quantity of the drug, whereas one who could not show himself to be an addict could be convicted. Addiction would become a defense of constitutional dimension to charges of drug use or possession.

Such a position is by no means morally indefensible. We could see it as resting on a policy of protecting people from themselves by punishing them for dangerous experiments, while they still retain the power of choice. Once choice is gone, punishment becomes gratuitously cruel and ineffectual and is therefore ruled out.

As is so often the case, the moral and constitutional propriety of the positions to be taken ultimately depends on answers to empirical questions. The relevant question here is: What exactly is the range of compulsion and deprivation of free choice contained in the concept of addiction? If the "addict" is a person who has truly lost the capacity to abstain from taking the drug, then *Robinson* ought to be extended to relieve him from punishment for taking it and possessing enough of it to continue his habit. But it may be that such a condition is characteristic of only some of those whom we call addicts. There may be others whose habit is sufficiently light, or whose makeup is such, that threats of strong punishment could be effective to cause them to give up the drug. If this is so, then a policy of pursuing the "addicts" themselves with rigorous prosecution and severe penalties, harsh though it may seem, might be the most effective way of controlling drug abuse. The dealer and trafficker have the lure of such enormous profits that no degree of rigor in law enforcement is likely to wipe them out of the picture. If the user himself could be deterred by threats of punishment, law enforcement might have greater hope of success.

But to inquire into the depth of the individual's addiction, into the degree to which he has lost the power to make a choice to abstain, would involve courts in detailed, lengthy, and finely spun investigations in each case where an addict was a defendant. This is no doubt one reason why the judiciary has stepped back from the implications of *Robinson*. Then, again, it could be argued that even though the addict has lost the power to break his habit by an effort of will, he has not necessarily lost the capacity to seek help from a program or agency that might assist him to get off the drug. His decision not to seek such help but to continue to use the drug could be regarded as a voluntary act, the punishment of which does not offend moral or constitutional principles.

The use of "hard" drugs is perhaps not an area where we should expect the courts to intervene in any radical fashion. There can be virtually no doubt that the properties of such drugs as heroin, cocaine, and the amphetamines carry sufficient dangers to confer a perfect constitutional right on the state to regulate their use, even to the point of banning them. Some may think that such a total ban is neither wise nor prudential, but it could hardly be doubted that it is constitutional. If basic changes are desirable, they must in this case come from the legislature. The most that can be constitutionally expected from the courts is that they throw some protection around the addict himself from a too aggressive pursuit by the criminal law.

"SOFT" DRUGS

With "soft" drugs, particularly marihuana, the constitutional arguments for intervention by the courts are more powerful. For decades marihuana has been classified, quite unscientifically, as a narcotic by most penal legislation and has often been included in the same degree of offense and the same penalty range as conduct involving heroin or cocaine. Since the overwhelming weight of published research and analysis demonstrates the insupportable nature of such equations, it is possible to attack some marihuana statutes on a variety of constitutional grounds.

It can be argued that the penalty for marihuana possession in some jurisdictions is cruel and unusual since it is equated with the punishment for possession of very dangerous drugs, such as cocaine, or very addictive drugs, such as heroin. Marihuana should more naturally be ranked with illegal drugs, other than narcotics, which are usually covered by separate statutes carrying much milder penalties. This argument has a double constitutional impact, for it amounts to a contention that the defendant is being denied the equal protection of the laws as well as being subjected to cruel and unusual punishment. It has, however, failed to persuade most courts, who have rejected it by holding that the legislature must be given the widest latitude to classify substances according to its own view of their danger. Judicial interference, the doctrine runs, is only proper and constitutionally mandated when there is no conceivable rational basis for the legislative classification.

But as evidence mounts about the properties of marihuana, some courts have been willing to regard this legislative classification as lacking any conceivable rationality. So the Supreme Court of Illinois in *People* v. *McCabe* (1971)[12] held that the joining of marihuana with narcotics for purposes of prohibition and punishment could not rationally be defended and that marihuana could not be reasonably distinguished from other drugs that were regulated in a more lenient fashion than narcotics. Accordingly, the court found that the great gap between the statutory sentences for marihuana offenders and those for other nonnarcotic drug offenders was in violation of the equal protection clause of the Fourteenth Amendment.

In 1972 the Michigan Supreme Court in *People* v. *Lorentzen*[13] held that the state's minimum twenty-year sentence for the sale of marihuana was cruel and unusual punishment. Punishment, in its traditional deterrent and retributive aspects, should always fit the crime. Though we cannot match the gravity of an offense with the severity of a punishment on any very precisely graduated scale, still we can properly demand that a rough tariff be set up by which heinous offenses are punished more severely than lesser ones. The Michigan court in *Lorentzen* held, in effect, that so gross a departure from the tariff principle as was apparent in the marihuana prohibition amounted to a cruel and unusual punishment. They reinforced this position by appealing to evolving standards of decency, in the light of which the marihuana penalty again appeared obnoxious.

The Constitution clearly does not entrust courts with a license to strike down laws that they may regard as unpopular. But when laws do become unpopular, it is generally because impressive arguments are perceived against their continuance. The marihuana laws may, indeed, be not at all unpopular with a large section of the community, but there can be no doubt that a significant minority, among whom are numbered many young people and many highly educated people, view them as both absurd in their prohibitions and barbaric in their punishments. Judges are well aware of this substantial body of opinion and are better placed than legislators to observe the harsh operation of the statutes against some of the offenders who are brought before them. It is hardly surprising that some courts would eventually turn to the growing body of sophisticated discussion in this field to pluck out arguments that give an unconstitutional face to certain aspects of the marihuana statutes.

But the examples so far given from the Illinois and Michigan courts once again display no more than a cautious and partial intervention. The degree of the offense and the range of the permissible punishment were declared subject to constitutional control, but there was no suggestion that it was constitutionally impermissible to forbid the use of marihuana at all. Such arguments, though much more radical, are possible. It can be contended that there is a fundamental right to use marihuana in private, which is part of the constitutionally protected enjoyment of liberty that cannot be removed without a compelling state interest which, in this case, cannot be shown. Alternatively, the right to use marihuana can be viewed as an expression of the penumbral concept of privacy which, as our earlier discussions of sexual conduct and abortion showed, takes life from the emanations of several Constitutional amendments.

As yet no court has squarely struck down a marihuana statute on such grounds. But some have come very close to such a position. In 1972 the Michigan Supreme Court in *People* v. *Sinclair*[14] nullified a marihuana statute on a variety of grounds, relied upon by different judges, including cruel and unusual punishment, irrational classification, and invasion of personal liberty. In the same year the Supreme Court of Hawaii in *State* v. *Kantner*[15] upheld the local marihuana statute only on technical grounds to do with the proceedings in the particular case, and appeared to offer plurality opinions that the statute was unconstitutional. In that case Judge Levinson expressed the question to be "whether a person has a constitutionally protected right purposely to induce in himself, in private, a mild hallucinatory mental condition through the use of marihuana."[16] He took the view that concepts of liberty in the Fourteenth Amendment and concepts of privacy arising out of several guarantees of the Bill of Rights did extend such a right.

Even so elevated a court as the Federal Second Circuit Court of Appeals has not dismissed out of hand the argument that the federal marihuana statute could be unconstitutional. In *United States* v. *Kiffer* (1973)[17] the appellants had been convicted of being in possession of approximately two tons of marihuana. The Court of Appeals noted that the appellants had argued that cases of this kind should be regarded in the same light as *Griswold* (the U. S. Supreme Court case invalidating a conviction for the use of contraceptives) and *Stanley* (invalidating a conviction for the private possession of pornography). Those cases, and others, held that where a state action *prima facie* infringes on a constitutionally protected or fundamental right, then the state action can only be validated if it is necessary to further a compelling state interest. In *Kiffer* the appellant asserted the existence of a fundamental "right of the individual to control of his own body and to indulge in private in what may be condemned in public or deemed immoral or unacceptable to society at large."[18] The Court of Appeals was not impressed with this contention since, as the court pointed out, the case concerned not private possession or use of a small quantity of marihuana but possession of two tons with intent to sell.

Since the prohibition on sale did not involve the *prima facie* invasion of a constitutional right, the legislation, the court said, must be presumed to be valid unless the defendant could show it to be utterly arbitrary and unconnected with any rational legislative purpose. Reviewing the testimony at the trial with respect to marihuana, the Court of Appeals was unwilling to conclude that the prohibition on sale could not have any rational purpose, and accordingly affirmed the conviction. But at the same time, the court was careful to say that the issue of private use or possession of a small quantity for use was not before it, thus leaving that fight to be fought another day.

Striking down completely all legislative prohibitions on the private use or possession of small quantities of marihuana would not, as the *Kiffer* case shows, necessarily amount to "legalizing" the drug in the full sense of that concept. Sale could still be prohibited, and so could public use. But even the validation by the courts of private use would be a major step, involving an overriding of legislative judgments in the interests of what lawyers call "substantive due process." We have already seen how this has been done with respect to the right of a woman to have an abortion and how such a position also may be building up with respect to the rights of consenting adults to engage in erotic activities in private. Can the desire and interest of an individual to partake of a mild hallucinogenic or euphoric substance be equated with the pursuit of sexual drives or with the autonomy of a woman over her own body? If not, what is the difference? And if a constitutional right can be perceived to use marihuana in private, then why not a constitutional right to use heroin in private? We shall be better equipped to face these questions after the discussion in the next chapter.

VII

Why Regulate Drug Use?

The characteristics of drugs that are fashionably used outside medical prescription and the legislative history of their criminalization, together with the response of the courts, form the contours of the present scheme of regulation. Now it becomes necessary to consider carefully the moral and social arguments for and against the existing penal emphasis. Several introductory cautions and distinctions need to be entered.

In the first place, it obviously makes no sense to think in terms of *one* appropriate solution to the drug problem. The properties and effects of marihuana, barbiturates, cocaine, and heroin are so different that widely differing schemes of regulation may be appropriate for each of these drugs. For our purposes we shall select heroin and marihuana for special consideration.

Second, as we have already seen, the alternatives are not as simple as a stark choice between criminalization and decriminalization. There are many habitable way stations between these terminals. One would be to make the use of marihuana and heroin, and possession of small quantities for use, no crimes at all, while retaining criminal penalties for dealing in the drugs. A slightly more generous step would also lift the criminal ban from "casual transfers" (at least of marihuana), by which we mean transfers of small amounts for personal use that do not indicate a pattern of dealing for profit.

Third, we must bear in mind that the abandonment of penal measures with respect to the heroin addict does not mean that he would necessarily be immune from the reach of the law. "Civil" (noncriminal) statutes exist or may be enacted that treat him as a sick person and set up procedures for his compulsory commitment to an institution. These deserve a scrutiny just as careful as that applied to penal statutes, for they share the essential quality of confining a person against his will.

Heroin

A threshold difficulty about any discussion of the morality and wisdom of criminalization of heroin use is that, though we can say a good deal about the state of affairs produced by the present system of criminal law enforcement, it is much more difficult to know what would be the consequences of a total or partial lifting of those penal laws. Here we have to make an effort of imagination that involves much speculation and conjecture. As in so many social situations, apprehension about the debatable results no doubt accounts in part for clinging to the status quo.

We can begin by looking back to the inception of criminal prohibition of the drug. We know little of the fate of the opiate addicts who found themselves in the early years of this century cut off from their supply of morphine or heroin by the curtain of criminality that swept down. Some must have managed to give up the habit; it is likely that many continued to carry on with supplies from illegal sources. What is clear is that with the passage of time, the character of the drug-using population changed significantly. Opiate addiction no doubt declined dramatically for some decades and, in this narrow and short-term sense, the penal legislation was most successful. Use of opiates became largely confined to exotic cult groups, musicians, and others, and a comparatively small number of medical professionals. Cocaine became a drug of fashion in certain special circles in the 1920s, and marihuana slowly but steadily gained in popularity. Though it is impossible to estimate with any precision, an enormous increase in the use of barbiturates took place. But, apart from a certain amount of hysteria about marihuana, it must have appeared by the 1940s that the drug situation was in hand and that penal policies were working well.

In view of the very small demand for heroin at that time, the street price was very low. An average habit could be maintained for perhaps two dollars a day. Even without a good income, one could afford to be an addict without devoting one's life to "ripping and running," as the argot now puts it. But in the late 1950s and early 1960s, a sudden escalation in the use of heroin began that rapidly seemed to threaten to engulf the whole country.

It became fashionable to speak of it as an epidemic. The response has been a constant winding up of law enforcement to new pitches of high tension.

We do not know exactly why the 1950s and 1960s gave birth to this new fashion. Modern studies have largely discredited the old notion that it was a result of a sinister combination of big-time criminals and low-level pushers who seduced young people into taking drugs and in this way turned them on. Organized crime may be adept at taking advantage of illicit markets, but it probably has never been creative enough to invent them. For a complex of reasons, young people who spent much of their time on big-city streets got interested in heroin, began to take it, and the incidence of its use spread rapidly. We may note here, parenthetically, that use of heroin now appears to be on the decline, and this may be attributable to equally complex psychosocial reasons that may have something or nothing to do with a long policy of tough law enforcement. Indeed, one of the besetting difficulties in this whole area is to arrive at any just estimate of the impact of law enforcement on drug-using fashions. Some consequences of criminalization, on the other hand, are only too clear.

It is a proposition of mere logic that penal laws about drug use create a vast area of criminal conduct with a stroke of the legislative pen. If possession and use of coffee (a substance containing the moderately addictive and dangerous drug caffeine) were to be made criminal tomorrow, many people would no doubt give up coffee drinking, but millions of others would become criminals, and a vast new market for organized crime would have been created. The legislation on opiates in the early years of this century certainly produced that result with the passage of time. In itself this is not a decisive argument against criminalization, since independently good reasons may be found to justify the imposition of penal sanctions. For example, if we were to make possession and use of tobacco a crime, great social misery and hordes of new criminals would be created, but this is not to say that a plausible case could not be made out for such a move. But it remains of great importance to put into the scales of our final judgment an awareness that criminalization has transformed a respectable and law-abiding addict population into one that, for the most part, leads a disorganized and unproductive street life in constant contact with the outcrops of organized crime.

More controversial, because of its cloudy empirical foundations, is the question of the extent to which penal drug laws contribute to an ancillary increase in crimes of theft and violence. We now know well enough that nothing in the impact of heroin on the body and mind of the user is particularly likely to drive him to otherwise unmotivated crime. But when a heroin habit may cost fifty to a hundred dollars a day and the addict is unemployed or marginally employed, the purchasing power must be largely drawn from illicit activities. Some of this income is generated by addicts acting at the same time as small-time dealers—an economic system of a kind referred to in Britain as living by taking in each other's laundry. In the case of some female addicts, a good deal of the necessary funds may be acquired by the very victimless crime of prostitution. But this still leaves a substantial proportion of heroin-buying income to be derived from crimes against property, which may often also be crimes against the person in the form of the familiar mugging.

Some recent studies have indicated that most addicts practice comparatively peaceful stealing (shoplifting, burglary of unoccupied dwellings) and stay away from crimes of robbery involving a confrontation with the victim.[1] Granting this, it remains true that a large volume of thefts is connected with addiction and a certain, indeterminate percentage of crimes of violence against the person. This kind of observation makes it seductively easy to rush to the conclusion that the big-city crime wave, which so rightly frightens many Americans, could be much alleviated by decriminalizing the use of heroin. We might argue that, if law and order were really our first priority, the most effective move to make would be to set up free heroin dispensaries in slum and ghetto areas in our large cities. But, quite apart from the strong moral objections that could be made to such a plan it might also not be very effective in cutting back on crime.

The etiology of violent street crime is profoundly complex. Only some addicts commit such crimes, and we have little warrant for believing that they would cease to do so if they somehow could obtain the drug without cost, or if they were weaned of the habit.

With many people a disposition to commit violent crimes may be one of the features of their personality, which also disposes them to addiction, so that a removal of the economic motive to sustain the habit would not necessarily appease whatever drives them to violent behavior. Again, it is a commonplace that addiction is much connected with the alienated, marginal existence led by young people, often belonging to racial minorities, who live in city slums. Their addiction is in some ways a search for some meaningful pursuit in their lives. As one writer has pointed out, "taking care of business" (the addict phrase for the stealing, fencing, and purchasing of the drug that consumes his time) is a busy way of life.[2] To take away this occupation without providing the substitutes that our morality regards as a decent way of living—reasonable education, job opportunities, and housing—will not necessarily remove the incentive for the alienated to commit crimes. Indeed, for many, the tranquilizing effect of heroin may hold violent impulses at bay. It has been suggested that the marked decline in juvenile street gang warfare in the 1960s was in part due to the rising popularity of the heroin habit. If the streets were swept clean of heroin, it is not at all unrealistic to guess that an increase in violence might result.

The nature and effectiveness of law enforcement in the drug area also properly give rise to troubling questions. Certainly a huge expenditure of resources now flows into pursuing drug offenders and into the detection of economic crimes that are sparked off by addict behavior. The enormous sums of money that big-time drug dealers and importers handle also inevitably lead to a certain amount of corruption among some police officers who cannot resist the financial temptations dangled before them. Again, the process of detecting drug offenders often involves extensive use of undercover agents who make drug purchases, and of informers often "wired" for sound. Wiretapping and bugging of premises are commonplace.

It is very difficult to estimate how efficacious these law-enforcement practices are in reducing the incidence of addiction. Until recently they probably made little impact since, while there were thousands of arrests of users and small dealers, large-scale importers and dealers were rarely touched. Of late there has been a much more energetic and successful pursuit of importers and important distributors. This has been accompanied by what most observers believe to be a falling off in the number of addicts. But so many other factors are at play on the scene that it would be rash to conclude that a cause-and-effect relationship exists between energetic law enforcement and a drop in addiction. Certainly it is logically possible to conceive of international law enforcement eliminating opiate use altogether. If the growing of opium poppies could be entirely stopped and the production of synthetic substitutes similarly eradicated, then there could be no more addicts. But such total success seems a remote possibility, and, if it were to be achieved, we can only wonder what new drugs of abuse, perhaps much more dangerous than heroin, might come into fashion.

Even if the enforcement record in the narcotics area were poor and largely ineffectual, this would not in itself be a good argument for repealing criminal prohibitions. Suppose it were the case that the police catch very few murderers or rapists or robbers, and that the efforts they make in those directions consume an enormous amount of police time and money. That would hardly be a good reason for abandoning legal prohibitions on murder, robbery, and rape. We all agree that those crimes are such grave moral infractions that we must continue to pursue those who commit them, no matter how ineffective the pursuit may sometimes seem to be. The question is whether heroin use falls into the same category. Can we say that the use and sale of heroin, the addiction to it, are harms of such gravity that there are prevailing moral reasons to continue the legal fight, no matter how difficult that may be and no matter what bad side effects it may have?

If the inquiry is confined to the punishment of the addict himself, then the arguments for criminalization seem very thin. Our earlier discussion suggested moral and legal principles that might amount to a defense of coercion or irresistible impulse if the addict is charged with use and possession. On such a charge his punishment might also be regarded as unconstitutional under the cruel and unusual punishments doctrine. In any case, what primary justification could there be for punishing him? Could it be that he is dangerous to others? We have said that he is not dangerous by any reason of the operation of the drug on his person. He may of course become dangerous because of his overwhelming need to acquire the funds to buy the drug, but then we have no moral warrant to convict him until he actually commits a crime of theft or violence, and we should convict him of that crime, not for using drugs. The addict's great need for funds is itself created by criminalization, since the drug would otherwise be available cheaply. To create an artificial scarcity and then punish those who are driven by an irresistible craving to pursue the scarce commodity partakes of a certain *Catch-22* logic.

Since the danger to others is an artificial product of legislation, we have to demand an independent and powerful justification before we could approve morally the present practice of punishing the addict for crimes of use and possession. The most obvious candidate for election here is the contention that the use of drugs is so dangerous to the user that people must be deterred in the most frightening fashion, by the threat of serious criminal penalties. This connects with our general discussion earlier of protecting people from themselves. Here, again, we must be careful of the false logic that the present system of criminalization nudges us into. Of course it is true that under the present scheme of prohibitions the life of the addict is miserable, perhaps "nasty, brutish, and short," unless he or she happens to be rich or a doctor. But if harm to the addict is to be the justification for prohibiting people from using heroin under criminal penalty, we are only entitled to consider that kind of harm that would ensue if there were no penal prohibitions. The harm caused by the operation of the penal law cannot be used to justify the existence of the penal law.

First we must remember that experimenting with or the occasional use of heroin does not inevitably condemn a person to addiction. It only creates a risk of addiction, just as consistent cigarette smoking only creates a risk of lung cancer or heart disease, though no doubt the risk of addiction, when using heroin, is statistically much greater. Until much more research is done, it is very hard to say with any confidence what exactly are the harms and miseries that addiction would impose upon the addict in a society where heroin was readily and cheaply available. We may imagine that some addicts would be able to lead reasonably stable lives on regular and constant doses of the drug. Others would find themselves plagued by the tolerance factor and might have to go through miserable periods of abstinence to reduce the intake. Some would become so enslaved to the very experience of use and its affects that they would be unfitted to do much else in life.

But of course this is precisely the condition in which many addicts now find themselves, except that presently they must cope also with the enormous additional miseries of use in a syndrome of illegality and crime. Would decriminalization produce more misery for more people than the present policy of prohibition? The great question mark here is whether decriminalization would significantly increase the number of users and thus ultimately the number of addicts. This can never be answered finally without making the experiment. Further comment on it awaits a later discussion on the different degrees and forms that decriminalization might take.

Civil Commitment

When the Supreme Court in the *Robinson* case outlawed punishing an addict for his addiction alone, it dangled a tempting alternative before executives and legislatures by suggesting that there would be nothing unconstitutional about locking up addicts by civil process in the same way that we lock up people who are seriously mentally ill. The two most populous states in the nation, New York and California, both burdened by hordes of addicts, accepted the invitation with alacrity. A New York civil commitment statute was enacted in 1968,[3] after a bellicose message to the legislature by Governor Rockefeller, in which the chief executive called for total mobilization and a declaration of war against narcotics dealers and users. The new scheme was proclaimed as a "crusade" that would lead to the final solution to the drug problem.

Essentially the New York statute is applicable to those who are addicted to an opiate drug or who are "in imminent danger" of becoming addicted. Such persons, after a due process hearing to determine the fact of their addiction or imminent danger, may be committed to an institution for a period as long as three years. The institution is avowedly designed to rehabilitate the addict, and the whole of the language of the statute is studiously couched in nonpenal and nonpunitive terms and along the model of a statute for commitment of the mentally ill.

It still, however, involves locking people up for a long time against their will. Does prison by another name smell any sweeter? We certainly do make a proper distinction between the enforced confinement of the seriously mentally ill and imprisonment. Some critics now question the propriety of the extent and scale of our compulsory commitment of those who are mentally ill, but nobody would question that such a procedure is necessary for some and that morally it is utterly distinguishable from punishment for the commission of a crime. But can we equate the opiate addict with the seriously mentally ill person for purposes of justifying his involuntary civil commitment? We are apt to condemn the Soviet government for calling people mentally ill and locking them up, when they simply disapprove of their expressions of political dissent. We must be careful not to expose ourselves to a justified similar charge that we lock up addicts just because they are an inconvenient nuisance to have around and because other methods of dealing with them involve too much imagination and effort.

Is addiction a serious mental illness or somehow substantially equivalent to it?[4] Certainly some addicts are seriously mentally ill. They may have been so before they became addicted, or the business of life as an addict may have contributed to their illness, but these are not quite the questions. We are asking rather whether addiction in itself can be equated with serious mental illness. By definition addiction does involve the concept of being unable to break a particular pattern of behavior by a simple effort of will. In that sense the addict is unable to help himself to stop doing something that he may very much want to stop doing. (This, again, is a syndrome very familiar to confirmed cigarette smokers, who so far have escaped civil commitment.) But, as students of the subject have pointed out, it is not at all true that addiction necessarily involves the loss of all power to make rational decisions about important and necessary aspects of daily living. Indeed, it does not even involve loss of power to make rational decisions about one's habit, as is evidenced by the fact that thousands of addicts have voluntarily committed themselves or sought help through public or private agencies and programs. The equation with the seriously mentally ill person thus falls lamentably short, since the only distinctive and singular mark of the addict is his incapacity to stop using the drug without outside help—if it may be possible even then. This does not make him dangerous to others, and though it poses some danger to him, it is a danger about which he retains the rational power to do something by going to seek help.

If the analogy with serious mental illness is a frail reed to support a theory of civil commitment, one can of course fall back on the concept that the addict is dangerous to others. Indeed, a close reading of Governor Rockefeller's message recommending the New York statute to the legislature, and of the preamble to that statute, reveals that this was seen as the strongest justification for that enactment. In the discussion of criminal punishment we have already seen that danger to others is open to serious attack if it is taken to justify punishment for use or possession of heroin. But at least in the context of a prosecution and punishment, it must be shown, after the *Robinson* decision, that the addict has done some prohibited act. The whole purpose of civil commitment is to avoid this necessity and to lock the addict up on the sole ground that he is an addict without any more proof.

Now it may be true that addicts as a class of people are much more likely to commit criminal acts than those who are not addicts, though, as we have seen, this result is itself an artificial creation of our structure of prohibitions. But such a statistical projection contains no necessary logical implication that any particular addict has committed or will commit any particular crimes. Suppose he were a millionaire addict who could support his habit financially without the least difficulty? In such a case he would present no more of a danger to others than if he were not an addict. But he would still be liable to involuntary commitment under the laws of New York. No doubt a statutory provision that exempted high-income addicts from commitment would fall a victim both to popular outcry and to the equal protection clause of the Constitution. But strict adherence to the logic of a civil commitment statute would lead to making such an invidious discrimination.

The whole notion of confining a group of people on the basis of a statistical projection that a high proportion of criminals is likely to be contained within their number commits fundamental aggression on principles that we have traditionally regarded as sacred. It amounts to a kind of preventive detention of people who cannot be shown to have committed any crime at all. We might say with accuracy that there are sections of a city where the crime rate is enormously high. It may be several hundred per cent higher than in other parts of the same city. We may therefore confidently predict that a certain substantial percentage of people living in that part of the city will commit some crime or other in the next few years. To lock up all the residents of that neighborhood for a few years would thus undoubtedly make a very practical contribution to reducing the crime rate. But no moral person could support such a solution, since it would involve a total abandonment of the principle of personal responsibility and the maxim that punishment is only justified as a response to the doing of a prohibited act by someone. To dub such a procedure "civil commitment" is to sweeten only its title.

The defenders of civil commitment, if pressed in this fashion, may fall back on another argument and another analogy. The addict, they may say, carries around with him a fearful contagion. We have always thought it right to impose compulsory quarantine on people who suffered from smallpox or were carriers of some other highly infectious and dangerous disease. The same reasoning applies with justice to the addict. We may lock him up for just so long as it takes to purge him of his contagion. But this position, too, is fatally flawed.

The analogy with contagious diseases on analysis turns out to be little more than a metaphor. When a person has smallpox, we know beyond a shadow of doubt, by medical experience, that there is the gravest risk of a direct physical transmission. Clearly we cannot mean that heroin addiction is transmitted in that manner. If we talk of contagion in the context of addiction, we mean something much more subtle and elusive, that while loose on the streets the addict may have motives (perhaps inner, psychic ones or perhaps cruder economic ones) to turn other people on. There may be some truth in this, but it is hard to say how much. The literature on addicts gives complex answers to this question. Certainly it appears that some addicts some of the time do try to turn other people on. There is also some evidence that some addicts do their best to convince their friends not to take up the habit. In the early stages of heroin use, before the user is fully addicted, he may find the experience so euphoric that he genuinely wishes his friends to share the joy he is experiencing. When the honeymoon is over and addiction has become a sour routine, he is much less likely to persuade others of the benefits of the life he is leading. And the objective picture presented by the life-style of the confirmed street addict is not likely to be one that in itself attracts others to emulation.

The analogy with contagious diseases also suffers from a tremendous disparity in the length of the confinement necessary to free the carrier of his taint and in the certitude of achieving such a purge. A few weeks at most is the time period we have in mind with traditional quarantine, and the brevity of this period, coupled with the tremendous risk of allowing the carrier to be free, justifies the compulsory confinement. But with opiate addicts, as experience bitterly recounts, months or years of confinement offer only a small hope of final liberation from the chains of the habit. If a contagion is a valid ground for the segregation of addicts in confinement, then it could only be truly effective with a lifetime term. Recoiling from the harshness of this solution, we compromise with a period of enforced isolation that is of dubious moral validity and of even less reliable efficacy.

If all the arguments just laid out could be surmounted, procedures of civil commitment, such as that under the New York statute, remain subject to another devastating stricture. If they are to be defended, they clearly must rest on some thoroughly reliable test for determining who is an addict. But no such test exists, or at least none that is constitutionally defensible. It is easy enough to determine whether a person has recently used heroin, but we know that the concept of addiction is much more complex and extensive than the notion of recent use. Needle tracks on the person's body may reveal that he has used heroin regularly, but there is no way of determining how many marks are so fresh as to indicate that the person has used heroin habitually in the recent past. And there is certainly no way of discovering what dosage he has been taking. The only way of ascertaining whether a person is addicted to an opiate would be to keep that person confined under observation in drug-free surroundings for a sufficient length of time to observe the kind of withdrawal symptoms from which he suffered.

Even this would be unsatisfactory, apart from the fact that it would probably be constitutionally indefensible. Withdrawal symptoms vary enormously from person to person. It is sometimes alleged that the heroin obtainable on the street in most American cities is so "cut" (diluted) that it is very difficult to build up a habit heavy enough to induce acute withdrawal symptoms. Some English studies suggest that withdrawal symptoms are often largely psychosomatic and can be markedly reduced or made to disappear if the addict is deceived into thinking that he is still receiving doses of an opiate.[5] Not only is it, therefore, very difficult to tell whether a person is an addict, because of the inherent vagueness of the concept itself, but it may also be the case that, under a strict definition of addiction, there are very few addicts in the United States, in view of the attenuated nature of the heroin available to them. And if it is often impossible to determine with justice that a person is an addict, then how futile must be the inquiry into whether a person is in "imminent danger" of becoming addicted. Yet the New York statute makes this a sufficient basis for commitment.

The civil commitment statute has received the blessing of the New York courts, but has never been subjected to the scrutiny of a high federal court. The Supreme Court did suggest in *Robinson* that civil commitment may be a proper procedure, but they did not have to decide that question, and their remarks may not have been well considered. All the criticisms laid out above could be translated into constitutional attacks. The difficulty of identifying an addict and the vagueness of the concept of "imminent danger" amount to due process arguments; the central argument that the compulsory detention does not serve a compelling state interest is another due process line of attack.

Yet a third due process approach is possible here. If civil commitment is justifiable at all, it is because of the predicate on which it rests—namely, that people are not being punished, are not being sent to prison. They are being sent to what is described in the statute as a "facility" to receive "treatment." The courts have begun to say in the 1960s and 1970s, in cases to do with commitment for mental illness, that where the provision of treatment is the vital factor distinguishing the incarceration from punishment, then the state is under a burden to prove that treatment is actually afforded.[6] Government cannot escape the constitutional restrictions on criminal proceedings and the infliction of punishment by simply shifting provisions into a different section of the code and affixing new labels. Prisons may be called "facilities," the accused may be called the "respondent," the sentence may be called "commitment," and so on, but without some substantial change in the reality of the process to which the person is subjected, this is no more than Orwellian Newspeak. If a showing could be made that the facilities to which addicts are sent do not offer any meaningful treatment, that in reality inmates are simply stored there with no more than a minimal façade of pretended therapy, then such custody would be in defiance of the Constitution and the release of the inmate could be obtained by a writ of habeas corpus. A civil rights action for damages against the state officials might also be possible.

To topple the statutes on this "lack of treatment" ground is not, however, a very likely avenue to success. The courts have advanced the principle, but in practice they have been willing to be persuaded by even very slender evidence from state authorities that some kind of therapy is being offered. The state of many public institutions for the confinement of the mentally ill is such that an energetic application of this due process principle by the courts would result in a general "jail delivery." No doubt frightened by this possible consequence, the courts are currently flirting with the principle, using it chiefly as a goal to encourage state authorities to improve at least minimally the quality of such institutions.

If the moral and constitutional justifications for the compulsory commitment of heroin addicts are dubious, the record of empirical success is no better. The New York scheme, introduced with such fanfare in 1967, has been so spectacularly unsuccessful that it appears to be quietly lapsing into obsolescence. In 1972, confessing the failure of all previous approaches, Governor Rockefeller of New York presented to the state legislature a new statute that returned with a vengeance to the old road of criminalization.[7] Savage escalations of penalties for dealing in drugs (including marihuana) were enacted, coupled with provisions that restricted the possibility of plea bargaining or parole. The principle acted on appears to be that if something new has failed to work, then one should try even more of what failed to work earlier. It has apparently as yet not occurred to anyone in high places that the problem of drug abuse may be one that legal regulation can do very little to affect, one way or the other.

Marihuana

While heroin remains for most Americans (and with some good reasons) a drug that inspires fear and revulsion, cannabis, in the smoking version known as marihuana, has become as familiar to millions as alcoholic drink is to others. The chasm between official legal condemnation and popular attitudes may not yet yawn as wide as in the days of Prohibition, for there is a generation gap, with middle-aged and older people, who grew up on a diet of whiskey and martinis, remaining suspicious of the new-fangled psychoactive substitute used by their children. In many rural areas this popular suspicion and, indeed, distaste may still be very strong. But unless fashion veers off in another direction, each year is likely to see more widespread community contempt and disdain for the marihuana laws.

Cannabis has come under the most intensive scrutiny by public commissions of inquiry in Britain (1968), Canada (1970), and the United States (1972). The commissions examined with considerable thoroughness every contention of harmfulness that had been made with respect to using the drug and every argument that could be advanced for decriminalization. They all came to the conclusion that, while cannabis use should not be encouraged, there was no good case for making its use or possession of small quantities and casual transfers offenses of any gravity. The British and Canadian commissions recommended that use and possession of small quantities be a very minor offense, while the United States commission advocated the complete removal of penalties for private use. All three studies, however, were in favor of continuing severe penalties for private trafficking or possession of large quantities with intent to sell.

No professional authority would assert that there is a finally proven case that marihuana is a totally harmless substance. Majority scientific opinion holds that there is no convincing evidence of any harm to the user from regular moderate use; but there remains a substantial element of doubt about the possibility of deleterious effects from continued heavy usage. In the *Kiffer* case, in the Second Circuit Court of Appeals, discussed in the previous chapter, the court, on the question of the constitutionality of the marihuana laws, considered evidence on the harmfulness of use. The principal witness for the defense was Dr. Lester Grinspoon, a clinical professor of psychiatry at Harvard Medical School, who is the author of a leading text on the subject of marihuana. The court said:

"In addition it was stipulated that five other experts would have supported Dr. Grinspoon's conclusions, which were, in brief, that marihuana is neither physically nor psychologically harmful to most users and not particularly susceptible of abuse, and that those few who might suffer ill-effects through overindulgence probably have personality disorders that would lead them to abusive use of whatever drugs they might succeed in obtaining."[8]

In rebuttal a government witness, also a professor of psychiatry, testified that use of high-grade marihuana by volunteers in a study in which he was engaged often induced psychotic episodes. Dr. Grinspoon himself conceded that an article in a British medical journal asserted that long-term use of marihuana led to brain damage. While Dr. Grinspoon did not believe that article to be credible, he agreed that "the effect of marihuana regarding brain damage is not known."[9]

One writer has pointed out that what we know about marihuana would give us considerable pause if it were a new substance that a drug house was wanting to release for medical use:

> Suppose a pharmaceutical firm proposed to release a drug with the possible side effects reported at Stockholm (a symposium on cannabis in 1971) or in the World Health Organization Technical Report No. 478, 1971—accumulation in body fat, interference with microsomal enzymes, tachycardia, teratogenecity, serious effects on driving skill, amotivation which may be related to actual brain damage and sometimes unpleasant psychotic effects. Although some of this evidence is based on animal work, some on humans, there would be quite enough warning signals to resist approval.[10]

These comments are obviously important, but the analogy with the release of a new drug by a pharmaceutical firm is most misleading. We may agree that we should scrutinize with a supercritical eye any new substance that a commercial house or a profession wishes to launch into the world solely for claimed therapeutic purposes. But marihuana occupies a quite different social setting. Nobody claims that we ought to discount the possible harmful effects of long-range use of marihuana because we need it for medical reasons. Marihuana is a substance already in use as a drug of choice for reasons of pleasure by a substantial minority of the population, who seem strongly disinclined to give it up in spite of the existence of criminal penalties. This existing practice and expression of public choice call for an evaluation and a response of a different nature.

All experts agree that whatever may be said about the possible harmful effects of overindulgence in marihuana or its long-range use can be topped by much more horrifying pictures of the damage done by cigarette smoking, the use of alcohol, and perhaps even caffeine. Cigarettes, alcohol, and coffee are legal, so how, some ask, can we without hypocrisy and injustice ban marihuana and punish its users? But, from the other side of the debate, this, in its turn, is too simple a response. Cigarettes, alcohol, and coffee are deeply ingrained in our culture and are used by millions of people. Though we now know enough about at least cigarettes and alcohol to realize that it would be much better for most people if they did not use them at all, or used them very little, it may be too late to go back and attempt by penal legislation to wipe out such familiar and cherished accoutrements of our way of life. But marihuana use has hardly yet reached such an entrenched status. Even if its use is less dangerous than that of cigarettes and alcohol, the argument might run, there is no warrant for reversing an existing situation of illegality when there is still considerable doubt about how harmful its use may be. The doctrine of equal protection, after all, is not a doctrine that demands that government must continue to make equal mistakes.

Apart from the possibly harmful effects stemming immediately from cannabis use, a hallowed argument of the defenders of the status quo has been that marihuana smoking has a tendency to lead to the use of more dangerous drugs, notably heroin. It may well be true that most heroin users smoked marihuana before they first used heroin, but, as someone has pointed out, most of them also drank milk before they used heroin. A sequence of events in itself tells us nothing about cause and effect, especially when the observation can be made that the vast majority of those who use marihuana do not go on to use heroin. Most researchers have not been impressed by the claim that the use of marihuana leads people to heroin in any meaningful way. The truth is more likely to be that certain people have a disposition to experiment with drugs and to become imprisoned by them. It is natural for such people to work their way up the ladder of available substances. But it would be rash to assume that if marihuana were unavailable, the move onward and upward could be frustrated. To put this more strongly, one might assert that the sort of person who is likely to experiment with heroin is very unlikely to be diverted in his progress by knowledge that the use of marihuana is prohibited by a criminal penalty.

The affirmative arguments in favor of legalizing at least the private use of marihuana are impressive. Advocates point to the fact that the drug is widely used and accepted and is, at the least, probably less harmful than legal drugs such as alcohol and tobacco. Its use is certainly a victimless crime, and the only possible justification for continuing criminal liability is the fragile one of protecting the user from himself. Young people, it is said, are led into contempt for the law and also into contempt for Establishment guidance when they discover the apparent harmlessness of a substance they have been told must be prohibited because it is so dangerous. This cynicism about teaching on the subject of drugs may positively encourage young people to use drugs (such as barbiturates and amphetamines) that are extremely dangerous, simply because officially disseminated information about these drugs will have lost credibility from the marihuana experience. The present state of the law also opens an extra market for organized crime and induces young people to make contact with criminals in order to obtain the drug. Law enforcement in the marihuana area is expensive and resource depleting as well as extremely ineffectual. A few unlucky users and some dealers suffer disgrace and punishment, while the vast majority remains untouched.

As with the use of heroin, legalization of marihuana may mean many things. The most modest proposal, that of the United States Commission, would legalize only private use, while retaining penalties for dealing and possession of large quantities. The most radical advocates would allow legal sale. So sweeping a change would involve finding answers to a host of subsidiary questions, such as who should control the commercial distribution (free enterprise or a government monopoly), what the quality of the substance should be, what regulations should surround the commerce in the nature of licensing, age of purchasers, etc.

The problem here is in one sense very different from the difficulties that surround heroin law reform. With heroin we are dealing with addicted persons, and much of the discussion has to do with affording them some legal access to the drug or a satisfactory substitute. With marihuana, the claim is not that it is cruel or useless to deny addicts access to what they crave, but rather that people have a legitimate claim to pursue a pleasure that is not vicious or self-destructive. In that light the claim for legalizing the sale of marihuana appears stronger than a similar claim with respect to heroin, which is rarely made. Whether a satisfactory solution can be reached by legalizing only use without at the same time legalizing sources of distribution will be one of the themes of the next chapter.

VIII

Other Approaches to Drug Abuse

The punishment of heroin addicts who are not engaged in trafficking attracts less and less support. Many still advocate a civil process of confinement for addicts, but, as the earlier discussion showed, this procedure is also open to the gravest doubts, both as to its moral acceptability and its efficacy.

To give up compulsory confinement of addicts, under whatever label, need not involve abandoning efforts to stem addiction nor the offer of assistance to addicts who ask for it. Indeed, a variety of techniques and programs is available that may help many addicts. These programs have radically different goals, for some are designed to get the addict off all opiates in a short space of time, while others aim to substitute a legalized and more manageable addiction that will give opportunities for great improvements in the addict's way of life. Recently, techniques of combating heroin by the use of other drugs (pharmacological intervention) have become increasingly fashionable, as we become more skeptical about the capacity of law enforcement or civil commitment to master the problems. Fighting drugs with drugs may take several forms.

Pharmacological Intervention

DETOXIFICATION

By detoxification we mean a comparatively brief period of alleviating the addict's real or imagined withdrawal pangs by weaning him off heroin with a tapering down dosage of a heroin substitute such as methadone. Other drugs such as tranquilizers may be used to help the addict cross the dreaded hurdle of withdrawal. The logic of detoxification implies a resolve and purpose to give up opiates. Since opiates are administered only briefly with the aim of helping the addict to abandon them, it is difficult to imagine any rational objections to such a program. However, simple detoxification without any further treatment or therapy is very unlikely to succeed in terminating a heroin habit. Relapse into drug use will be the usual development.

MAINTENANCE (METHADONE)

During the Second World War, when Germany was cut off from supplies of the opium poppy, its ingenious scientists put together a synthetic opiate substitute known as methadone. Though not a true opiate, it closely mimics the action of opium and, for this reason, is called an opioid. It is itself a powerful pain reliever and sedative and is highly addictive.

In the 1960s, Drs. Vincent Dole and Marie Nyswander of New York began to advocate, as a result of their research, the use of methadone to stabilize heroin addicts and remove their need to pursue illegal heroin on the streets. After much controversy, this methadone proposal gained many converts and, by 1972, became the most favored and most vigorously pursued of government programs for addiction. It is not difficult to see why, for methadone has much to promise officialdom. It offers what to some may seem to be a quick, technological solution: It is cheap and apparently uncomplicated; it produces very visible results and, by alleviating the misery of addicts and reducing street crime, it may at last convince the public that a workable solution has been found. So it is not surprising that early complaints that the use of methadone simply transferred addiction from an opiate to an opioid were soon stilled, at least in official circles.

Methadone undeniably has remarkably useful properties in improving the life-style of the addict. Dr. Frances Gearing, who has monitored a methadone program in New York City, listed in 1972 the following advantages of this form of maintenance.[1]

1. Methadone is a longer acting drug than heroin, and a patient can be maintained on one dose a day, as compared with the four to six injections of heroin that he might find necessary.
2. Methadone is very effective when given orally. It is normally taken in a drink and, in the form in which it is now customarily

furnished to patients in the United States, is not injectable. This is certainly a somewhat more convenient form of administration, but it is not obvious that it is an overwhelming advantage. It is true that many of the illnesses associated with addiction (hepatitis, endocarditis, tetanus, malaria) stem from unsterile injections. But this is a symptom of street illegality and would not arise from clinic injections. The real importance here may be that the "needle" has acquired a peculiar symbolic horror for the American public and medical profession. American observers of the British maintenance system have sometimes expressed shock at the practice in some programs there of allowing addicts to inject methadone or heroin.

3. Many patients on methadone can be built up to a steady, stabilizing dose on an ambulatory basis. This permits them to seek jobs and to lead a more or less normal life-style apart from the sheer fact of their continued addiction to an opioid. The importance of this claim is challenged by some critics. There is continued disagreement about whether methadone is inherently superior to heroin as a stabilizer that avoids the potent tolerance factor. Any orally ingested opiate or opioid is slower acting and longer lasting than an injected dose, though its impact is less potent. Some British doctors have suggested that methadone has no inherent superiority to heroin as a stabilizer and that the American programs have achieved some success in this direction simply because they administer extremely large oral doses.[2]

4. Methadone maintenance, it is claimed, produces a heroin blockade. By this is meant that an addict, receiving regular maintenance doses of methadone, will experience no increased euphoric or tranquilizing effect from taking heroin and therefore has no incentive to seek a supply of the illegal drug. Again, some students of the subject, particularly in Britain, question this as an inherent virtue of methadone. They argue that the blockade effect is simply a factor of the large doses administered in most American programs. A similar effect could presumably be obtained by administering a correspondingly large dose of heroin itself.

5. The long-term medical side effects of methadone maintenance do not appear to be harmful in any significant respect. For some addicts, maintenance has gone on long enough to make

this a meaningful judgment. It is hardly a surprising one, since what we know of opiates leads us to believe that the same judgment could be made of maintenance on morphine or heroin itself.

6. Dr. Gearing concludes that methadone maintenance programs have a considerable rate of success. But the nature of this conclusion is only that among patients who accept methadone treatment and remain long enough in the program to be stabilized, the retention rate is in the range of 80 to 85 per cent after three years.

This is certainly in itself encouraging, but many caveats must be interjected lest we become too optimistic. The figures refer only to addicts who were initially accepted into the program and remained long enough to be stabilized. In the early days of methadone treatment, great care was used to select patients who gave promise of responding well. The figures thus tell us little or nothing about what percentage of the general population of addicts is likely to be successfully stabilized for a long period. The raw figures also tell us nothing about how great a return to "normal" living was made by those who were successfully stabilized. As methadone maintenance has become the treatment of fashion and programs have vastly expanded, it appears that the success rate, even under Dr. Gearing's rather narrow criteria, may be diminishing considerably.

But with all the qualifications and reservations, it is undeniable that methadone maintenance does mark something of a breakthrough in the American approach to addiction. It signals a partial withdrawal from the penal approach, a recognition that the addict is a person who needs support and treatment, and a healthy admission that for many addicts, treatment must mean long-range, and perhaps lifetime, opioid maintenance, since "cure," in the sense of completely dropping the habit, is for many impossible. In this way a significant number of addicts have been able to achieve a dramatic improvement in their life-style. They may now be bound to opioids by hoops of steel, but at least they can step off the treadmill of the street pursuit of the illegal drug. Some are able to return to productive work and the support of their families. These most successful patients are liberated from the need to steal, so that there is some reduction, though we cannot say how large a one, in the volume of drug-connected crime.

There can be no doubt that methadone maintenance must be continued until, if that should ever be, improved treatments are discovered. But this recognition of the value of methadone should not blind us to dangers in the ideology and practice of some of the present programs. In the first place, we need totally to disabuse ourselves of the cant and hypocrisy contained in the suggestion, express or tacit, that methadone treatment is a cure for addiction. It is quite simply and literally the substitution of one opiate addiction for another. Continued and subtle research is needed to measure the success rate of these programs. Some studies point out that many methadone patients are unable to return to work or a life-style at all resembling normality. Many, while no longer seeking heroin, continue a pattern of drug-taking behavior and supplement their methadone doses with barbiturates or alcohol. Some patients do not respond favorably to methadone at all and drop out of the programs. Many addicts are so little attracted by the programs that they never apply for acceptance.[3]

Some programs are to be faulted for being too crudely preoccupied with the number of addicts who can be regarded as stabilized and paying too little attention to other important criteria of success. Too little attention is often paid to the follow-up services of a social and therapeutic kind, which may be necessary to pursue the personality traits or social deprivations that have pulled the addict into his relationship with drugs. Not enough effort is made to give the stabilized addict an entrée back into the normal world. It should be emphasized that if there is blame here, it usually should not be placed on the hard-working and preoccupied administrators of particular methadone programs, but rather on the higher-level drug program planners who may sometimes be too beguiled with the impression of success displayed by mere enrollment figures.

Some political spokesmen for minority groups have attacked all opiate maintenance programs and, in their most bitter language, have called them a form of genocide. If such attacks are overexcited, they do contain a kernel of truth in their perception that methadone maintenance programs are not always accompanied by a serious effort to wean away from the drug those who might be candidates for kicking the habit. American methadone maintenance was born with the intention of administering "saturation" doses to addicts so that their desire for illegal street heroin would be stilled. It was a response framed and controlled by the official perception of the use of illegal heroin as a cause for anxiety bordering on panic. Cynically, one could regard the whole scheme as an enormous perversity, allowing as it does massive administration of an opioid to go on legally, while at the same time expending huge sums of money and volumes of energy to prevent people taking an opiate. Methadone, for obscure reasons, has become the clean opiate while heroin remains par excellence, the dirty one.

But in the end, the defensibility of maintenance programs turns on the prospects of achieving complete "cure" by some other technique. If there were some ready and effective means of liberating addicts altogether from their addiction, then no maintenance program could be morally justified. In the present state of knowledge, it seems agreed that complete liberation is a likely prospect only for a minority of addicts. If this is so, then maintenance is eminently justified, even if the fullest measure of its success can be to reduce crime and offer the addict an improved way of living. But there can be no excuse for a maintenance program that simply accumulates addicts on its rolls without striving to identify those who wish to be drug free and might succeed in that endeavor.

MAINTENANCE (HEROIN)

The main principled justifications for heroin maintenance are the same as for methadone—that it is a humanitarian measure designed to enable addicts to lead a better life, that it will cut down on crime, and that in some cases it may allow a measure of medical supervision and other therapy that can wean the addict off the drug altogether. But it is not at all clear whether we need a heroin program side by side with a methadone program.

The prevailing opinion in the United States seems to be that anything heroin can do, methadone can do better. However, voices are raised, contending that there are many addicts who do not find methadone an adequate substitute for heroin and so drop out of methadone programs. Others do not even initiate themselves into methadone clinics because of the singular attachment they have, or believe they have, to heroin. A heroin maintenance program, operating as a backstop to methadone programs to absorb the addicts who do not take to the other drug, might fulfill a vital supplementary role. Or so some argue.

The British experience may be instructive here. Until 1968 the British permitted private physicians to prescribe heroin to addicts, either in the hope of curing the habit or as a program of maintenance. (It may be observed parenthetically that while heroin has no legal uses in America, it is prescribed by doctors in Britain for ordinary medical purposes.) In the late 1960s there was, in British terms, a steep escalation in the number of addicts, though the addiction figures have always been ludicrously small in comparison to the American picture. Part of this increased use of heroin was traced to the irresponsible actions of some doctors who, either for profit or for reasons of principle, were prescribing large quantities of heroin rather freely. In response, the British removed by legislation the power of the private physician to prescribe heroin to an addict patient (it may still be prescribed for other medical purposes to nonaddicts), and transferred the care of addicts to treatment centers, which are usually attached to hospitals.[4]

In perhaps typically British fashion, there is no statutory or administratively prescribed single mode of treatment at the clinics across the country. This is left to the professional judgment of the medical administrators. The result is that some treatment centers will offer heroin maintenance by injection, some will have nothing to do with heroin but will offer methadone by mouth or injection, some offer methadone by mouth only, and some will administer no opiates at all except for detoxification. Not unnaturally, this has produced a variety of competing claims, and it seems probable that each of the methods has worked well for some people. While some British experts contend that for some addicts no treatment other than heroin maintenance can have any efficacy, others disagree. Many British doctors apparently regard the regular administration of moderate doses of heroin as more defensible than the massive doses of methadone orally administered in some American programs.

Perhaps the sharpest lesson of the British experience is that we still do not know very much about the etiology of addiction nor about the relevance of different treatment methods to a taxonomy or typology of addiction. If we are to find out more, Britain is the most promising laboratory, since it has in operation a variety of different treatment programs, most of which are being studied with patient scientific scrutiny. Though the detailed answers are not at all clear, it might be fair to prophesy that we shall have to accept that no single method of treatment is likely to work for all or most addicts. A flexible and varied spectrum of treatment offerings will have to be put forward. This lesson is perhaps slowly sinking home in the United States. With respect to drug abuse, one of the American mistakes has been the single-minded search for the perfect solution—the one program that would stamp out the evils of illegal drug use. At first, it was to be law enforcement and, when that was less than wholly successful, methadone maintenance was offered as a method which, if it could not eradicate addiction, could at least divert it into less antisocial channels. But a single technological counterblow to addiction is unlikely to succeed. More imaginative construction of multifaceted programs tailored to special types of addicts will have to be devised. Among these, heroin maintenance may have a place.

Opiate maintenance was once briefly tried in the United States. After the passage of the Harrison Act and similar state legislation, some authorities recognized a need to do something for the suddenly deprived addict, and in some cities clinics were set up to dispense opiates to addicts. By general agreement, the New York clinic, which received the most attention, was disastrously mismanaged, making little effort to check the identity of patients or the reality of their addiction. Through this neglect, the clinic became a source of spillage of morphine onto the streets and cannot be viewed as a serious attempt to maintain addicts in conditions of careful scrutiny and medical supervision. The clinic was eliminated in the early 1920s, as the administration of the narcotics laws was pursued more harshly, and it has often been pointed at since as an example of the disastrous failure of opiate maintenance programs. Modern studies have indicated that the failure had more to do with the unplanned and unsupervised nature of the New York operation. Clinics in some other cities were managed much better and seem to have been moderately successful.[5]

Heroin maintenance may appear to contain an inherent perversity. We would not think of prescribing a fifth of gin a day for an alcoholic. Then why heroin for addicts? The answer is that alcoholism and heroin addiction are very different problems that may demand unrelated solutions. The alcoholic is in the grip of a destructive substance that gravely impairs his normal functioning and may make him dangerous to himself and others. We could not find any warrant for lending official encouragement to his own destruction while there is any hope of restoring him to a better, alcohol-free way of life. In any event, there is no need of an alcohol maintenance program for the ironic reason that the alcoholic can simply walk out and buy the substance that is destroying him at the corner liquor store. But heroin is not in itself an inherently destructive substance. Stabilization may be possible that permits the addict to lead a much better life than he does while he pursues the drug illegally, and, for some addicts, a better life than he is able to lead without the drug.

If the addict wants to get off the drug, we have the strongest obligation to work with him to help him to live free of it. But when the addict has come to a serious and final awareness that he cannot function without opiates, and when a realistic medical appraisal, unclouded by sentiment, agrees with that judgment, the only question left is which regime of maintenance can afford this addict the best life. For some this may be a methadone program; for others, it may be heroin maintenance. To shut off the latter because of an emotional response to the word "heroin," which we are apparently able to escape with the word "methadone," is only to act with stupidity and cruelty.

OPIATE BLOCKADERS

While methadone, if administered in sufficient quantities, may block out the effects of heroin, this is because it is substantially affording equivalent satisfaction. It is an interchangeable source of appeasement for the habit. Experiments have been made with other drugs, not opiates or opiate equivalents at all, but pure blockaders of opiate action. They provide no assuagement of the craving for opiates, but they interpose a barrier to the impact of opiates on the tissues, so that opiate administration has no effect on the user. The expected euphoria or tranquilizing effect simply does not arrive. The two drugs of this kind on which most research has been done are nalaxone and cyclazocine.

Present disadvantages of these drugs are that they are very short acting and have unpleasant side effects for many patients. Very possibly both these drawbacks may be overcome by future research, which may develop a long-acting blockader without side effects. Such a drug could offer valuable support to the person who believes he has broken the habit and can live tolerably well without opiates but needs insurance against temptation. Used in such a voluntary fashion, no moral or legal objection can be perceived. The patient who finds that, after all, he cannot function with reasonable effectiveness without opiates could always cease to use the blockader and apply for admission to a methadone or heroin maintenance program.

But suggestions have been made that, if effective blockaders were developed, addicts could be subjected to court orders to adopt a blockading regime, subject to the threat of imprisonment or commitment if they refused. In the light of our knowledge of the ferocity with which opiate addiction embraces many lives, such a proposal has chilling aspects of cruelty. Addicts under such a regime might live in perpetual depression and acute anxiety from which they could find no escape at all. By the pharmacological intervention of the state they would be condemned to eternal exclusion from the one substance that could afford them tranquility and perhaps a reasonable degree of normality. Since such a scheme would condemn people to worse lives than they would otherwise lead, it could only be viewed as a self-righteous and puritanical condemnation of others to suffering because of what is seen as their weakness. Powerful constitutional objections could also be raised. The scheme could be seen as state action that withholds the best and most appropriate medical attention from sick people and so as a denial of equal protection of the laws and a violation of due process. It could also be regarded as a most emphatically cruel and unusual punishment. Research should indeed be continued on opiate blockaders but, unless they can also afford relief from the symptoms of opiate deprivation, they should be regarded as suitable only for volunteers, or as very short-term aids to detoxification.

Pharmacological intervention, in the form of maintenance, appears at the moment to offer the best promise of improved life for the majority of addicts. As already demonstrated, we must be careful not to call it a cure. But the very nature of addiction to opiates involves the proposition that, for many, cure is impossible. That assertion is, of course, contingent on the present state of medical science. Further research may so increase our knowledge of the physical process of addiction that a treatment may be discovered that removes the craving for opiates without the need to continue to administer them. If such a treatment consisted of the regular administration of some other drug, we could be pushed into the semantic corner of having to rebut the charge that we had simply replaced dependence on opiates by dependence on another drug. Indeed, that would be an appropriate comment to make on the continued administration of the existing heroin blockaders. What must be avoided is the sterility of the position that dependence on a drug that imprisons the addict in a continuous state of discomfort is a morally acceptable cure, while dependence on a drug that maintains him in a state of reasonable comfort is an impermissible perpetuation of a condemned habit.

Therapeutic Communities

At the same time, we must acknowledge that some addicts have been able to make a final break with their drug habit. Why exactly some are able to do this while others are not is a subject of considerable mystery. It may have something to do with physiological differences that cause opiates to impose a harsher chemical tyranny on some than on others; more likely, it more often depends on the psychic and emotional composition of the individual. Some of those who break the habit may, in truth, never have been in the grip of a very real addiction, in view of the heavily diluted quality of heroin generally available on the streets. The observation has also been made that for some people the grip of addiction appears to loosen as they get older, so that many addicts seem to drop the habit more or less naturally as they pass into middle age. On the other hand, this is clearly not true of some who remain fiercely addicted even with advancing years.

Some of those who escape from addiction do it unaided. Others have received the invaluable assistance of the various therapeutic communities (TCs) that have existed for some time. The one common feature of these programs is that they are drug free, except in some cases for a brief initial period of detoxification. Otherwise, they may differ greatly: Some are residential, while some receive their members only in the daytime and permit them to live outside; some require residence or attendance for several years, while others aim at success in a shorter period; some rely on an austere regime of discipline, while others stress a warm, loving, and supportive atmosphere. While there can be no doubt that most of these communities have achieved at least enough success to amply justify their existence, it is often difficult to gauge the measure of that success with any precision. They are for the most part highly selective in their admission of patients and sometimes demand that addicts pass arduous tests of their suitability and then serve a probationary period, after which they are subjected to further review. Such procedures may be eminently proper, since these facilities cannot afford to waste their scanty and precious resources on those who are unlikely to benefit. But the necessity for such procedures and the rejection of many addicts as unsuitable immediately demonstrate the limited role to be played by the TCs.

Addicts who are admitted may do well in the supportive atmosphere of the TC, particularly if it is one that requires full-time residence. But community directors often admit that there is a significant relapse rate among addicts after they have left the community. Pronouncements of cure based simply on the addict's remaining free of drugs while still attached to the TC may thus be rash. Even by the most rigorous standards, however, a significant number of permanent cures is probably achieved.

Even if the number of cures were very small, it would still be of the greatest importance to have available a number of TCs in areas where addiction is high. The merits of such programs are enormous. They are voluntary, and addicts are not committed to them, though they may sometimes find their way into them as an alternative to going to jail. They are imbued with the aim of getting the addict away from his habit and are the only programs in the nation seriously devoted to this end. They generally provide the addict with psychiatric counseling, domestic counseling, job training, and an atmosphere of concern and support that is not easily to be found elsewhere. In short, the best TCs restore to the addict a sense of his personal worth and dignity and demonstrate to him that there are people who are concerned about him and will work with him to reach a goal that he could not attain without help no matter how passionate his desire.

Evaluation and Recommendations

One cause for regret is the internecine warfare that has sometimes broken out in the ranks of those who are in the addiction-curing business. As heroin use has spread and become a major national concern, part of the response has been a startling growth in the number of officials engaged in combating the problem. A bureaucracy has evolved that defends itself with all the zeal and tenacity ordinarily associated with the protection of jobs and the aggrandizement of administrative empires. Roads to salvation are discovered and sanctified to the exclusion of all others. Competing programs may even be anathematized as immoral, dangerous, or ineffective. So some methadone people fulminate against heroin maintenance and sneer at the TCs. Some of those deeply involved in the administration of communities roundly condemn methadone or heroin maintenance as a surrender to addiction or even as the deliberate enslaving of minority groups. Advocates of one particular kind of TC are sometimes given to condemning others as cruel or ineffectually soft, as the case may be.

No program has any proper exemption from thoughtful criticism, and present imperfections need to be underlined so that they may be excised. But, in principle, we know enough already to assert that a coexistence of different types of maintenance programs and different kinds of TC is an essential part of any rational response to heroin addiction. There are many different kinds of addicts, the genesis of whose addiction varies considerably. Some may be helped in one way, some in another, and some hardly at all.

A recognition that addiction is often incurable and that maintenance programs offer the best hopes for most addicts while TCs may help some to escape the drug altogether provides a foundation for the construction of a sensible response to the needs of the addict himself. It still leaves open a whole range of questions about the general regulation of opiate drugs. Should sale of heroin continue to be an offense? Should possession or use of heroin be an offense for the person who is not yet an addict?

Before trying to fashion answers to these difficult questions, we might usefully summarize the most relevant considerations, many of which have been revealed in the discussion so far:

1. Though we do not know all we need to know about the effects of the use of heroin and other illegal drugs, we know enough to be giving honest and useful information to the public and particularly young people. Drug education has gone on for many years, but it has often been misconceived and less than helpful. Lurid and inaccurate warnings about the dangers of marihuana have made young people, who are familiar with the comparative innocuousness of this drug, contemptuous about official statements on other drugs. Information about heroin too has often been misleading. There has been exaggeration of the physical dangers of the drug itself and the agonies of withdrawal, while on the other hand the prospects of cure through commitment procedures or other programs have been painted too rosily. Better results would probably be achieved by being painstakingly honest about heroin. This would involve telling people that: (a) the drug is not in itself particularly damaging to the body; (b)

withdrawal can be extremely unpleasant but is not likely to be hideous or fatal, especially with the comparatively readily available detoxification programs that now exist; (c) the drug is extremely addictive and, once a strong habit is built up, many if not most users may never be able to shake it off; (d) many will never attain an easy relationship with the drug but will be so obsessed with its use that they will be largely unfitted for other activity; (e) while criminal prohibitions remain, the pursuit of the drug will be expensive, utterly time-consuming, and will almost inevitably lead to criminal conduct and trouble with the law; (f) the illegality of the drug may also lead to dangerous and perhaps fatal illnesses arising from impurities in the supply or from unsterile equipment.

If there is to be drug education at all, it should be along these lines of purveying soberly accurate information within the frontiers of existing knowledge. It is quite possible, though, that it might be more productive to mention drugs as little as possible. The high frenzy of the official excitement about drugs in the past decade may in itself be a contributing factor to the growth of addiction. Certainly research needs to be done on the comparative merits of intensive drug education as compared with benign neglect in this direction.

2. The old despair about the condition of the addict has been alleviated to some extent. Methadone maintenance, the knowledge of different maintenance schemes operating in Britain, and the small but significant success of the TCs combine to demonstrate that a substantial number of addicts can be, if not cured, at least helped to lead much easier and sometimes reasonably normal lives.

3. But a substantial number of addicts remain who cannot be attracted into or satisfied with any of the treatment programs. In the end, if they do not die first, illness or weariness or ultimate disillusionment may bring them in, but for years during the early and middle phases of their addiction, they may stay out.

4. In addition to existing addicts, it is virtually certain that for the foreseeable future there will be a significant number of new users of heroin appearing each year. This number is probably diminishing because of more effective law enforcement, or better

awareness of the dangers of addiction, or some complex and subtle shift in fashion, or some combination of all these reasons, but it surely will not wither away altogether for a long time, if at all.

5. Because of the last two factors, while the law remains as it is, there will continue to be an illegal market: addicts who will not enter programs, and new users, will be forced into seeking out the criminal supply and probably into criminal activities to finance their purchases. At least this will be so unless criminal law enforcement becomes so effective that it eliminates the supply altogether. But this just does not seem a practical prospect in the near future.

With this platform of knowledge and reasonable forecast, a final determination about the appropriate degree of criminalization ultimately depends on a judgment about the acuteness of the danger that the use of the drug poses to individuals and society. But such a judgment is infinitely complex. There are no doubt some people who can live better with opiates than without them. They are by disposition beset by tensions and anxieties that make normal functioning close to impossible. A steady maintenance intake of opiates or opioids may keep them at a level of relaxation where they can function with reasonable efficiency. But there may not be many such people, and it is too dangerous to experiment to find out who they are, since the experiment would inevitably involve the implantation of addiction.

Most people who use heroin are not likely to be very happy people at the onset of use. They may be socially very deprived, with little education, bad housing, and poor job prospects; they may suffer from very distressing intrafamily situations; or they may be naturally of a depressed or disturbed disposition. Probably for most such people, heroin use brings initial relief and some euphoria. This may not last long as addiction sets in and the demands of an illegal market impose more and more mordantly a disorganized and criminally connected life-style. But even the sordid constraints of the new way of life afford their own perverse satisfaction. Life has, in a sense, become simple: All other concerns and anxieties are dissolved in the overwhelming simplicity of the search for a single substance. Tension and anxiety certainly do not disappear, but at least they now appear understandable in their apparently concrete connection with a hunger of the body. In this way absorption in addiction becomes a channel in which all the dimly apprehended fears and miseries of an unhappy life can be metamorphosed into the easily understood search for a white powder. It is an excuse and an explanation for failure and unhappiness and, in a way, a great relief from having to grapple with the awful complexity of the forces that were creating that failure and unhappiness in the absence of addiction.

If this is true about very many heroin addicts, we have little warrant to expect that their lives would have been dramatically better if they had never sampled the drug. Perhaps alcohol would have taken its place, and it is hard to say whether that would have been more or less absorbing and destructive. In a few cases there can be little doubt that, in the absence of heroin, violent and antisocial behavior would have developed at some point.

The social institutions of modern life create conditions that ineluctably produce a sense of deracination and alienation in many people. It may be that the unnatural aspects of modern living have developed farther and faster in America than in almost any other place in the world, so that, without fundamental social change, impulses of irritability, confusion, or depression will continue to drive a significant number of people to seek modes of escape from the unconfrontable realities that life thrusts before them. If we squeeze hard to choke off one escape route, the driven and the hopeless will surge harder through other established ones or else break out new ones. How could we ever measure how much social good rigorous enforcement of heroin laws has done or could do, unless we could know exactly how many people have been driven by these laws into becoming alcoholics and heavy barbiturate users? We can never know this exactly and, in the absence of such knowledge, we can only move carefully, humbly, tentatively, and with a great expectation of making mistakes and having to change direction.

Let us try to imagine living with a legalized system of opiate sales. Perhaps people could purchase morphine or heroin at drugstores. The containers might be marked clearly with bold-type warnings that opiates are strongly addictive and should be taken only occasionally and most cautiously. The proposal has certain immediate attractions and apparent benefits. Among them we can note the following: The illegal market in opiates would presumably immediately collapse. Organized crime would be deprived of a great source of revenue. Addicts and users would have no need to contact criminals for their supply and no need to commit crimes to raise the money for the drug. Vast expenditures of time and money by law-enforcement systems, prosecutors' offices, the judicial system, and legal aid systems would be eliminated immediately. The congestion in the criminal courts would be much relieved, with great benefit to the rational conduct of their business. Those addicts who presently cannot adjust to maintenance programs would be able to obtain a cheap supply of the drug of their choice, which might greatly improve the life-style of some of them. By offering a pure product that could be used in sterile conditions, lives would be saved and health preserved.

But before we yield too easily to these blandishing appeals, we ought to list the accompanying evils that might ensue. In the first place, it can be argued that the very act of legalizing a previously prohibited substance will inevitably, no matter what disclaimers are made, leave a strong impression with the public that the substance cannot after all be so dangerous. A natural expectation might then be that a large number of new users or experimenters will emerge. Once legalization has come, not only will there be no obstacles to obtaining the drug (except for regulations as to age, etc.), but also there can be no effective control over the amount consumed by individuals. It is true that rationing systems are theoretically possible. The Scandinavian countries have tried them with respect to liquor purchases but not with much success. It is hard to see how, on the American scene, any effective rationing of individual consumption of a drug could be imposed once its general sale is legalized.

This would mean that there might be a very large increase in the number of people truly and deeply addicted. At the moment the quality of street heroin is so poor that most street addicts have in fact very frail habits that offer promise of cure, at least for some of them. But the characteristic tolerance factor associated with opiate use would no doubt mean that, under conditions of legal availability, most users (new or old) would build up their intake to enormous doses when compared with the present average street habit. This would not necessarily destroy life or health (since the habituated organism can tolerate huge quantities of opiates), but it would certainly plant addiction so firmly that it might never be uprooted. The over-all danger thus becomes a significant rise in the number of deeply addicted opiate users.

This prospect is so alarming, risking as it does the creation of a whole new generation of addicts whose habit could never be eradicated, that we surely should shrink back from legalization unless we are clearly persuaded beyond much doubt by either of two propositions or justifications. The first justification would be that addiction to heroin is not a condition of sufficient danger to permit us to identify paternalistic or other utilitarian warrants for fending it off by prohibition of the drug. The alternative justification would be that, although heroin may be a substance of sufficient danger to justify its criminalization if other things were equal, there are special circumstances here to overbear that conclusion. The special circumstances would be that the business of law enforcement and the syndrome of behavior surrounding criminalization do, in the end, more harm than good.

It seems that at the moment neither justification could be convincingly made out and that, therefore, it is at the least premature to advocate the legal sale of opiates. With respect to the first argument (that heroin addiction is not so dangerous a condition), we are carried back to our earlier discussion of paternalism as a good reason for criminal prohibition. If everyone were a middle-aged, highly intelligent, and emotionally stable person, then perhaps we could safely let each individual make up his or her own mind about running the risks of sampling heroin. But the reality is very different. The presence of cheap, legal heroin in every drugstore would be a constantly dangling temptation to all depressed, anxious, and unhappy people, old and young, to purchase some immediate relief from their condition without a meaningful appreciation of the risks they run; for, though opiates will not destroy their bodies, they may well so capture their whole existence that all prospect of living what is normally accounted a happy life will be irredeemably forfeit. If freedom should not include the liberty to sell oneself into slavery, then there may be a good case for the continued prohibition of heroin on the ground that it takes possession of many people in a way that may be illuminatingly compared with a condition of slavery.

Neither can we be in the least sure that the evils of criminalization are obviously worse than the bad consequences that would flow from legalization. The case is simply not made out, even under the present regime, and there are many ways in which the bad aspects of criminalization could be considerably alleviated without proceeding to legalization. As we have seen, this would principally take the form of dropping a policy of law enforcement with respect to the addict himself.

The reasonable conclusion appears to be that the best we can do with respect to heroin use is to make marginal improvements in the present structure of law enforcement and treatment. Such a program should include at least the following measures:

1. The dissemination of sober and accurate information about the nature of opiates and addiction to them.

2. The repeal of any criminal laws that make possession of small amounts of heroin by an addict for his own use a crime.

3. The repeal of laws that provide for compulsory commitment of addicts.

4. The provision of varied and sufficient voluntary treatment programs for persons who are presently addicted. Some of these programs should aim at "cure"; some should aim at maintenance (on methadone or opiates); all should include supportive social service programs and therapeutic counseling. Diligent efforts should be made to identify the most suitable program for an individual addict, with the understanding that the best possible efforts will be made to help any addict who wishes to eliminate his addiction.

5. Law-enforcement efforts should continue, with a concentration on large-scale importers and dealers.

With such a program we shall have to continue to live with heroin addiction for a very long time and perhaps indefinitely.

The program is after all nothing more than a plan for containment, since the roots of the problem are immune from the touch of simple measures of regulation and treatment. If the containment effort fails (as such efforts often do), there are only two ways in which we can move. One would be to legalization, which would involve the benefits and dangers discussed above. A last and quite contrary possibility would be to conclude that heroin is such an inadmissible menace on our social scene that its use must be kept to an absolute minimum by a policy of harsh punishment of the addict himself. The Supreme Court has held that the status of addiction cannot constitutionally be made an offense, but the law already makes simple possession a crime. In most places law enforcement has shifted its emphasis from pursuing addicts themselves, holding only small quantities, to the pursuit of importers and dealers. There might be a deterrent rationale in reversing the emphasis and making the most vigorous efforts (within the bounds of legality) to apprehend addicts carrying small quantities. If this were backed by a statute or sentencing policy that imposed prison sentences in all such cases without possibility of plea bargaining, it would be at least possible that there might be a marked reduction in the use of heroin.

But this is no more than a speculative possibility and is attended by so many ethical objections that it seems a last and desperate resort. The use of heroin confronts the makers and administrators of the law with a social problem to which they would do well to bring a great deal of modesty about the powers of their trade.

Marihuana

The case for decriminalization of marihuana is at once both simpler and more complex than with heroin. It is simpler in that marihuana lacks the powerful chemistry with which heroin may impose addiction and enslave the user. This disposes us to regard marihuana as much less dangerous than heroin and to incline us toward legalization. But this very lack of a powerful addictive property, in another aspect, speaks against legalization; for we cannot view the marihuana user as being a sick person, driven by an irresistible impulse to pursue the drug. This makes it seem more defensible to punish him.

There is a range of substances, among which may be included alcohol, tobacco (nicotine), and marihuana (cannabis) that, to varying degrees, exhibit the following qualities and properties. Many people have come to find them supportive, tranquilizing, relaxing, and thus a prop and a shield when confronted with the discomforts and tensions of ordinary life. Alcohol and marihuana in addition have the capacity to induce euphoria and alteration of mood, the extent of which depends on the amount ingested. Regular users are able, through experience, to control the extent of this mood alteration to a point where it is usually pleasurable. None of these drugs appears to be significantly harmful if used in small quantities occasionally. But the regular use of them in substantial quantities poses different degrees of danger. With tobacco such use markedly increases the risk of contracting heart disease, lung cancer, or other pulmonary afflictions. Alcohol, used in such a way, may cause a variety of illnesses and lead to debility and death in extreme cases. Less is known about the long-term heavy use of marihuana, but some researchers suggest there is a possibility of brain damage. Other studies point to the fact that substances contained in marihuana are built up over a long period of time in the body and may cause genetic damage to offspring, if not disease in the user.

To this we must add that of the three drugs, the most powerfully addicting is tobacco. Alcohol is not per se physiologically addictive, though psychological dependence on it may habituate a minority of users to such regular intake of large quantities that they become in fact addicted and can suffer severe withdrawal symptoms. Marihuana has no addictive properties, though a small minority of users may become so dependent that their lives become largely devoted to the drug.

If mankind were clamoring for a tranquilizing, mildly euphoric substance and only one of these drugs could be legalized, which would we choose? Imagine that a national commission has been set up to respond to the public need for such a substance, and it studies all that is known about tobacco, alcohol, and marihuana, with a view to selecting one for legal production and distribution. It is difficult to see how the choice could rationally not be marihuana.

Tobacco has little to commend it. It has no euphoric effect and little capacity to induce mild and pleasant alterations of mood or consciousness. Its tranquilizing effect has to be learned, and for many users wears off after a time as use becomes a mere satisfaction of a physical need, as with heroin. It is extremely addicting and very dangerous to health in its long-term effects. Surely this would not be the winner of the contest.

Alcohol appears more attractive. It is tranquilizing and euphoric and may be pleasantly effective in altering consciousness. Its use is surrounded with agreeable and elaborate social rituals that have to do with food, conversation, and erotic encounters. For the majority of people who are able to maintain a controlled relationship with the drug, alcohol has a soothing, humanizing, and enriching impact on their lives. But against this must be set the fact that the powers of alcohol are great for evil as well as for good. Occasional excessive use may lead to accidents or violence; regular use of heavy amounts leads very many people to the disease of alcoholism, which works huge amounts of social damage. An authoritative decision maker surveying the harm that alcohol has caused would probably strike it from the list.

Marihuana we admittedly know much less about, precisely because it has no history of legal use. But what we do know about it tends to show that it has considerable powers for tranquilizing and producing pleasurable states of consciousness. A minority of users may become heavily dependent on it (as with alcohol), but there is no evidence that marihuana destroys their bodies nor that occasional excessive use of it has the potential that such use of alcohol has to lead to violence. The Commission of Choice on the existing evidence ought to pick marihuana.

But we are not starting with a clean slate. Tobacco and alcohol are legally distributed and used, while marihuana is not. This received position is in itself an important element in decision making. Perhaps regular use of marihuana contains terrible dangers that we as yet know nothing of. Its apparent harmlessness may be only a factor of comparative ignorance when compared with our long love-hate relationships with tobacco and alcohol. Again, marihuana is to many people a strange and unknown substance, vaguely associated with supposedly unpleasant foreigners or people of a different color. They find it difficult to fit it into a scene of social pleasantry and grace, as they are quite accustomed to doing with cigarettes or whiskey.

The use of marihuana may have a longer Western history than many suppose, but it has been a submerged, working-class one, never breaking through into circles of fashion until recent years. The seventeenth-century Dutch peasants who are depicted in the paintings of Adriaen Brouwer as being "drunk on tobacco" had probably added a little of the hemp plant to the contents of their pipes. Much more important is the fact that it is now the drug of choice of a great many people.

We suggested earlier that we ought not to legalize marihuana only because it is less harmful or no more harmful than tobacco and alcohol, which are already legal. But we should now add that, given the fact of actual use by many people, then the comparative harmlessness of marihuana does become an argument that should count for something. The claim to use a drug of pleasure no more harmful than others that are legal may not be ripe for constitutional recognition as a claim of equal protection, but it is a social argument of some cogency for a legislature to ponder. The drug of choice of the young, of many minority groups is banned, while the drugs of the white, middle-aged, middle class are legal. This is one of those exaggerations that contains an uncomfortable grain of truth.

So, on the one hand, we hear the clamor of those who claim a right to have their pleasure in a way that is not demonstrably more harmful than other people's ways of getting their pleasure. From the other side comes the reasonable-sounding caution that the licit presence of dangerous drugs on the social scene is not a very good reason for liberating another substance of some unknown degree of danger. But it is not impossible to accommodate both sides of the argument in a compromise that may be the most reasonable temporary solution.

The claim to use marihuana is a justice-type claim, based on the notion that it is unfair to punish its use when we permit the use of alcohol and tobacco. This is a persuasive claim, and we ought, therefore, to abolish penalties for the use of marihuana and possession of small quantities for the purpose of personal use or casual transfer. But the warnings about the unknown dangers and the unknown number of people who might be turned on if there were full legalization have good utilitarian roots and deserve some accommodation. This can be done by retaining the penalties for sale of marihuana or possession of substantial quantities for sale.

Certainly this would leave the situation in a somewhat perverse posture. It would be legal to use a drug for which there is no legal source of supply. In practice this would mean that the user would have to go to some trouble to obtain the drug and have to pay a somewhat inflated price. This may have precisely the desired effect in inhibiting an increase in use and a growth in the number of users. The formal paradox of the solution may be a price worth paying for the practical sense of the outcome. At least in the short run. But such a position should only be retained for a stipulated number of years, while marihuana research is vigorously pressed. In a reasonably short time, we should know enough about the drug to make a final decision on legalizing sale and distribution.

Conclusion

Because of a change in fashion, or pressure from the law, heroin use may appear in the future as a less sharp and pervasive problem than it does today. Growing recognition of the comparative harmlessness of marihuana will no doubt in time dilute our perception of that danger, too. But drug abuse in general is not likely to diminish, only to change its forms. For some time now a trend has been apparent to indulge in multidrug use, perhaps of barbiturates combined with alcohol, spiced with the occasional and newly fashionable sedative-hypnotics (such as methaqualone). A renewed interest in alcohol by young people, often mingled with the use of other drugs, raises perhaps the greatest danger. Opportunities remain rife for physical harm and damaged lives.

If life in America leads many young people to experiment foolishly and dangerously with drugs of destructive potential, certainly some organized public response is called for. This can be best shaped by dropping the obsession with heroin and marihuana as particular substances and concentrating instead on the provision of services to deprived and disturbed people. We should remember that there are ways in which drugs for a time do help people to cope with or escape from their problems. In the long run the remedy is usually worse than the disease, but while we offer no alternatives, it is natural enough that this foolish self-medication will be tried. Considerable success has been gained with the operation of "crisis centers" for young people, that offer counseling, treatment, and practical help with legal, medical, educational, housing, and employment problems. Such centers have managed to divert many young people from drugs into happier and less disturbed lives. Public and private fundings of such centers should be vastly increased. While penal law enforcement has a place of some importance in the over-all attack on the danger from drugs, it should be much less central than the provision of services to help the unhappy and bewildered members of our society.

PART 3

Disobedience and Disruption

IX

Civil Disobedience

We recognize a general duty to obey the commands of a lawfully constituted government. But Western society has always managed at the same time to accommodate a theory of justifiable revolution. Even when the concept of the divine right of kings flourished, the Catholic Church was still able to acknowledge a right and, indeed, a duty to depose a godless and tyrannical prince. This notion of the just revolution was strengthened by the development in the seventeenth and eighteenth centuries of a social contract theory as the foundation of legitimacy in government. Early explanations of the social contract posited a historical act by which men, recognizing the brutal and anarchic nature of ungoverned life, voluntarily gave up freedom in return for protection by a ruler. The price they paid was the assumption of a social and moral obligation to obey his commands. Even in this form of the theory, the obligation dissolved once the ruler failed to discharge his elementary duty to bring order and protection from illegal violence.

In the sense of a direct compact between presently living citizens, the social contract does not exist at all. Portrayed as a single historical incident, it grossly oversimplifies the slow and subtle way in which human societies evolved into systems of law and government. But these are insufficient reasons for dismissing the theory from any relevant role in the debate about the obligation to obey the law. The social contract may be viewed as an allegory that retains vitality because it contains moral lessons about the kinds of claims that government may reasonably make upon us. The lessons go both to the form and the content of laws. With respect to the form of legislation, the social contract demands that government adhere to the valid procedures prescribed by the constitution. With a modern democratic gloss this can be seen as involving periodic renewal of the consent of the governed through the electoral process. With respect to the content of laws the social contract requires, at the least, that government does not violate the fundamental requirements of justice in its dealing with citizens.

If government ignores the constitutional forms of law making, it is itself committing a revolutionary act that legitimates resistance. If government formally complies with valid law-making procedures, but at the same time does fundamental injustice, a point may be reached, which cannot be precisely defined in advance, when such transgressions become so diffused and so morally offensive that a right to revolt is generated. Recent history is replete with examples, as with Hitler's Germany, where we would think that government had become such an instrument of organized evil that a right to revolt could not be questioned.

The moral problem is comparatively uncomplicated when we are confronted with such tyrannically oppressive regimes, though the prudential calculations may be agonizing. The regime may have forfeited all moral claim to allegiance, but the costs of revolt may be heavy, and these must be considered, together with the chances of success and failure. Revolt in arms may appear impossible of success or likely to lead to bloody reprisals. In such a dilemma one alternative tactic that may be pursued is civil disobedience. The civil disobedience in India, under the example and leadership of Gandhi, may be viewed as a tactical move toward the revolutionary objective of removing a foreign, colonialist regime that was perceived as lacking any legitimacy. Though the campaign failed to reach its objectives in the short run, it no doubt had an enormous educative impact, which helped to pave the way for the eventual British withdrawal. But against the most vicious tyrannies civil disobedience is unlikely to be a successful revolutionary tactic. Civil disobedients in Nazi Germany were heroic and often saintly figures whose sacrifice may continue to provide inspiration, but foreign planes and tanks were necessary to dislodge Hitler.

Those who practice civil disobedience are by no means always revolutionaries employing what seems for the moment to be the most promising tactic to achieve the overthrow of a government seen as illegitimate. Indeed, civil disobedience as a major phenomenon on the American scene in the past two decades has rarely proclaimed itself as aiming at revolution. Its goals have been more modest but at the same time more complicated to justify; for if a government is not bad enough to deserve expulsion, then how can it lose its moral claim for compliance with its constitutionally framed regulations? Can we recognize its general legitimacy but yet claim a right to break laws in special circumstances? The justification of civil disobedience within a constitutional democracy carries with it special difficulty.

Why Obey the Law?

One way to approach the problem is to ask why we have any moral obligation to obey the law at all.[1] Where the content of the law overlaps universally accepted moral prohibitions (as with crimes of murder, rape, and other kinds of violence to the person), it is clear that we do have a moral obligation to comply, but it could be said that this is because the conduct is independently immoral, quite apart from its being proscribed by statute. We would have a moral obligation not to murder and rape even if there were no law at all. Some further justification is required where the conduct is not of this kind, but is of a regulatory nature designed to enforce some policy of the government of the day, or where the conduct appears quite innocuous in the circumstances, even though the general existence of the regulation can be seen as necessary in most circumstances.

A particular example may assist the discussion. Suppose I am driving an automobile, and I come to a crossroads with a traffic light, which is red as I approach. The countryside is flat, visibility is perfect, and I can see that there are no vehicles or persons approaching in any direction. Would it be wrong for me to drive through the red light? Though the traffic laws with respect to complying with signals such as red lights are generally necessary for public safety, in this particular case I can claim convincingly that I endanger nobody by disobeying. It could not even be said that I am setting a bad example for anyone else since, in the hypothetical situation, there is nobody there to observe me. And even if there were someone to observe me, it is not clear why it is a bad example to present someone with the spectacle of my driving through a red light when no danger at all is attached to the act. There is of course an argument from prudence, that one should not generally disobey the law because one may get caught and suffer unpleasant consequences. But, in the hypothetical, there are no police around to observe me, and, in any case, the argument about getting caught would not establish the immorality of my act but only its lack of attention to self-interest.

Must we, then, accept the conclusion that my driving through the red light is morally unobjectionable? Modern writers on the concepts of fidelity to law and civil disobedience have argued convincingly that we are not compelled to such a judgment. The wrongness of my act can be perceived once we state in general terms the principle on which I would rely to defend it. That principle would have to be that, whenever in my considered judgment breaking a law would not involve any risk of causing the harm the law was designed to prevent, I may properly do so. Under general notions of fairness and justice, I can only assert such a claim with any propriety if I am willing to accord everyone else the same privilege. I might respond that I am quite willing to let anyone go through a red light when it is perfectly safe to do so. But such a principle would not exactly fit the claims of fairness here. The concession that is needed would have to be much broader—that I would be willing to permit anyone to drive through a red light when *in their judgment* it is safe to do so.

If I am a prudent person I would do well to pause before making so large a concession, for, when pressed, the issue becomes one of considerable substance and gravity. Can we envisage an orderly society if people were exonerated from social criticism when they broke public rules and regulations simply because of their honest assertion that in the circumstances it did not seem dangerous to them to do so? Certainly such a plea might temper the harshness of our criticism, but part of the underpinnings of a regulatory system is that the rules must apply to all cases. The reason for this is that stopping at red lights has been established as a uniform public standard of careful behavior. To confer a privilege on individuals to exempt themselves from the obligation in particular cases, on the basis of their personal evaluations of the absence of risk, would strike at the very policy of the law that seeks to ensure safety through regularity and uniformity. The reason why the law cannot allow such a defense is precisely, therefore, the same reason why we cannot view the explanation as a good answer to social or moral criticism. Public safety could not be protected if such a privilege were extended to everyone, and I am therefore in the wrong when I claim a privilege that a reasonable person would have to acknowledge could not be universal. The fact that it was perfectly safe to go through the red light in the particular circumstances makes no difference at all to this judgment.

Nature of Civil Disobedience

The person passing through the red light would not of course make any claim that he was a civil disobedient. He would claim only that under the circumstances it did not seem necessary to obey the law. The example, though, is of great importance in demonstrating that such a claim is not a moral justification and that a quite different argument would have to be advanced before we could think of a theory of justifiable noncompliance.

Another example may move the inquiry further. Suppose a married couple live in a state that makes a wide variety of modes of sexual gratification criminal even when practiced between husband and wife. (Our earlier discussion showed that such a statute may well be unconstitutional, but for the moment we will ignore that complexity and assume the law to be formally valid.) The husband and wife are drawn to and take pleasure in one of the proscribed varieties of sexual intercourse, but, being moral people and good citizens, they are troubled at the thought of breaking the law. After reflecting on the matter, they decide that the law is not only indefensible from a utilitarian standpoint but also oppressive in the way that it seeks to regulate the private relations of husband and wife in the bedroom. They decide to indulge in the prohibited mode of intercourse and believe themselves not to be wrong in so doing.

This example is significantly different from the traffic light one. The legal prohibitions involved are not of the same kind. The traffic provision involves no natural judgment on the badness or wrongness of conduct; in nature there is no reason why a red light should be more of a signal to stop than a green one. It is simply that some uniformly accepted system of signals must be devised to further the orderly and safe flow of traffic, and we have selected red as the stopping color. Legal penalties for sodomy or fellatio or whatever are clearly grounded in some other notion. They seem more like prohibitions on murder or rape in that the conduct in and of itself is thought to be intrinsically wrong. And yet they differ also from prohibitions on murder and rape, for there is universal moral agreement that acts of unjustified personal violence are bad and to be condemned, while the moral consensus about the wrongness of certain sexual activities has disappeared, if it ever existed. The sexual prohibition may thus be seen as the certification of a certain moral position by the state in opposition to a considerable and perhaps majority body of opinion. When applied to the private acts of married persons, there are additional aspects of intrusions into privacy and attempts to regulate intimate married behavior that raise the strongest arguments against the justice and wisdom of the law. The married couple who choose to ignore such a law would thus not claim that, while it is generally necessary, they see no reason in utility for obeying it on this occasion. They would claim rather that in its general application to them it is unjust and that they have no moral duty to comply.

Claims of an injustice kind are clearly in a different category from claims of immediate disutility. Under the red light example we argued that an orderly society is hard to conceive if people claim a privilege to make personal judgments on each occasion about the need to comply with a law that they concede is generally necessary. If they act on such a principle they therefore deserve social and moral criticism as well as legal penalties. It is not so obvious that the goal of a by and large orderly and safe society necessitates the rejection of claims to ignore laws when the individual conscientiously believes that the law impinges on him or her in a way that does deep injustice. Certainly we might concede that the existence of a legal duty imposes what has been called a *prima facie* moral obligation. In social contract terms we could express this by saying that any person who participates in a society and derives benefits and protections from the scheme of mutual forbearances erected by the legal system has a *prima facie* obligation to comply with the duties that are imposed by laws validly made under the rules of the system.

But there is no reason in logic or moral principle why even a system that functions with perfect, formal democratic validity should be able to make *any* demand on a citizen or to call for *any* sacrifice from him simply because he has derived benefits from the system. The social contract is not after all a business of selling one's soul to the devil. What is required is that disobedience be justified by some compelling ethical argument. Part of the burden imposed by the social contract is to comply with laws even when this may be personally inconvenient or contrary to one's own prudential judgment. But if the citizen, after serious reflection, should take the view that compliance with the law would result in his submitting to fundamental injustice or, perhaps worse, in his having to do fundamental injustice to another, it is by no means clear that he does not now have a good reason for refusing to obey.[2]

So far we have established only that injustice-type claims by lawbreakers deserve a more serious consideration than claims of a utilitarian type and call for a different response. Even the second of our examples still does not reach fully into the topic of civil disobedience. The husband and wife, privately practicing the prohibited sexual act in their bedroom would think it strange if they were characterized as civil disobedients. They certainly *are* disobeying a law because they think it unjust; but further elements seem necessary to fill out the usual notion of what it is to be civilly disobedient.

The core of the concept of civil disobedience, not contained in the above examples, is that it is not only conscientious but also at the same time has the character of a public refusal. In order to have this character, the act must not be deliberately concealed or hidden. Private defiance of sexual prohibitions may be defended conscientiously, but the reason for the law-breaking is the pursuit of pleasure. One explanation for the difficulty of challenging the constitutionality of certain sexual laws is the dearth of candidates for litigation. This might be expressed by saying that while many people are perfectly willing to break such laws (and would conscientiously defend so doing), they are not willing to disobey them "civilly" in the sense of offering themselves as public challengers to the alleged injustice involved.

Two Kinds of Disobedience

It is almost inevitable that public refusals to comply with the law will take on the character of a protest or appeal, and these aspects are of the essence of civil disobedience. But there remains an important distinction between two basically different modes of executing such a project. The law that he disobeys may be one that in itself makes a direct demand upon the disobedient that he finds intolerably unjust. Such disobedience has occurred throughout the ages with respect to laws requiring compulsory attendance at church, the compulsory taking of oaths, submitting to vaccination, etc. Refusal to be inducted into the military service during the war in Vietnam has been a recent example. What was rejected there was seen as a call to suffer injustice or to do injustice. This is not logically necessarily connected with the notions of reform, for it is possible to imagine that the disobedient has no hopes or aims of changing the law. He may refuse to obey simply because his conscience will not allow him to, and he may have no interest in what others do or care little for what the law may now do to him. But in practice this is an unlikely situation. If a person perceives the demand that a law makes upon him as unjust, then he must see the law as unjust in making such demands, though he may think it quite proper for people who are so disposed to do the required acts voluntarily. His disobedience, when the supporting reasons are uttered, has an inevitable tendency to take on the character of a protest and an appeal for change in the law; for the disobedient is clearly sacrificing himself, and sacrifice is always a mute appeal to the conscience of others.

For many disobedients in this first category, the purpose of protesting and appealing to the conscience of the public is fundamental. In the evangelical sense they offer themselves as a "witness" to the wrongfulness of the law and hope that they may sufficiently stir the conscience of their fellow citizens to make them press for change. And the law disobeyed may be perceived as unjust by a disobedient even though its particular application to him would not result in a violation of *his* conscience. Suppose that, to take an example from other times, a law requires all people to attend the established church every Sunday. If X is by conviction a member of that church and believes further that attendance every Sunday is desirable, compliance with the law, though it might sometimes be inconvenient, would not violate his conscience. However, he may recognize that there are others in the community who are by conviction not believers in the doctrines of the established church and whose consciences would be bruised by going to church. X might refrain from attending church on Sunday in a spirit of civil disobedience to protest the ways in which the law inflicts injustice on others.

Examples of this first variety of civil disobedience have become less frequent in modern times as legal systems have become gentler and have generally provided "conscience" exemptions, as with military induction or taking oaths. It may occasionally recur in a bitter form, as happened with the war in Vietnam, where the statutory provisions for conscientious objection were not wide enough to embrace the claims of those who asserted that they were not conscientiously opposed to all wars but only to unjust ones. When such disobedience occurs it makes a powerful appeal for understanding and lenity, since there are unpleasant overtones of barbarism about punishing those whose consciences will not allow them to do what we ask of them. As later discussion will show, there may still be persuasive reasons why punishment (and even severe punishment) is justified.

There is a second kind of civil disobedience, which has become the most frequent mode in recent years. This is where the law that is broken does not in itself make generally unjust demands on the disobedient or anyone else. Indeed, it is probably in general terms a quite necessary and unexceptional law. It is broken, though, because the disobedients find this an effective way to protest against some public or private social practice or set of arrangements that they believe does inflict injustice. Suppose it is felt that a private employer is discriminating grossly against minority groups or against women in his hiring practices. To protest against this, a group of people intrude upon his premises and sit-in there. The law that they are breaking is a trespass law, but they are not trying to make the point that laws against trespass are unjust. They use the breach of the trespass law as an indirect or collateral attack on the unjust practices of the employer. Some of the people who sit-in may believe that they themselves have been deprived of jobs because of the employer's practices. Their aim would be to publish to the world the injustice done them in the hope that either law or public opinion may cause the employer to reform his ways. Some of the trespassers may not themselves have been deprived of jobs but are impelled by conscientious desires to seek redress for the injustice done to others.

This second variety of disobedience is somewhat harder to justify than the first, for it lacks the element of conscientious refusal to comply with a law that itself offends the conscience of the disobedient. It looks more like a tactic to achieve social change, and we must scrutinize such tactics carefully when they involve law-breaking. We would want to be satisfied that political means of persuasion or application for judicial relief had been given a reasonable chance to succeed before we can see even the beginnings of a case for law-breaking here. Again, actions of this kind almost inevitably involve imposing social costs on others in the community, some of whom at least are quite innocent of the acts of injustice alleged. Consider the example of sitting-in on the premises of the employer who discriminates. If the sit-in disrupts his business, he may suffer financially. If he is truly guilty of discrimination, then we may feel that he deserves this loss. But his employees, not themselves guilty of discrimination though some of them may have profited from it, will also suffer, and so may his customers and the general public, who may depend on the product he manufactures.

Where the sit-in or obstructive activity is in a public place and directed against a policy or practice of the government, then innocent private citizens will almost certainly suffer through being delayed or prevented in going about their business. This element of interfering with the rights of the innocent hardens the burden of proof on those who seek to make out a moral justification for this kind of disobedience. This is not to say that such a case cannot sometimes be made out convincingly. If the injustice is sharp, if peaceful and legal methods of seeking redress have failed, then the infliction of inconvenience on some innocent people may be a price worth paying to rectify the wrong.

Conscientious disobedience of the first model may also involve interference with the rights of others. During the civil rights activism of the 1960s, civil disobedience was committed on both sides. Those who believed that black people were being unjustly discriminated against often initiated trespassory activities to protest the injustice. But some state officials responded by direct refusals to carry out the orders of federal courts with respect to the redress of unconstitutional segregation. So there were those who stood in the schoolhouse door in order to prevent the entry of black children, in defiance of federal court orders. Now, state officials might have contended (and some of them did) that such actions were conscientious. Whatever the Supreme Court said, they may have believed that the law of God made it a sinful and deeply immoral practice to educate children of different colors together. Assuming, for the sake of argument, that such religious beliefs were sincerely held, we must concede that such state officials were acting from the promptings of conscience. But it must be overwhelmingly obvious that this amounts to no moral excuse nor to any prudential reason for treating them gently in their law-breaking. The reason is that, however conscientious their acts, they were trampling on both the constitutional and the moral rights of others.

Whether disobedience be of the first or second models, then, the extent to which it interferes with the rights of others must always be considered in evaluating its moral justification and in assessing the appropriate response. Mild and temporary inconvenience to the physical liberty of movement of others may be justified in the moral calculus if it is imposed with the aim and some hope of redressing substantial injustice. But substantial interference with the moral and constitutional rights of innocent citizens can never be justified and should be vigorously prosecuted, no matter how conscientiously motivated.

How to Respond

The discussion so far has all been in terms of moral justification, as opposed to a legal defense that might be raised by the disobedient. That a law is disobeyed because the disobedient perceives it as violating his conscience cannot be thought of as a legal defense, unless, as we shall shortly see, it may be translated into equivalent constitutional terms. When the disobedience is not of the direct "conscientious" kind but instead is collaterally aimed at an unobjectionable law in order to attack some other practice or policy, it is even clearer that it should not be a legal excuse. The justification we have been speaking of lies in the realm of ethical judgments. It is nonetheless practically important for that.

Once civil disobedience is viewed as having some moral justification, a number of inescapable questions are posed to persons in authority. They include the following: (1) In the case of conscientious disobedience, should the law in question be abolished or revised in order to avoid intolerable impositions on conscience? (2) In the case of collateral disobedience, should the policy or practice protested against be changed? These first two questions are primarily for legislative bodies. (3) Do the motives of the disobedients remove them so far from the ordinary concept of blameworthy lawbreakers that prosecutorial officials should exercise their discretion not to bring a charge? (4) Should a jury, when civil disobedients are prosecuted, exercise its untouchable privilege of acquitting, even though nothing has been raised that amounts to a defense in strictly legal terms? The jury's power of "nullification," as it is called, by which we mean returning an acquittal against the strict law and the evidence, is an important way of demonstrating public sympathy for the position of the disobedients and of registering criticism of the law or policy that brought the disobedients to trial. (5) If the disobedients are convicted, what significance should judges attach to their motives and aims when imposing sentence?

If the criminal law is an institutionalized and public apparatus of social criticism, then it must not only itself be open to review and criticism but may also be used as a vehicle to level criticism against other social practices and institutions. The civil disobedient is seeking to do exactly this. To prevent the law from falling into disrepute, legislators, prosecutors, juries, and judges must always remain sensitive to the voice of protest that is raised when civil disobedience occurs. This does not mean that the disobedient is always right; we may think him entirely wrongheaded and very dangerous. But if, after reflection, we perceive moral force in his position, a response that goes beyond a wooden and mechanical application of criminal sanctions is called for.

For prosecutors and judges, the dilemma may be an acute one. Lawyers are professionally familiar with the notion that the law does not excuse participation in crime on the ground of purity of motive. But in recent experience, as with the Nazi regime, the legal system itself could be viewed as a deliberate and deadly attack on values cherished in our morality, and our applause was reserved for those who took the awful risk of disobeying. The enormity of evil expressed in modern tyrannies has undermined any simple faith in the overwhelming importance of fidelity to law. At the same time there has been ample evidence that skillfully organized campaigns of civil disobedience can be very effective in securing desirable social change. Those who have occupied the office of solicitor general of the United States are not prominent advocates of illegal behavior, but Professor Archibald Cox, a former holder of that office, and other prominent ones, has written:

> Social protest and even civil disobedience serve the law's need for growth. Ideally, reform would come according to reason and justice without self-help and disturbing, almost violent, forms of protest. . . . Still, candor compels one here again to acknowledge the gap between the ideal and the reality. Short of the millennium, sharp changes in the law depend partly upon the stimulus of protest.[3]

For all these reasons, even if the motive of a lawbreaker would not be a matter of defense at trial, entitling him to a verdict of acquittal, it remains a crucial consideration for prosecutors in deciding whether to prosecute and judges in fixing sentence. The motivation of an accused has always been recognized as a relevant consideration, as an aggravating or mitigating circumstance, when settling a punishment. But it is not always clear what significance we should attach to the circumstance that the defendant deliberately engaged in violation of the law as a response to what seemed to him to be pressing moral demands. In one aspect such a person seems less deserving of reprobation than one who breaks the law for personal gain and who would not even pretend to offer a moral defense of his behavior. If we are satisfied that the defendant was indeed moved by conscience, we can perhaps sufficiently vindicate the ideal of fidelity to law by the denunciatory impact of conviction, coupled with nominal or light punishment. The infliction of a severe penalty on a person who has been morally impelled to do what he has done is only cruelty. Such a notion has been apparent for a long time even in the case of murder, the most serious of all crimes, where in euthanasia-type killings a variety of devices has been employed to secure a light sentence for the accused.

But, in another light, it is possible to regard civil disobedience stemming from moral conviction as especially dangerous to society. Those who have deep moral objections to the law's demands are likely to proselytize others to join them in their disobedience. They make a public appeal to the conscience of their fellow citizens, quite unlike the man who breaks the law for greed or in violence. They may be stubborn in their convictions and unlikely to yield to the threat of only mild punishment. If the demand made by the law and rejected by the disobedient is felt to be vital to the security or well-being of society, then it may be thought that harsh punishment is necessary to reduce the number of disobedients to those with unshakable certitude and unconquerable courage. This explains the traditionally severe punishments meted out to those who in time of war refuse to serve in the armed forces for conscientious reasons that are not accommodated in the statutory scheme for conscientious objectors.

To treat civil disobedients with great lenity runs the risk of making defiance of the law too easy. To treat them severely runs the risk of brutalizing the institution of punishment and undermining the respect for the legal system, for few of us can be happy about the imposition of severe sanctions on people whose motives we agree are honorable, even though we may question their judgment. The wiser course is surely to persist in lenient treatment until the social dangers of the disobedience are indubitably obtrusive. If there is a suspicion that moral positions are being advanced only as camouflage by those who wish to avoid the burdens of complying with the law, or if there is a belief that those who are disobeying have not, because of the lightness of previous penalties, reflected long and soberly enough, then this can be expressed by a gradual escalation of sanctions. Even when we are convinced of the honesty and reflectiveness of the defendant's stand but believe his rejection of the law's demand to be dangerous because of the vital nature of the duty involved, a slow hardening of penalties is still to be preferred. To assert that the most dangerous people in our society are those of strong moral convictions and courage is an unhappy admission to have to make. It is one that we should not be in a hurry to embrace.

Unconstitutional Laws

In a legal system, such as that of the United States, that includes judicial power to review and quash legislation or executive acts on constitutional grounds, it is necessary to isolate a situation that is only marginally, if at all, one of civil disobedience. This can arise when the protester deliberately violates a statute or executive ruling that he believes will be declared unconstitutional by the courts and when his predominant purpose is to engineer a test case for a review of the question of constitutionality. Sometimes the constitutionality of a statute may be effectively tested without any *prima facie* breach of the law being committed. But in certain situations the most expeditious method of bringing the question before the courts is to act contrary to the statute. In the wave of civil rights disobedience in the 1960s, black people frequently sat-in on segregated premises. Local courts were ordinarily ready to convict for breaches of trespass laws in these cases, but the protesters were often able to obtain review in the Supreme Court of the United States of the statute or practice that excluded them from the premises.

For complex legal reasons those constitutional attacks were sometimes successful and sometimes not. When the attacks were successful it is plain that, in the outcome, the protesters were not disobedients at all, since the law they seemed to break in fact turned out to be no law at all. Their convictions would accordingly be reversed. The situation is less simple when a court decides that the statute is constitutionally acceptable. In a sense here the defendant has made a mistake of law (he hoped to show that a statute was unconstitutional, but a court disagreed with him), and lawyers are familiar with the notion that a mistake of law is generally not a defense in a criminal prosecution.

But, even as the law now stands, mistake of law is recognized as a defense in special situations. It has been admitted as a defense in cases where the defendant's mistake proceeded from bad advice from an official concerned with the administration of that branch of the law. In 1957 the Supreme Court opened up new doctrine in this area in the case of *Lambert* v. *California*,[4] by holding that ignorance of the existence of a criminal prohibition could be a defense when the statute required a positive act on the part of the defendant, and government had failed to take adequate steps to bring the law's requirements to the notice of persons to whom it applied. In that case the defendant had been found guilty of failing to register as a person earlier convicted of a felony, having claimed in her defense that she never knew that the law imposed any such requirement. Nothing in the existing cases, however, would warrant the argument that the mere presence of a belief in the defendant that the violated law was unconstitutional should be a defense, even if the belief were based on the opinion of attorneys. But the development of such a doctrine is certainly within the power of the courts and might be salutary, if confined within careful limits.

The restrictions on such a defense would have to include at least the following: (1) that the defendant had the purpose of demonstrating the unconstitutional character of the law; (2) that there was legitimate doubt about the constitutionality of the law, as perhaps evidenced by expert testimony on the current state of professional opinion; (3) that there was no way, short of disobedience, by which the defendant could have obtained a determination of the validity of the law; (4) that the disobedience was nonviolent.

The contention here is that a declaration of the constitutionality of a statute by a court does not logically entail the conclusion that a person who has broken the law should be convicted and punished. Other factors are relevant to guilt, and it would be quite proper to hold that, although the law is now found to be constitutional, the defendant shall not be convicted because of the exculpating circumstance of his honest and reasonable doubt as to its validity. Such a defense would be, however, quickly exhausted since once the Supreme Court had made a definitive pronouncement on the constitutionality of the statute, presumably no assertion of its unconstitutionality could afterward be regarded as reasonable for purposes of justification.

But if a continued assertion (in the teeth of a court's opinion to the contrary) that a statute or executive order is unconstitutional cannot be seen as a full defense to criminal conduct, it may still be possible to see it as a circumstance of excuse, significant for the exercise of prosecutorial discretion and the judge's determination of sentence. Ronald Dworkin has pointed out that in cases of conscientious disobedience the arguments of injustice made by the disobedient are always capable of translation into constitutional terms.[5] Those who refused induction into the military service during the war in Vietnam certainly condemned American participation as immoral and unjust, but at the same time they regarded it as unconstitutional, as being in violation of treaties and international law, and also as usurping the reservation of the war-making power to Congress.

Some tried to take these matters to the courts, arguing that the unconstitutionality of the war should serve as a defense to any criminal prosecution based on refusal to be inducted or to obey orders to proceed to Vietnam. The Supreme Court and lower federal courts turned aside these attempts by ruling in effect that the constitutionality of the war involved political questions on which the courts should not rule. This "political question" doctrine throws a shadow over a pillar of the American constitutional system, for its very nature remains not fully elucidated. In some contexts it appears to mean that the courts have no competence to rule on certain questions, since their determination has been reserved by the Constitution for resolution by some other branch of government. Questions arising out of the impeachment of a President might be an example of this kind. But in other contexts the application of the political question doctrine appears to signify no more than that a court (and particularly the Supreme Court) does not find it timely or propitious to seize an issue, perhaps for reasons of political sensitivity, among others.

Applying these theories to the issues surrounding the war in Vietnam, the Court's application of the doctrine could, therefore, be given either of two interpretations. These would be: (1) that the question of the exercise of the war-making power was a matter for political resolution between President and Congress and that the express reference to this power in the Constitution should not be understood as conferring any capacity on courts to decide questions under it; (2) alternatively, that, although the Court had the competence and capacity to decide questions about the proper exercise of the power to make war, it was refraining from such resolution in the instant case for reasons of prudence.

Under either interpretation, those who challenged the constitutionality of the war in Vietnam might have felt that they could with some propriety continue to pose the challenge; for if the constitutionality of the war was a matter that the courts *could* not touch, then every citizen remained entitled to his opinions, a least until the legislature and the executive could issue some agreed-on and authoritative clarification. And if it were a question that the courts simply *would* not touch, then there was a real absence of resolution coupled with a possibility of future determination that justified continued assertion of the claim.

It may well be that the grave constitutional crisis that might have arisen from a judicial attempt to restrain military action ordered by the executive was a sufficiently awful danger to justify the abstention practiced by the federal courts over the questions of the Vietnam war. But the abstention left disobedients in a posture in which they could continue to argue with some force that the law was on their side and that those in office were the lawbreakers. Only in the complexities of a constitutional democracy are such dilemmas possible. The Vietnam war example is a particularly sharp one, framed as it is in the difficulties of judicial abstention under the political question doctrine, but it contains a lesson of some general import. When a person is cast by official action in the role of a disobedient but protests that in fact he is the one who is being faithful to the highest law of the society, we should at the least pay respectful attention to the arguments offered; for it may well be that we ourselves in years to come may conclude that the disobedient was right after all. Respect for the moral foundations of his position and an accompanying slowness and moderation in using the weapons of prosecution and punishment are for these reasons generally desirable.

X

Disruption

The civil disobedient makes us face up to moral dilemmas and examine our consciences. In this way he is often an uncomfortable and disturbing figure, but rarely a frightening one. Traditionally his aura has been that of gentleness and sacrifice, and his lineage one of martyrs and saints. The term "disruption" has quite different connotations. It evokes images of violence, of running bodies, screaming faces, and swinging fists. It may make us afraid for our safety and awaken impulses of suppression and revenge.

But disruption is evidently not a concept that can be distinguished from civil disobedience with any precision. Certainly extreme examples can be offered that fall decisively into one classification or the other. The person who quite passively refuses induction into the military for reasons of conscience is a civil disobedient. The mob who break up the meeting of a learned society by making an intolerable din and who act purely out of hooligan impulses are disrupters. But the two concepts converge on each other to form a borderland of large dimensions. We have seen that some forms of civil disobedience involve obstruction that interferes with the rights of innocent third parties. In recent years some outbreaks of disorder and disruption have been purposefully aimed at exposing injustice and stirring the conscience of the community. There are family resemblances here that lead one to believe that civil disobedience and disruption can in some respects be helpfully compared.

Once civil disobedience goes beyond a pure assertion of personal principle by the disobedient, once it aims at change and reform, then it will always be beset by a tendency to evolve into disruption. At first it may be hoped that the pure appeal to conscience through sacrifice may convert others. Then it may be observed that if enough like-minded people join together in the disobedience, they may have a considerable nuisance value in harassing government. The nuisance may reside simply in the embarrassment to which government will be put by the public knowledge that so many oppose their program or in having to take legal steps against a substantial number of people. But the nuisance may be more serious in that it may actually obstruct the execution of the program expressed in law that the government wants to enforce. So if enough people could be persuaded to refuse induction, it would be difficult to fight a war. Once civil disobedients band together and proselytize with the aim of impeding the execution of government programs, they have already moved from a pure expression of conscience into a kind of disruption, however passive and nonviolent.

From this starting point, a scale could be charted that might move through intermediate stages to the apex of a violent revolution. So the obstruction by passive refusal to participate is less disruptive than obstruction by physical interposition of bodies however limp and noncombative. Lying down on a roadway in front of army trucks would be an example of nonviolent physical obstruction. The next stage might be noisy and insulting, though still nonviolent, disruption, such as attempts by defendants and others to break up the orderly conduct of judicial proceedings. Higher on the scale might come the forcible seizure of buildings and other pieces of property and holding them against those who have a lawful right of presence. The student disorders of the late 1960s provided a legion of examples of this kind of conduct.

Violent conduct, involving risk of injury to persons and the actual destruction of property, takes us one step farther, as with "trashing" buildings or hurling missiles. Even more terrifying modes of protest are now sickeningly familiar, such as kidnaping and assassination. At this point we have clearly left civil disobedience far behind, though such actions may still be presented or characterized as political and aiming at change and reform, perhaps accompanied by the punishment of oppressors.

It is not, of course, the case that the spectrum of conduct outlined here represents an inevitable progression, either of practice or principle. The pure civil disobedient is no more likely to "progress" to kidnaping and murder than the person who occasionally smokes a marihuana cigarette is likely to become a committed heroin addict. Nor is the conscientious civil disobedient properly to be charged with countenancing or tacitly approving the commission of violent acts of protest. Nothing in the principles he espouses binds him to such approval. He may with perfect consistency defend his refusal to act against his conscience and at the same time abhor acts of violence or even passive physical obstruction.

But historical and recent experience in many parts of the world with the violence of political and social movements of protest do impose two urgent moral duties on anyone engaging in even the most peaceful form of law-breaking for even the most conscientious reasons. The first is a duty to engage in the most grave and meticulous examination of the moral justifications for his action. This, in turn, involves consideration of the possibility that his conduct and government response to his conduct may be seen by others (though not by himself) as justifying an expansion into harsher and violent modes of protest. One segment of human history, claims for national independence, has been sadly characterized by progressions of this kind. The national group, denied its autonomy, often first makes its claims known peacefully by argument and petition, perhaps supported by civil disobedience. Lack of a positive response by the colonial or occupying power is seen by some as justifying riotous assemblies, the destruction of property, and perhaps ultimately assassination and bombings. People who are seen as the enemy are killed, and inevitably innocent people, often members of the group that sees itself oppressed or denied its liberty, are also hurt and killed.

Freedom has of course been won this way, and new nations established, most of which we may feel have strong and valid claims to self-government. Whether such freedom might eventually have come by more peaceful means we can never know, and whether the gaining of political autonomy justifies violence is a hard question for moral philosophers. It is a question that we do not have to tackle, since violence of that sort is inseparably tied to a theory of justifiable revolution. It aims at the overthrow of a government seen as illegitimate. Revolution may of course be domestic and aimed at basic changes in the social order rather than the expulsion of a foreign power. But, in either form, the theory of revolution is outside the scope of this book. We are concerned here with the different, and perhaps even more perplexing, question of the extent to which disruptive activity may have some moral justification outside the aims of revolution.

We may start with the assumption that any system of government is flawed. However excellent its principles, its constitutional foundation, and its organization, it will be subject at all levels to the taint of human imperfection. The legislators will be less than wholly pure and selfless in their motives; some officials will be stupid or venal; segments of the bureaucracy will be inefficient or inert; some judges may be harsh or corrupt or discriminatory. Individual citizens will suffer from these flaws, and certain groups are more likely to suffer collectively than others. These will be groups who have historically been little represented in circles of power. This may be because they were workers or because of their color or religion or national origin. The combination of their low social status with their concomitant lack of power makes it easy for those in authority to ignore their claims and to allow a situation of injustice to continue with respect to them.

Such a society, like every human one, is evidently a society in which injustice is being done. It is not so easy to say whether it is an unjust society. We might of course settle the question by stipulating that every society in which injustice is done through the instrument of government is an unjust society. But this would do some violence to ordinary usage, for it would call unjust every human society at all times. It might be better to say that a society is properly called unjust only when social arrangements expressed in or sanctioned by the laws result in continuing or recurring patterns of injustice to individuals or groups in that society.

Even in this more limited sense, many societies would properly be styled unjust, and some would argue that all human societies have always been unjust, even in this stronger sense. To condemn a society as unjust in this sense is not the same, however, as finding a justification for violent revolution. Before the threshold of justifiable revolution is reached we should want to know that the patterns of injustice are deep and hard, that those who have power have been stubbornly deaf to pleas for change, that the society as a whole shows no impetus to move to right the wrongs. We would have to be convinced too that the attempt at revolution had at least a fair chance of doing more good than harm.

Many people who live in societies where injustice is done, societies that may even be called unjust, are far from being convinced that the case for revolution is made. They may see their government as flawed, even deeply flawed, but as on the whole preferable to the risks of the unknown or the disturbance and violence involved in radical change. Nevertheless, and especially if they are the victims of injustice, they may wish to press keenly for fundamental social change. When persuasion fails, civil disobedience is one technique to which they may resort. They may ask themselves too whether forms of disruption going beyond the quietism of classical civil disobedience may not be justified. Here they confront the morality of disruption in a nonrevolutionary posture. A study of the case for disruption in one area of American public life may serve to clarify the issues.

Disruption in the Courts

Disruption in recent years has reappeared in one American forum where it had not visited for a long time, the courtroom. The disruption of the judicial process has caused particular trauma for lawyers and judges who may be anxious to behave with fairness but who also cherish order and decorum as not only gracious adornments but absolutely necessary aspects of judicial proceedings. It is a good example on which to concentrate and to analyze with some care.

How should we react to defendants who will not co-operate with the judicial process, to radicals, black or white, who shout insults at judges or mount guerrilla theater in the courtroom? Can we rest content with the gag and the nightstick as the inevitable countermoves or even with more sophisticated suggestions of plastic cages or closed-circuit television relay of the proceedings to a defendant outside the courtroom free to communicate with his counsel by telephone?[1] Most discussion so far has been in terms of a choice among such alternatives, and there can of course be no escape from debate about the rival merits of restraint and separation once disorder is on the scene. But to accept disruption in the court as just another of the seven plagues that annually visit our sick society while neglecting serious discussion of the roots of the disease would be a serious error.

We need to examine the impulses and motives that drive disrupters to behave in the way that they do, for it is in the first place of primary importance to know whether these people feel themselves to be acting in a *justifiable* manner or whether they are simply savages who live outside our realm of discourse. Their own justifications and any others that might be supplied for them will then deserve the most serious examination, for any conclusion that disruption in our courtrooms might in some circumstances be justified would be a startling one, inevitably entailing urgent duties to reform institutions and practices so as to remove the causes.

An initial clarification is desirable at this point. Even if it should turn out that some reasonable justifications for disruption can be advanced, this is not to argue that disruption should be tolerated. To tolerate disruption in the courts would be to commit institutional suicide, and it is not necessary at this point to decide whether institutional morality ever includes a duty to self-destruct. But any showing of justification for disruption, while permitting steps to be taken to allow the trial to proceed in tranquility would clearly be a cogent reason for dealing mildly with the disrupters in the context of sanctions and, as indicated above, an urgent reason for curing whatever institutional inequities constitute the justification.

CORRUPT COURTS

To begin with a hypothetical model, it is possible to imagine a situation in which refusal to co-operate with the judicial process would be the *only* kind of disobedience that would make much sense. Suppose a society where all the laws are generally acknowledged to be wise and just, where the legislators are prudent and incorruptible, the police and prosecutors gentle and humane, and where no great economic inequalities exist. This utopia is, however, marred (and perhaps made more believable) by the circumstance that some of its courts are staffed by corrupt and arbitrary judges whose improper and unpredictable conduct of judicial proceedings is left uncorrected by a weak and also corrupt appellate court system. Any defendant brought before these courts can have no reasonable expectation that his case will be decided by a rational application of the rules and principles of law to the facts. If efforts to unseat such judges through constitutional means should fail, then it seems that refusal to co-operate peacefully with their processes becomes at the least a moral right and perhaps a moral duty for the good citizen. This is only to say simply that where the judicial process as a whole or some part of it loses all integrity, then it forfeits all claim to respect and submission.

And yet such a situation might well not be one where a general revolutionary policy would be justified. A dictatorial and brutal regime could conceivably (though not probably) coexist with reasonably fair and impartial courts. South Africa may be such an example. Here revolution may be justified even though the judicial process is comparatively unexceptionable. Conversely, a reasonably fair and just society might in some aspects be saddled with grave abuses in its judiciary and courts. Here, although revolution might not be justified, nonco-operation with courts might be.

So the argument begins to develop that disruption in the courts *could* be (in certain given circumstances) a justifiable form of disobedience that does not depend on the prior identification and justification of a generally revolutionary position. Would such a posture be justifiable only when the iniquity protested against was in the judge himself and his conduct of the courtroom? Or could it extend to situations of more diffuse failure of integrity in the legal system? We might begin here by offering a concrete illustration in a comparatively trivial area without obvious connotations of radicalism and certainly far removed from traditional contexts of civil disobedience.

DISCRIMINATORY ENFORCEMENT

Suppose that a state has a very broadly drawn statute that prohibits all forms of gambling. Local law-enforcement authorities have long been in the habit of ignoring public gambling activities conducted by religious groups for charitable or church-related fund-raising and also ignoring fairly overt social poker playing for money. However, a rigorous policy of enforcement is pursued with respect to dice games played for money. Now, it so happens that while middle-class WASPS, Irish, and Italians commonly play cards, dice games are usually played by blacks and Spanish-speaking Americans. These minority groups thus bear the brunt of prosecutions and naturally feel aggrieved. They try to redress this grievance in an orderly and democratic fashion by addressing arguments to the police and local prosecutors, urging a change in the selective enforcement policies. These are of no avail. When prosecuted for gambling offenses they appeal the convictions and make constitutional arguments that the selective law-enforcement policies are infringements of their rights to equal protection of the laws and due process. These arguments fail, and the convictions are affirmed.

At this point there are plausible grounds for contending that, with respect to gambling laws, an unjust and unequal enforcement policy has been countenanced by law-enforcement officials and the courts, so that on this issue at least the usual moral arguments in favor of co-operating with judicial processes have been overborne by countervailing arguments derived from principles of justice and fairness. Here again we begin to find a case for starting civil disobedience in the courtroom, but again this is not at all the same as a general case for revolution or a general argument for behaving criminally or even a general argument for always violating the tranquility of the courts. It asserts only that in one small and very particular context the administration of justice has generally deteriorated into arbitrary caprice and deserves no respect. It would be a perfectly proper position to be maintained by a generally law-abiding and orderly group.

The courtroom disruption that has emerged in recent years has not of course been in the low-level context of gambling offenses. For the most part it has taken place at the trials of political radicals, black and white. Writing at the height of these disruptions Haywood Burns commented on the doubt expressed by President Kingman Brewster of Yale University as to whether black revolutionaries could get a fair trial anywhere in the United States.

> Many black revolutionaries have answered the question firmly in the negative. Having made this assessment of the legal system and their chances within it, many revolutionary defendants have ceased to look upon the courtroom as an arena in which a contest for and against their exoneration is waged, but rather as a platform to expose the failings of the legal system, to educate and politicize a larger public—to indict the system. What has so often been characterized as disruption is often less a calculated attempt to impede the progress of their trial than it is a refusal to sit silent while being subjected to personal affronts.
>
> If such defendants believe someone is lying about them, they say so. If they believe their constitutional rights are being abridged, they say so. If they believe the judge is behaving in a racist fashion, they say so—and in their own terms. This refusal to accept the rules of the judicial game stems from a judgment on their part that the game is fixed.
>
> In their minds there is no reason to sit passively by or to participate co-operatively in a process that is designed for their own destruction. As revolutionaries they believe it is their obligation to behave as revolutionaries wherever they find themselves—in the streets, in the courtroom, in jail. If this conduct is calculated at all, it is calculated to make manifest the latent bias which the defendants believe is rife in the legal system, to bring to the surface the vicious antipathies that would otherwise be masked by the niceties of legal rules.[2]

This summation of the disrupter's point of view will very likely come as something of a shock to the white judge or attorney, no matter how impeccable his credentials for deploring racism and advocating equality. For, Mr. Burns contends:

> Whereas white Americans are accustomed to viewing the law as a historic vehicle through which liberties have been progressively expanded, black Americans have experienced law in quite another fashion. From the very first, American law has been the handmaiden of American racism. It has been the means by which the generalized racism in the society has

> been made specific and converted into the particularized policies and standards of social control.[3]

This is a sweeping charge that, fortunately, does not have to be affirmed or denied to carry the present discussion further. We do not have to be convinced that the whole of American society is fundamentally shot through with racism, or that the legal system has been the executant of racist policies in order to find some justification for disruption in the courts. Mr. Burns was writing about black revolutionaries, and the beliefs and state of mind he outlines are necessary to support a revolutionary posture. But, as we have suggested earlier, less gross defects might be found in the legal system which, while not amounting to a true bill on charges of general racism, might be sufficient to forfeit claims to respect and co-operation.

ABUSES AND REFORM

Courts cannot cure all ills that blacks and radicals are heirs to. What those who presently attest to grievances have a right to expect is that senior officers of the legal system will institute rules and policies to curb abuses of discretion and will then vigilantly oversee subordinates who execute these policies. A concentration on the merits of glass cages versus closed-circuit television quite misses the truth that co-operation with the legal process is ultimately secured only when people accept the process as by and large fair and just, albeit imperfect.

Discretionary aspects of the administration of criminal justice in the United States bear down with particular hardship on political radicals, members of minority groups, and nonconformist people generally. The American system has lavished obsessive care and scrutiny on the investigatory and trial stages of the criminal process but has virtually ignored the discretionary procedures by which a small number of defendants is selected from the host of candidates. A leading work on criminal procedure comments:

> Arresting officers commonly exercise considerable discretion in determining whether to make an arrest. Quite frequently in situations involving minor misdemeanors, e.g., assault, an

> officer may refuse to make an arrest even though the offense was committed in his presence. . . . The prosecutor will decide against charging in a substantial number of cases. Not infrequently 30 to 50 per cent of the persons arrested in a major city on felony and misdemeanor charges are not prosecuted.[4]

In such a climate it is small wonder that some have contended that the criminal law in the United States is not in the least a body of prohibitions that evenly and equally admonishes all citizens but rather an arsenal of weapons in the hands of officials who will use them remorselessly against their enemies but with considerable mercy or perhaps indifference against others.

Kenneth Culp Davis points out a curious paradox of police discretionary powers. They become most extensive and most potent as we descend the chain of command so that the man on the beat, usually without a college education, is the one who often makes the most crucial decisions.[5] No matter how much respect and admiration we may wish to accord the police for doing an unpleasant, difficult, and not very well rewarded job, there is clearly cause for grave disquiet when hundreds of thousands of decisions on which liberty may depend are made secretly, without any public proclamation of relevant standards, and in circumstances that generally make review impossible. At best this may lead to selective law enforcement, which often owes much to an officer's sensitive awareness of the mores of his own cultural and racial group and a nonmalevolent but nevertheless critical ignorance of the customs and folkways of other groups. At worst it may lead to systematic harassment of racial groups, political radicals, and other unpopular characters. Since the criminal process in many of our large cities moves with all the swiftness and efficiency of a paralyzed tortoise, it is often a sufficient punishment for the guilty and a horrendous fate for the innocent just to have a criminal process initiated against them, even if the outcome is an acquittal.

When selective law enforcement is combined with unshakable certitude in the minds of political radicals and minority group members that the police routinely practice wholesale perjury, then nonco-operation with the judicial process becomes at least understandable. Indeed, the wonder is that there has been so little disruption in the courts when there has so often been good reason for it; for in these areas, where police and prosecutorial discretion bear down most heavily on radical and minority groups, constitutional doctrines seem of little avail as protection. The Constitution, which has spun a Byzantine web around so many aspects of the investigatory and trial processes, has understandably run into an impermeable curtain when the discretionary practices of the police on the street are in question. Even in the area of the discretion exercised by prosecuting attorneys, courts have been very hesitant about interposing constitutional supervision. The Supreme Court has admittedly said that selective law enforcement may amount to a denial of equal protection if "an element of intentional or purposeful discrimination" is shown, but this dictum has borne very little fruit.[6]

The California case of *People* v. *Gray* (1967)[7] is an interesting illustration of the problem under discussion. In that case the defendants had been convicted of violating a section of the Los Angeles Municipal Code that prohibited marking or writing on or affixing any sign to private property without the consent of the owner. The sign that the defendants had put up ran "B---, B---, B---!," which might be thought to stand for "Burn, Baby, Burn!," though the defendants contended (somewhat implausibly, in view of the number of hyphens) that it stood for "Bring Back Brown!." The incident occurred at the time of primary elections in California, and the defendants produced many photographs of signs of every nature posted at random throughout Los Angeles in connection with the elections. They then produced testimony from owners of the properties involved to the effect that they had never given permission for the signs in question to be posted and that the police had never been in touch with them concerning the signs. Judicial notice was taken that between January 1 and July 31, 1966, the dockets of the Municipal Court of the Los Angeles Judicial District showed only two prosecutions for violations of the section in question out of about twenty-five thousand nontraffic misdemeanor complaints. One was the case in question, and the other involved an identical slogan.

The Supreme Court of California sent back the case for retrial on the ground that the trial judge had imposed too heavy a quantum of proof on the defendants with respect to their defense of discriminatory enforcement. The court clearly recognized the existence of such a defense, but pointed out that discriminatory enforcement is something more than selective enforcement, though the opinions are not helpful in establishing the nature of the additional elements that must be shown. Certainly the court was of the mind that a mere showing on a statistical basis of comparative desuetude (that is, that the law was very rarely enforced in terms of the number of breaches known or that reasonably might be supposed to be known to the police) was insufficient to establish discriminatory enforcement. Presumably the thrust of this comment is that the defendant would have the burden of showing the specifically arbitrary reason or motive that the authorities had in singling him out for prosecution, clearly a difficult burden to discharge.

The defendant did make an attempt at such a showing in the New York case of *People* v. *Walker* (1964),[8] where she contended that her prosecution for violations of the Multiple Dwelling Law was a reprisal for her exposure of corrupt practices in the Department of Buildings. The Court of Appeals reversed her conviction and ordered a new trial on the ground that she was unduly restricted at the trial in her attempts to establish her allegations. Chief Judge Desmond dissented and protested at what he regarded as the introduction into criminal law of a "novel and mischievous defense."

In commenting on *People* v. *Gray*, the editors of *Modern Criminal Procedure* ask the following questions:

> May a Negro prosecuted for violating a gambling ordinance defend on the ground that the law is enforced only against members of his race? . . . May the police justify their conduct on the ground that, since *most* of the city's gambling was believed to be taking place in Negro residential areas, *all* of the "gambling squad" was assigned to duty there? Is this different than a state justifying its exclusion of *all* Negroes from jury service or the voting rolls because *most* Negroes did not possess adequate educational qualifications? Is this different than a "burglary squad" patrolling only the high-priced resi-

> dential area since *most* burglaries are likely to occur there? Is the court in *Gray* correct in rejecting the "statistical method employed by the Supreme Court of the United States in a series of jury discrimination cases"? Even if the defendants cannot show why it is that the law has not been enforced against others, are there cases in which the statistics would show a disparity "too gross to be the result of mere chance?"[9]

Indeed, the position of the California court in *Gray* may be a good deal more sympathetic to the defendant's contention than that which obtains in many jurisdictions. A law review comment states that many state courts have taken the position that "the equal protection clause does not guarantee to those who violate the law equal protection from prosecution. Underlying this rationale seems to be the assumption that the equal protection clause forbids only the discriminatory deprivation of pre-existing rights, but does not create an independent right to nondiscriminatory penal enforcement, since there is no pre-existing right to commit a crime."[10]

If courts are reluctant and cautious to move decisively into the field of discriminatory law enforcement, they appear virtually paralyzed when confronted with wholesale police perjury. A prime example of this is the notorious "dropsy" evidence offered in criminal courts in narcotics cases, by which a quite incredible number of narcotics carriers appear to have in common the careless habit of dropping their narcotics on the ground whenever a police officer or agent happens to be passing by. In this way the police apparently acquire evidence lawfully without the unfortunate necessity of having to make an illegal search. In a case in the New York City Criminal Court, *People* v. *McMurty*, the defendant contended that he had been illegally searched by the police, contrary to the police testimony for the prosecution, which was to the effect that the defendant had let drop a plastic container of marihuana. Judge Younger, speaking of police "dropsy" testimony, said:

> The judge has no reason to disbelieve it in any particular case and of course the judge must decide each case on its own evidence without regard to the testimony in other cases. Surely, though, not in every case was the defendant unlucky

enough to drop his narcotics at the feet of a policeman. It follows that at least in some of these cases the police are lying.[11]

Judge Younger went on to hold that "dropsy" testimony should be scrutinized with especial caution and should be rejected if the policeman's testimony seemed "inherently unreal" or if there was some independent contradiction of his testimony. On the facts of the case before him, he did not find any of these conditions satisfied, and so allowed the evidence to be admitted.

This courageous judicial exposure of police illegality has of course been matched for a long time by a profound folk knowledge of the chasm that lies between the view of criminal procedure that might be gained from reading the decisions of the Supreme Court and the reality of law enforcement and prosecutorial processes. Discriminatory law enforcement and perjury are for the most part beyond the present effective scope of judicial action, as also is most police brutality. But it is by no means beyond the scope of judicial imagination to move more boldly into a posture of intervention in these areas. As the cases show, in the area of discriminatory law enforcement, only a slight shift in doctrines with respect to burdens of proof and the nature of evidence taken to be sufficient to establish the discrimination would be necessary to strengthen judicial intervention. Judge Younger's opinion referred to above points the way to a less trusting and more open-minded view of police veracity. Judges could be a great deal more zealous in investigating allegations of police brutality by defendants and in exhorting prosecuting authorities to look into such matters. Very much more may be done within the existing law in many jurisdictions by the attorneys general of states in supervising the activities of the local prosecutors and the police.

In large urban areas the courts have a particular duty to remedy the lengthy incarceration of defendants before trial, which is a consequence of the combined impact of crowded dockets and high bail. It is certainly true, as some apologists have pointed out, that delay in bringing an accused to trial is to some extent a product of complexities introduced into criminal proceedings by the Supreme Court's expansion of the rights of suspects and defendants, and in particular cases the result of an individual defendant's raising many of these issues in extensive pretrial motions that require lengthy pretrial hearings. But it would be a strangely perverse comment on legal institutions if defendants were made to pay a forfeit of long incarceration for insisting on their constitutional rights —a penalty exacted furthermore while they are still unconvicted. If crowded dockets cannot be cleared by reform of court procedures or if judicial lethargy or legislative parsimony are too-powerful obstacles to such reforms, then the only proper response ought to be increasingly liberal granting of bail.

Sixth and Eighth Amendment rights to a speedy trial and to bail that is not excessive provide clear signposts to judicial duties in this field. And where bail has to be denied or a defendant cannot make the bail that is set, there is surely good constitutional foundation in the due process clause for insisting that the facility in which he is detained be clearly distinguishable from a traditional prison facility in which convicted prisoners are housed. This is not of course to insist that a prison must be punitive or that a house of detention for defendants awaiting trial must be demonstrably more comfortable than the most enlightened open prison in the same jurisdiction. But it would involve the proposition that those persons awaiting trial in detention because they cannot make bail must be afforded the maximum freedom and minimal amount of restriction compatible with preventing escape and that the conditions under which they are housed must meet a standard of minimum decencies. Where these conditions are not satisfied, release from such detention ought to be afforded under the writ of habeas corpus.

There has, of late, been a growing recognition that prisoners of all kinds, whether awaiting trial or serving sentences, suffer profoundly from not having ready access to lawyers who might process their complaints or advise them as to their rights. An important recent study has suggested the setting up of legal services offices in prisons and detention centers.[12] This would be a step that might go a long way to remove legitimate discontent.

PUBLIC DUTIES

Disruption in the courts is, then, either the expression of a general revolutionary position or, in a less extreme posture, a kind of civil disobedience evincing protest against what are felt to be deep injustices either in the processes that have brought defendants before the courts or in the court procedures themselves. The disruption that has so far attracted most attention has stemmed from defendants who probably espouse a generally revolutionary position, though this would no doubt encompass the belief that there are basic injustices in the law-enforcement system and judicial procedures. Lawyers, in their professional capacities, cannot be expected to find general social remedies for revolutionary protests, except of course insofar as revolutionary positions owe something to basic injustices in the content and operation of the legal system itself. But where disruption is not so much a by-product of a general commitment to revolution but is rather an ad hoc response to scarifying malfunctions and inequities in the legal system, then lawyers have a peculiarly urgent duty to make the correct response.

For here there are two incipient dangers, both of which have already to some extent come to the surface. The first is that persistent indifference by the legal community to the legitimate grievances of defendants, particularly in large urban areas, will so deepen and sharpen the sense of injustice that disruption of legal procedures will become the norm and not the exception. Recent disturbances in houses of detention in New York City and elsewhere lend credence to this conjecture. Courtroom disruption may soon become the tactic not only of a handful of committed revolutionaries but also of hosts of the black and Spanish-American urban poor who find themselves thrown into the jaws of the so slowly masticating legal monster. Crisis reaction on the part of the legal community will then be seen by the consumers of the legal product for what it is—a coerced response to the violence of men whom the law has made desperate, and not the timely correction of perceived injustice. The second, and in the long run the more dangerous, consequence is that those who find the legal system so cynically wanting in qualities of humanity and concern, even wanting in simple efficiency, will soon be converted to a position of supporting general revolution. In this way, as has so often happened in history, a cold and cruel process of law will breed its own destroyers.

The claustrophobic effect induced by the mental furniture that a classical legal education and the practice of law often provide may lead to a response to disruption in the courtroom that may be tragically irrelevant to the present scene. When confronted by an incident of disruption or when contemplating its possibility, lawyers are apt to think in terms of the rending of the very basic fabric of law and order. The courtroom is likened to a temple, and disrupters are seen as almost committing sacrilege. The judicial process for the lawyer is the ultimate happening, in which all the argument and all the disputation are resolved by authoritative rulings. If this very sanctum sanctorum can be invaded, if rude hands, as it were, seek to dash the chalice from the priest, then all the rest is of no avail. An emotional response of shock is thus very understandable but is for that reason all the more in need of a cool analysis in the light of a reality that is not exclusively apprehended through the eyes of a keeper of the temple.

The first step is to perceive and acknowledge with due humility that some part of the response of outrage is due to the simple professional vanity of people who are accustomed to thinking of their life's work as carrying a peculiar dignity, status, and social value and who are therefore correspondingly filled with rage at those who demonstrate in the most brusque and pointed manner that they do not agree. Some of this is encapsulated in the traditional phrase "contempt of court," which suggests unhappily that the heart of the offense is an insult to the profession. In the only recent English case that has had to deal with disruption in the courtroom, Lord Justice Salmon made just this point:

> The archaic description of these proceedings as "contempt of court" is in my view unfortunate and misleading. It suggests that they are designed to buttress the dignity of the judges and to protect them from insult. Nothing could be further from the truth. No such protection is needed. The sole purpose of proceedings for contempt is to give our courts the power effectively to protect the rights of the public by ensuring that the administration of justice shall not be obstructed or prevented.[13]

As the English judge so rightly points out, there are patently legitimate public interests that demand that steps be taken to avoid disruption in the courtroom and perhaps in some cases to punish it. But if it is a public interest that is being protected, then the true nature and limits of that interest must be located. These are surely to be found in the interest of the public in having a tranquil legal process, *so long as that process is by and large just and humane.* When the process loses to a considerable extent the qualities of justice and humanity, at that moment the general public interest in its tranquility disappears.

Many or most of those who are brought before criminal courts in the large urban concentrations in the United States believe that that point has long since been reached. This belief is at the least arguably correct. The general public, which has been bombarded with tales of criminals who are pampered and led safely away from well-deserved punishment by the protections thrown around them by the Supreme Court, may find such a contention very hard to accept. But the fine web of constitutional law that now encases criminal procedure, admirable as it is in its demonstration of an American zeal to do justice in the most subtle and profound manner, unhappily makes all too little impact on the average urban defendant. In the world of police perjury, long incarceration before trial, and representation of the most perfunctory kind by the Legal Aid officer who bargains within the conventions of the Establishment for the acceptable plea, the body of developed constitutional doctrine may seem as remote, to borrow a metaphor from Judge Jerome Frank, as the manners at Buckingham Palace would seem on the New York subway.

The occasional instances of trial disruption from dedicated political revolutionaries will probably not present serious problems for the courts and are already on the wane. The emergence of large-scale disruption from ordinary defendants would presage a critical convulsion of the criminal-law system. To avoid this, an urgent and strenuous effort must be made by legislatures and the legal profession, both bench and bar. The nature of this effort must be to move swiftly to eradicate all the abuses noted here by adopting every remedy that innovative doctrine and practice can offer. The objectives are easy enough to state. The public must be made to see that the criminal-justice system can be even-handed in its pursuit of offenders of all social classes and races with respect to all manner of crimes. Police and prosecutors must behave with respect for the individual humanity of those whom they arrest and prosecute. The courts themselves must be purged of corruption, where it exists. Their preliminary procedures must bear the marks of a dignified search for good cause to commit a defendant for trial rather than the frantic maintenance of a conveyor belt, as they too often seem today. Plea bargaining must be tightly controlled by publicly proclaimed standards that neglect neither the protection of the public nor the equal treatment of defendants. Incarceration before trial must be drastically reduced and, where unavoidable, must be radically changed in its physical aspects. Judges must be educated on moral and social principles relevant to sentencing.

Difficult as these goals are to achieve, a serious and visible effort, attended by some measure of success, will be necessary before we can confidently dismiss the moral claims of those who disrupt the judicial process.

PART 4

Compensating the Disadvantaged

XI

Collective Responsibility

The poor have always been with us, but the disadvantaged have arrived more recently on the scene. "Poor" is a good, plain, descriptive word, but "disadvantaged," and the fashionably interchangeable adjective "underprivileged," are more subtle as well as more euphemistic. They hint at some assumption of guilt by the presumably advantaged or privileged majority; they suggest a moral duty to act in some way to rectify a situation of social injustice. But the nature of the moral duty involved, the weight of the burden of guilt that one ought properly to shoulder, and what measures of redress might be appropriate are very much in dispute.

That some should be comfortably affluent while others live in misery was, until rather recently in the world's history, accepted as a natural and given condition, imposing no duties except ones of personal charity. But for the last hundred years or so, political theory and moral philosophy have explored concepts of collective reponsibility, of a social duty to improve the way of life of the worst off and to seek to eliminate the presence of the harshest kinds of want and deprivation. In all countries the questions of poverty or disadvantage have been inflamed by concepts of class, and conflicts among classes. In the United States the divisions among degrees of social status and economic strength have taken on peculiar bitterness, since they have much to do with past or present racial discrimination.

Compensation

The simplest notion of responsibility to compensate other people, which is accepted by popular morality and law, applies in a situation where one person has harmed another by an act that is blameworthy. If X should injure Y, either intentionally or through reckless or negligent conduct, the law would say that X is at fault and is liable to pay compensatory damages to Y. The civil law of actions for damages for personal wrongs, the law of torts, is grounded in this principle. It accords readily with our intuitive sense of justice that an innocent party should be restored as best we can to the condition he was in before the other party's wrong adversely affected him. With most personal injuries such restoration is never perfectly possible. The loss of an arm or an eye is irremediable. So we give the only thing that can be given, money, and the jury in a civil suit must do the best they can to measure the plaintiff's pain and suffering or his loss of expectation of life in cash terms, which must be paid by the defendant.

In modern society fault has come to be too narrow a principle to accommodate all the situations of loss and damage where compensation seems appropriate. The processes of industrial activity and the distribution of products cause harm to many people through accidents that are not directly attributable to the intentional wrongdoing or negligence of the employer or manufacturer. A workman may be injured through an accident on the job; the buyer or user of a product may be injured through a defect that could not have been foreseen or prevented, no matter how careful the manufacturer might have been. Yet, for the injured party, the loss would be crippling if he were left to bear it without compensation. Impressed by these considerations, legislatures have enacted statutory schemes of workmen's compensation that rest not on a theory of fault but simply on the occurrence of an accident in the course of employment.

In a similar way, the common law of torts has enlarged its theoretical apparatus to hold manufacturers and distributors of products strictly liable for injuries caused to consumers through defects, even though no specific fault can be proved against the defendant. This approach is sometimes known as "enterprise liability," and it reflects a judgment that the capacity of a person or an institution to absorb a loss can sometimes be a consideration as important as the location of blame in working out rational schemes of compensation for injury. In effect the manufacturer or employer is able to pass on his liability through the agency of insurance, and the cost of the insurance is absorbed by suitably increasing the price of his product. In this way the accidental injury to the employee or consumer is spread over all users of the product or service in society, thus saving the victim from a catastrophic economic blow.

This enterprise liability or social insurance concept retains important elements of moral responsibility, even if it moves away from traditional concepts of personal fault. It asserts in effect that if we want to engage in certain social activities, if we want certain products and services, then we must recognize the inevitable risk that some innocent people will be accidentally injured, and we ought to make arrangements to disperse that damage in a bearable fashion. As an acknowledgment that social duties to compensate may arise independently of personal wrongdoing by guilty parties, it has an important connection with any discussion of compensating disadvantaged people in society.

There are other instances in life where people suffer loss but where responsibility, even in the broader sense of enterprise liability, is hard to fix. A child is born blind or retarded; a man is injured by a falling tree in a storm, and, in the absence of sufficient private resources to care for the sufferer, we may feel an impulse to argue that the state has a duty to give assistance. Such a duty would have to be based on broad notions of human dignity, of compassion, of empathy, and of sympathy ("there but for the grace of God go I"). We could express the idea loosely in terms of insurance by arguing that there is a whole continuum of risks inherent in being a human being in this world. All of us run these risks, and mutual help through a kind of state insurance scheme makes the loss, when the blow falls, easier to bear. The concept of need is important here too. We cannot satisfy every want or make everyone's condition exactly equal. But a point comes when a person falls into such an extreme condition of need that it degrades the status of a human being to let the deprivation go unattended.

This preliminary survey suggests, then, three circumstances where an individual, or society as a whole, has a duty to compensate a person: (1) where blameworthy acts are responsible for the injury; (2) where the injury occurred as an accidental incident of socially desired communal activity; (3) where the individual is in great need and unable to help himself.

The Disadvantaged

For some years now it has been fashionable in the United States to refer to some people or groups of people as being "disadvantaged." Such references are often coupled with assertions of corollary duties to compensate or pay reparations, or at least to take affirmative steps to improve the status and living conditions of such people. In the simplest sense "disadvantaged" may refer quite neutrally to objective measurements of people's income, or housing or education or whatever compendium of criteria is used to measure the good life. More often in current usage there is a suggestion, more or less explicit, that those who are disadvantaged have in some way been the victims of social wrongs. This approach in turn needs to be disentangled into three possible and distinct interpretations.

In the first place, to speak of an individual as being disadvantaged might mean that he or she has been or is now being personally treated in some unfair or inequitable way under the existing social arrangements, practices, and institutions that operate to confer wealth, power, and status. If this is so, equity dictates some kind of rectification that might involve a general political change in social institutions and might also call for compensation to the individual for past loss. In the United States, some situations of this kind may amount to an infringement of constitutional rights and could be redressed through a civil rights action for an injunction and also perhaps by an action for damages.

In a second meaning, the claim may be of a more subtle kind. An individual may not be able to point to any specific and concrete way in which he has himself been unfairly treated but may allege simply that he is a member of a reasonably identifiable group in society that is by and large unfairly treated. Most people who belong to minority groups in the United States might make allegations of this kind. Many of them of course would make the stronger claim of the first type that they themselves have been unfairly treated. Others, while unable to point to specific acts of discrimination (whether social or economic) directed against them personally, would claim that in a more oblique fashion they have suffered from being members of a maltreated group. For example, the average income of blacks is considerably less than that of whites in the United States. Suppose a black person points to the fact that his income is less than the national average. Even if unable to produce evidence of personal discrimination against himself, he raises a not altogether implausible point if he asserts that his economic position may have some connection with the generally low income level of blacks, which, he further asserts, has to do with past and present discrimination against black people. If claims of this sort can be shown to have some foundation, they raise difficult questions about the appropriate response. Should we be only forward-looking and seek only to eradicate the economic impact of racial factors for the future? Can we justly ignore claims to reparation or compensation for past loss? But, if we flirt with theories of compensation and reparation, grave complexities of morality and administration will arise. The first, which is already apparent, would be whether we should be thinking of compensation to be paid to individuals or collectively to groups.

Yet a third meaning could be given to the notion that people are disadvantaged. This would be that a person is a member of a group which, although not presently treated in any unfair way, suffers from a legacy of such discrimination in the past. We may think here of the American Indians, once the object of genocidal warfare, and of American blacks, with a history of servitude and long-continuing segregation and discrimination. Even if it were true that discrimination against these minorities had ceased, it might reasonably be contended that a generation or more would be necessary for equal opportunity and equal respect to do their work to bring them into a position of actual equality. For a considerable time members of the group (especially the older ones) would remain whose earlier denial of opportunity and maltreatment have not only piled up an accrued claim against society but also continue to condemn them to a low level of material comfort.

These three possible elucidations of the concept of being disadvantaged reveal a distinction that will be relevant at many points in the subsequent discussion. It is the contrast between what have been called "process injustice" and "product injustice."[1] Under the first two interpretations, there was ongoing unfair treatment, either of the individual complainant himself or, by and large, of the group to which he belongs. This is a continuing process-type injustice and, in the first example, clearly shapes a good moral claim for rectification. In the second version, there is also clearly some viable claim for correction, though it is arguable whether it should be translated into compensation for particular individuals. But in the third situation, we no longer have any process injustice but only a "product injustice" resulting from an earlier unjust process, which has now been rectified. How far society has a duty to respond to claims of product injustice is a difficult question. To propose such a duty involves a moral claim to redress the dead sins of the past.

Responsibility and Guilt

Making claims for compensation in all these situations raises questions about collective responsibility. The earlier discussion of enterprise liability revealed that collective or social responsibility is a more complex concept than the identification of personal guilt. But in the context of claims by minority groups in the United States, arguments about responsibility have tended to become entangled with questions of guilt raised through the linking concept of racism and allegations of racist behavior or unconscious racism on the part of the white majority. Overt racism is a clear enough idea, but what exactly is meant by "unconscious" racism? The question is important, because if many white people are indeed unconscious racists, they may in some sense be to blame and so would have a duty to improve their behavior and perhaps to make redress.

To say that X is an unconscious racist might be nothing more than a reference to the expression of racist attitudes in his dreams or fantasies, attitudes of which he is unaware because they do not appear to him in a racist light. X is certainly not to be blamed for the quirks in his unconscious, though it might indeed be better for him if he could be cured. Nor is there any sense in which he is to be held accountable if his dealings with other people are quite unaffected by these unconscious promptings. If X behaves with impeccable equality to all people in his public and private dealings with them, he is doing no harm and is exempt from blame.

But it may be that X is deceiving himself in thinking that he deals with all people in this equal manner. Perhaps a sophisticated observer could point out to X that there are really subtle differences in the way that he treats people of different colors and that these differences spring from racist attitudes of which X was not overtly aware. X is still not to be blamed, for until now he was unaware of the nature of his behavior. However, if it can be shown that this behavior has harmed some people by treating them with invidious discrimination, then it may be proper to say that X is accountable for the harm and ought to take steps to rectify the damage. And X will be at fault and to be blamed in the future if, with his new awareness of his sins, he does not take steps to improve his behavior.

There are other foundations of responsibility lurking in popular polemics about unconscious racism, though they are not very happily described by that term. Many white people may never behave in an overtly racist manner and may also be free of any detectable subconscious racist rumblings. But they do nothing, take no affirmative steps to redress the inequalities and unequal treatment that they know persist in society. One may protest and say: "It's not my fault. Whenever I have dealings with people in minority groups my behavior is unchanged. I know that other people don't always behave well, but what can I do about that?" The reply could be made that all religions and moral codes recognize sins of omission as well as of commission. To neglect steps that we might take to improve the lives of others who are not treated fairly may make us answerable to an indictment for moral laziness or indifference, sins that beset most people, white and black. They scarcely add up to a charge of racism, but this does not deprive them of significance. What is important here is the social and collective implication of such accusations rather than the question of individual guilt. To ascribe to an individual a duty to compensate others about whose plight he has been morally lazy might be a religious precept or a counsel of saintliness, but it hardly seems a workable standard for a secular morality. But to say that a polity that has neglected to intervene to ensure equal treatment for some of its members now has a duty not only to change things in the future but also to compensate those who have suffered through past indifference makes much more sense.

This is especially so if it is the case that a class or majority group in society can be shown to have taken a profit out of the deprivation imposed on a minority through unequal treatment.[2] Historically in the United States, as with the seizure of Indian lands and the use of black slave labor, there can be no doubt that many whites profited greatly from injustice to people of other colors. Certainly this would not be the case for all whites. Some whites are a great deal poorer than some blacks, but it may well be true that for the greater part of American history and still today, the standard of living of the majority of white people has to some extent ridden on the backs of disadvantage imposed on black and other minority peoples. Much has been done in recent decades to move toward equal opportunity for everybody, but a large legacy of deprivation still attaches to many minority group people. If the white majority can be seen as enjoying a corresponding legacy of advantage, then social duties arise to rectify and compensate.

But compensation, in political or juridical terms, comes down in the end to payments of money in some form or another. Let us suppose that 80 per cent of the population of the United States enjoy a standard of living that does not fall below X units of well-being, but that the remaining 20 per cent live at a standard that moves on a scale between X—1 and X—20 units of well-being. A continuation of present social institutions and practices might ensure the further upward movement of the standard of living of the comfortable 80 per cent but might even further depress the standard of living of the remaining 20 per cent, or at least indefinitely postpone the narrowing of the gap between them and the more affluent. But a change in social institutions and practices is conceivable by which the living standards of the depressed groups would move more swiftly toward the X point; such a change, however, would entail some lowering of the standard of living of the 80 per cent majority and might lead to some of them falling below the X point. Let us assume that this is a democratic society, so that general decisions about fundamental matters of policy are from time to time presented to the electorate. The comparatively affluent 80 per cent would thus be in a position to determine whether to adhere to present social patterns, which would ensure a continuation of their progressive affluence or, on the other hand, to assume a measure of sacrifice in order to elevate the position of those who were less happily placed.

Whether that is the actual situation in the United States or not, the model is a useful one to suggest an argument that needs to be developed, that the moral claims of justice can be such that sacrifices can be properly demanded in some situations. Utility may not dictate a sacrifice where justice may. We are not speaking here of sacrificial acts that spring from love or compassion. Parents make sacrifices for their children out of love, and outside the family there are no doubt countless instances of persons who from love or compassion willingly curtail their own material interests in order to help others. But this is not (except in a religious context) a demand that we can make on people; and it is not the way that minority groups would want to present their demands. Black people in America are not saying to white people, "You ought to help us because you ought to love us and make sacrifices for us out of charity and compassion." They are saying, rather, "You owe us something. Please pay your debt." This is in the nature of a claim and, like all claims, it needs to be scrutinized.

Justice Claims

If the claim is to stand up, it will have to be anchored to general principles of social justice. The most recent exposition of such principles has been put forward in the important study by John Rawls in his book *A Theory of Justice.*[3]

Rawls asks us to imagine rationally self-interested people living in a state of nature, without government or rules or regulations. Perceiving disadvantages in this state of affairs and hoping for considerable benefits from a communal union under a system of rules, they come together to discuss the possibility of setting up such socializing institutions. Their natural state of living leaves each individual unaware of his or her prospects of success in a social setting. The individual cannot measure his social assets, in the way of skills, talents, personality features that might lead to success, and so on. Everyone is thus taking a chance about what position he or she will come to occupy in the future society, whether it will be one of leadership or affluence or modest prosperity, or one of manual work and comparative stringency. In this sense the venture has something of the aspect of a lottery or a gamble for all the participants. They will thus wish to arrive at principles that will ensure that, whatever positions they occupy in the society, they will not have cause to complain. Rawls suggests that the principles they will arrive at might be expressed as follows:

> First: each person is to have an equal right to the most extensive basic liberty compatible with a similar liberty for others. . . .
>
> Second: Social and economic inequalities are to be arranged so that they are both (a) to the greatest benefit of the least advantaged and (b) attached to offices and positions open to all under conditions of fair equality of opportunity.[4]

Perhaps it can be convincingly demonstrated that the future society cannot function at all without some inequalities. This the prospective members may be willing to accept. But, unless they are foolish gamblers, willing to take a chance on the turn of the wheel, they will want to have some guarantees. The guarantees, Rawls suggests, that rational self-interest demands are that where inequalities are attached to different positions and offices, they must be open to all on the basis of a competition that relates to fitness and talent, and that the inequalities are only to be tolerated at all because in the long run they work out to everyone's advantage. But can it be to a poor's man's advantage that he is poor while another man is rich? Only on the assumption that a total equalization of income would depress *everyone's* standard of living by reducing incentives and motives for energetic activity and production by those who have specially needed talents. If the inequality is not necessary for the purpose of improving the position of everyone in the long run, then it is an unjust inequality, in Rawls' exposition, and ought to be remedied.

Rawls' theory, when pressed, runs into complexities of welfare economics, but its overwhelming merit is in presenting the principles of justice, not as intuitive perceptions or as religious ordinances, but rather as a natural and rational construct from the business of people living together in a social union. Some people of course may be foolish gamblers, and Rawls does not contend that this is not an aspect of human nature. His position is rather that, if people are imbued with a rational self-interest, then they must subscribe to the principles of justice, since these are exactly the principles that are necessary for the protection of rationally self-interested people.

An English writer, W. G. Runciman, has taken up Rawls' principles and extended them in a context very relevant to the present discussion:

> The parties to the contract are, after all, required to envisage a society whose general level of well-being is such that not only is nobody starving but a good many people are earning sums very much more than adequate for the current average level of wants. Many of those at or near the bottom of the income distribution may be in possession of consumer goods which would seem to the members of other or earlier societies to be beyond the dreams of avarice. But they may be conscious of being, for example, much less well housed than the majority of their society; and at the same time, they may be aware that a good many of their fellow citizens have a great deal more than the average income. They accordingly put forward a claim that those earning much above the average should be sufficiently taxed to bring them some way closer to the general level, the money so raised to be set aside in a fund to be used for raising the standard of housing among those whose incomes are least adequate to enable them to approach the average standard. There is no question of doing away with the rights of the greater contributors to earn more than others in accordance with the criteria agreed in advance. The claim is only that where marked inequalities exist in terms of whatever standard is current then justice requires that some priority should be given to needs (in this sense) over and above the other two criteria.[5]

This contractual model provides an argument for a partial redistribution of wealth when gross inequalities exist. It is an argument that might have a particular appeal to lawyers, since it has as its theme the notion of evaluating human institutions by the criterion of what terms in a hypothetical agreement would be equitable. At the same time, it is a way of presenting a judgment of injustice that should have an immediate appeal to the ordinary man, for it entails a question to which we can all respond without sophisticated argument: "Would you be willing to enter a lottery in which you had a random chance of being a black person in the United States?" We may guess that the reply of the white majority is going to be negative. It would also be negative, of course, if the chance in the lottery were to be healthy or sick, assuming that the person we invite to enter the lottery is presently healthy. But the point is that being sick is for the most part a natural accident, while the miseries that surround the business of being black in America are the products of past and present institutions and social practices. If these institutions and practices have resulted in a position where a person would not be willing to take a fair chance of being black, then they must be condemned as unjust, and a corresponding duty to rectify arises.

This analysis should not stand on economic inequality alone. Minority groups complain, and again with justice, of a lack of respect paid to them by the community as a whole. Here, again, a useful distinction has been made by Mr. Runciman between the concepts of "praise" and "respect." Praise is that which we accord to a man because of his demonstrated talent or virtue; there is no injustice in praising a great writer or lawyer more than a mediocre one. Indeed, it is quite proper to praise a class as a whole if we believe that most members of the class are members of it because they possess admirable skills and talents. So to praise writers or lawyers in general is unexceptionable. Praise may become an offense to principles of justice, however, when it is predicated simply on membership in a group without any evaluation of the individual's performance as a member of the group. This would be to accord respect to status irrespective of the merit of the individual. Now, to denigrate one's fellow man, irrespective of his personal merit in performance or virtue, on the ground alone of his membership in a racial group or an economic class, is clearly to step out of the permissible field of praise and to move into illegitimate respect for status. There may be inequalities of praise, but there must be equality of respect. Runciman writes:

> If we suppose the parties to the contract to be envisaging the possibility that different status may be accorded to them in their eventual society depending on the colour of their skin, it is obvious that they will rule out such a system on principle. If I do not know whether I shall have a black skin or a white one, I shall surely be unwilling to agree to any principle whereby either the one or the other will secure for me unequal treatment in the hierarchies of class, status or power. But suppose someone wishes to defend discrimination of this kind as no violation of social justice. It would be absurd for him to try to describe colour prejudice in terms of differential praise. Afrikaaners in South Africa, or white Southerners in the United States, can hardly be described as *praising* each other for the colour of their skins. What they accord to each other, and what the parties to the contract would stipulate against, is differential respect.[6]

Following this kind of analysis, we might then say that some racial minority groups, including blacks in the United States, have a well-grounded double complaint of injustice, based partly on their unequal economic status and partly on disrespect shown to them on the irrational basis of their race or color. Though the two claims can be separated analytically, it is evident that they are empirically much connected. Disrespect shown to people because of their color makes it difficult for them to advance economically, and continued economic depression makes it more difficult to eradicate irrational disrespect. But the resolutions of the injustices are not necessarily interdependent. Economic inequality might be eradicated without an accompanying elimination of unjust demonstrations of disrespect, though we can surely expect the removal of the one to have a substantial impact on the other.

Reparations

In the international sphere there are many precedents for reparations. Usually they seem to be more the mark of the imposition of victorious power than the setting right of past injuries, though the assumption of a duty by Western Germany to pay compensation to the victims of Nazi atrocities is compensatory in the relevant sense.

Domestically, it is not easy for government to make a public confession that one section of the community has been treated unjustly and has a good claim to reparation. But American legislative history does have a recent precedent of this kind. A federal statute of 1946 set up an Indian Claims Commission, with jurisdiction to hear and resolve claims arising from the seizure of Indian property and breaches by the United States of its treaties with the Indian nations and tribes.[7] In subsequent proceedings it was held that the government of the United States was liable to pay compensation for, among other places, the whole of Kansas. If we are willing to applaud this tardy effort at reparation, we might ask whether there are not good arguments for its extension. If a proper sense of shame at our forerunners' dealings with the Indians prompted the statute of 1946, can we feel any less sense of shame at their dealings with the black population of America? There is not very much to choose between the sporadic outbursts of genocidal rage that were displayed toward the Indians and the settled, institutional policy of slavery that was applied to blacks. So if a public confession can be made in statutory form of the just claims of American Indians for compensation (a phenomenon uncomfortably close in time and nature to postwar Germany's reparation payments to Jews), why should we not initiate similar schemes for reparation to black Americans?

Other statutory remedies of a different scope, resting on the general concept of the invasion of an individual's constitutional rights, are also relevant here. In particular we must take notice of Title 42 of the United States Code, Section 1983. This statute, sometimes known as the "Ku Klux Klan Act," provides that:

> Every person who under color of any statute of any state subjects any citizen of the United States to the deprivation of any rights secured by the Constitution and laws shall be liable to the person injured in an action at law.

Pressed hard, this statute, providing as it does a civil rights action for damages, could be taken to have extraordinary implications. It could be construed to mean that every state official who has participated in maintaining a segregated school system is liable to pay damages to every minority group member who at any time suffered damages as a result. Viewed in this way, the statute could be seen as an extensive scheme of reparations or compensation for any inequitable treatment that could be construed as a violation of the United States Constitution or laws. These examples show a fragile foundation of legal precedent for compensatory treatment, but for the reasons that follow, it is not one that can be translated into a broad reparations approach, either in the courts or by legislatures.

The first major difficulty with a reparations concept on the American scene is in identifying proper plaintiffs. The Indian statute escapes this problem, since it has to do with seizures of land and breaches of treaties, and identifies the subjects of the compensation as tribes and nations. Blacks in America were never organized into tribes or nations. What would an individual black have to show to have a proper claim for reparations? That one of his ancestors had at some time been a slave? This would disqualify a black whose family came to America from the West Indies some fifty years ago. (There was slavery in the West Indies at an early date, but it was British slavery, juridically speaking, and not American.) Does such a disqualification make sense? Shouldn't blacks be entitled to reparations just as blacks? But then would we have to include even blacks who occupy professional positions or are making substantial incomes? To avoid this apparent anomaly, we might confine the ultimate beneficiaries of the reparations scheme to those blacks whose income falls below a certain low level. On what principle can we then exclude whites whose income falls below this level? Shall we say that there is a *prima facie* presumption that when a black has a low standard of living this has some some connection with a past history of discrimination, while a low standard of living for a white is *prima facie* his own fault? But while poor blacks generally have suffered from discrimination, it would at the same time be nonsense to exculpate society from collective fault for the condition of many poor whites.

Quantifying the measure of damages would be a second source

of well-nigh insuperable difficulty. Again with the Indian statute, seizure of land and breach of treaties seem reasonably susceptible of measurement in cash terms. With black or Spanish-speaking Americans the problems would be more complex. It is not that the law is unfamiliar with freezing elusive kind of injuries in cash terms. Pain and suffering and loss of expectation of life are converted into money every day by juries, and nothing could be harder to measure. The problem here is rather to know what to count as an injury at all. The denial of a job to an individual on account of race is simple enough and is already covered by civil rights statutes. But where the individual points to such factors as descent from servitude, membership of a group historically discriminated against, income below national average, or poor education in a segregated school, we may be reasonably confident that unjust social attitudes toward people of his color have something to do with his disadvantaged position, but we shall be hard put to measure the amount of compensation against that due to another black person who can point to only some of these facts in his history. If a person went to a segregated school, but now has a very good job with a high income, is that person entitled to any compensation? In other words, are we to try only to trace the impact of past discrimination in terms of present economic loss, or should we look also to emotional injuries imposed by lack of respect? Does it make any difference whether the discrimination in the past is of a kind that we now recognize as unconstitutional, as with segregated schools?

In a strictly legal context, operating under existing statutes, such as 42 U.S.C. Section 1983, further technical barriers interpose themselves in the way of general compensatory remedies. Section 1983 is couched in terms of an action for damages against a state official. It does not plainly give any right to sue the state itself. In fact, the courts have interpreted Section 1983 as giving such a right in some situations, but the precedents are complex on this point.[8] This is not of course a difficulty of principle, for once a duty to pay reparations was recognized, the state could simply assume the necessary obligation by legislation.

Another technical problem under Section 1983 does, though, underline again the delicacy and complexity of any reparations scheme. The statute gives a remedy where a state law has been used improperly to deprive the plaintiff of his federal constitutional or legal rights. In this way it reveals its origins as a post-Civil War remedy for freed slaves who might be harassed by whites in the formerly rebel states. But the interpretation of federal constitutional rights is constantly changing. It was not until 1954, for example, that the Supreme Court plainly decided that segregated public schools were unconstitutional. How, then, should we view the claims of those who went to segregated public schools before 1954? With hindsight we may be willing to concede the social immorality of the practice of segregation at any time, but the state officer, if made defendant in a Section 1983 action, could always point to the apparent legality of such procedures before 1954, even under federal law. These limitations of Section 1983 certainly do not bind our imaginations in devising larger schemes of reparation, but the confines of the statute underline the question whether we should be seeking to measure only the denial of constitutional rights or rather all legacies of deprivation imposed by practices that now appear socially unjust.

A final difficulty in any scheme for reparations to minority group members would be selecting the channels for distribution to recipients. This connects back with the earlier question of whether we should attempt to identify individuals deserving compensation with precision, or more bluntly concede that racially identifiable groups in general are proper beneficiaries. The context in which demands for reparations have been put forward in recent years has certainly been one of collective demands by groups, or on behalf of groups. Suppose, for example, that we decided in some rough fashion that the black community in the United States was entitled to one hundred billion dollars of reparations. How should we divide up that sum? We could count the number of black people and give each individual his or her quotient. Or we could make a gargantuan effort to examine each individual case and see how much each person has suffered, if at all, and then make payments commensurate with individual injury. Then again we could employ intermediaries and hand over all the money to black organizations charged with the task of ascertaining the wishes of the black community and putting the money to uses that advance the welfare of black people in accordance with those wishes.

Reform

Compensation or reparations look both to the past and the future. They look to the past in that they depend on a finding of responsibility to invoke them. They look to the future in that they are designed, in part, to enable the plaintiff-victim better to bear the deprivations inflicted on him. But in grappling with social inequities, there are necessarily great differences between the quasijuridical model of compensation and the freer-ranging approach of social reform effected through legislation. The juridical model is beset by all the vexing needs discussed earlier to identify particular plaintiffs who can make out specific cases of illegal or unconstitutional treatment by particular defendants. The legislature can accommodate more spaciously aims that are partly compensatory but that look principally to eradicating unequal treatment in the future.

Wrongs done to the dead cannot be made good. Our concern has to be with the future of the living and those still to be born. Good and moral government should surely be preoccupied here with two themes. One is to reform social practices and institutions that are unfair to certain groups or individuals, either by depriving them of equal opportunities or by distributing rewards and burdens inequitably. This first concern has to do with that aspect of justice, analyzed by John Rawls, that turns on the notion of fairness. But, as we saw earlier, claims may be made that do not depend on charges of unfairness. People may be in need through misfortune, bad luck, or incapacity, which have nothing to do with unfairness in social practices and institutions. The relief of intolerable need, whether it proceeds from accident, old age, mental illness, or whatever, is a second moral obligation of good government. We may view it as another aspect of social justice anchored in the concept of human dignity and the duty to protect the human personality from degrading deprivations that cannot be overcome through the individual's reasonable efforts.

In America, deprivation stemming from unfair practices, as well as deprivation stemming from simple need, are by no means confined to racial minority groups, though, proportionate to their numbers, these groups may have suffered most keenly. In an absolute sense, the number of white people whose social and economic background gave them a poor start in life, and the number of whites who are in sharp need of health care, reasonable housing, and nutrition exceeds the number of blacks in the same straits. For this reason any large-scale scheme of reparations tied to the index of color alone would be in itself a gross inequity. In twentieth-century America, a stark confrontation with the issue of racial discrimination was inevitable and altogether necessary. At the same time, its transcendent priority in any listing of social problems over the past two decades has had the unfortunate result of diverting attention from deep injustices in the social system that impinge with equal force on many blacks and whites.

If the relief of need and the elimination of inequity are honestly and diligently pursued, what room is left for a theory and practice of reparations for past social wrongs? A group might remain, who are not in such need as to have a claim for relief under that principle, but who nevertheless contend that they are demonstrably less well off than the majority and that this has something to do with early lack of opportunity or early discrimination. Should their demands be answered? One aspect of this topic is the question of preferential treatment in the context of education and employment. A later chapter is devoted entirely to this particular theme. In general terms the identification of some level of present disadvantage as being distinctly attributable to an inequitable social practice would be so tenuous, so elusive, so immeasurable, and probably applicable, if at all, to such a large percentage of the population that any scheme of cash compensation would seem to be quite impractical. If the difficulties of identification and attribution could be overcome, the scheme would no doubt be financially ruinous to the economy.

The narrow limits of present legal remedies, giving actions for damages only when a violation of constitutional rights can be shown under color of state law, are thus probably preferable to any wider scheme of cash compensation for past discrimination. Minority groups are understandably preoccupied with a history of discrimination based on color, which has been so conspicuous a feature of the worst aspects of American life. But the accidents of birth have inflicted losses of opportunity and an unfair distribution of rewards and burdens on millions of Americans, for reasons that have nothing to do with color but much more to do with class. Persistent efforts to remove inequities and impediments would of course require reforms in education, in the provision of housing, in health services, in wage and tax structures, and so on. Struggle in this direction will be much more rewarding than a claim for reparations tied to the question of color.

This is not to say that a principle of compensation should be abandoned. People are certainly not to be written off because they are no longer young and cannot now get the benefit of new and more equitable practices. But compensation should be embraced within a more general principle of offering all people every service that may assist them to develop their potential and improve their way of life. Such services might take many forms including adult education, job retraining, housing improvement, special medical care, and so on. Simple cash payments are best reserved for cases that are appropriate for consideration under the principle of relief of need, and need should be met whether or not it is the product of past social inequity.

XII

Equal Educational Opportunity

In a just society, as John Rawls tells us, offices of profit and advantage must be open to all. This is a modern conception, quite at odds with a medieval view of the world, in which rank and status settled by the accident of birth rigidly determined privileges and duties. The idea of such equal opportunity, at least for white people, has been one of the cherished dogmas of America's image of itself. At one time there was a body of visible evidence to give it some support, though no doubt it has always had something of the quality of a comforting myth. More than in European countries, Americans could look at their successful statesmen, businessmen, and professional leaders and find among them a reassuring number who had fought their way to the top, armed only with talent and determination, from humble or even poverty-stricken origins.

But by the mid-twentieth century, America and Europe in this regard had moved closer together. While rigid class distinctions were slowly breaking down in Europe, the road to success in America came to be more and more squeezed into a conventional trail of educational qualifications. Some people of great energy and acumen may still crash through into spectacular business success without academic trappings, but there are not many of these. For the great majority, the difference between affluence and a modest standard of living has to do with the gap between the doctors, lawyers, and executives, on the one hand, and the clerks, assembly line workers, and secretaries on the other. The diploma and the degree have come to be the talismans that offer the prospect of entering the ranks of the moderately affluent.

The likelihood of a child's achieving academic success is usually evident at an early age, at least by the low teens, if not before. Many people thus see their children ineluctably tagged as hewers of wood and drawers of water, while other children seem to be moving ahead to academic accomplishment, with all its promises. If this distinction could be quietly accepted as the irresistible designation of fate, people might remain unhappy, but protest or calls for change would be pointless. But many suspect that the difference in the academic performance of children has something to do with the quality of the educational system in which they are enrolled. If this is the case, then parents of children in bad schools rightly become angry, for their children are being condemned to second-class prospects because of the inequality or inefficiency of the system. In this way teachers and school administrators may become the targets of an understandably virulent indignation.

When demands are made for improvements in educational systems, they often seem to involve taking something away from or at least effecting changes in schools that are concededly of a high order. The demand for equality may take the form of a call for changes in school financing, so that there is equalization on a per capita pupil basis throughout a state, instead of the vagaries of the local property-tax basis now so widely employed. But this might result in less money being spent in certain school districts than at present. Or the demand may be that schools be more racially integrated, which may involve busing of children from schools in affluent, middle-class neighborhoods to schools in poor neighborhoods. In these situations an equally understandable backlash usually appears from parents who fear that the good quality of the education their children are presently getting will disappear or be diluted. For these reasons among others, the most passionate battles for equality in the United States have recently been fought over the schools. As we go along, we shall see that the positions espoused may sometimes rest on relative ignorance or misapprehension of the influences that contribute to academic success and on an exaggerated faith in the power of educational systems to change the performance level of children. But whatever the truth of these matters, a demand for equal educational opportunity is clearly in general terms a powerful justice-type claim.

We must also remember here that prospects for gaining lucrative and prestigious jobs are not the only good reasons for demanding equal education. Education can be a key that unlocks a whole storehouse of ways and opportunities for people to enrich their lives in spiritual and cultural directions. It may enlarge our intellectual horizon, open new fields of effort and appreciation, and so enable us to spend our leisure in more stimulating and creative ways. This double dimension of education's potential for shaping our lives, coupled with the slender hopes of reversing in later life the damage done by poor education, gives the debate a quality of peculiar urgency.

Education, Inequality, and Race

The problem has taken on a special bitterness because of its intimate connection with racial divisions. Minority groups have at times ardently embraced the notion that a principal reason for their continued comparative lack of affluence is an unequal system of education. Some students of the problem have thrown doubt on this. They suggest, for example, that blacks do not necessarily get good jobs just because they are as well educated as some whites. Old-fashioned racism may still play a large role in the allocation of jobs and offices of profit and prestige.[1] If this is so, better or more equal education would not be a panacea even for the economic manifestations of racial divisions. This is, indeed, a disquieting message, for many have come to believe that the problems of racism would be enormously alleviated if minority group members made substantial economic progress and that this can be best achieved through equalization of education.

Talk of unequal education itself suffers from an inherent ambiguity, as recent studies have pointed out. The ambiguity resides in a failure to indicate whether the reference is to the educational process or the educational product.[2] Process inequality assumes that, if we take two broadly identifiable groups of students, perhaps inner-city blacks and surburban whites, it could be demonstrated that the education offered to the two is by some measurable standard different in quality. The most obvious example would be that more money is spent in the predominantly white schools than in the predominantly black schools. The money may be used to attract more skilled teachers by paying higher salaries, or to provide technological learning aids, or to enrich the curriculum. This would be an inequality in the educational process; alternatively, it has been called an "input inequality." Logically, such an inequality would not necessarily result in children emerging from the poorly endowed schools less well educated than from the well-endowed schools, though we might guess that very likely this would be the result.

But let us suppose that this kind of demonstration cannot be made, that schools are roughly equal by these measures of input, so that we do not have process inequality, at least in terms of expenditure of funds. It may be that there is nevertheless a marked difference in the average educational attainments of pupils from the one school district as compared with the other. Here we would have a "product" or "output" inequality, but one that could not be directly linked to a process inequality. It is of course product inequalities that in the first instance worry parents and community leaders, for these are the simplest indices of prospects of future success in life.

Where product inequalities exist among school districts (or among schools within a district), they are evidently susceptible of a number of different possible explanations. A logically possible one is that one set of children is simply less talented or less possessed of academic skills than the other set of children. Put more crudely and less euphemistically, one might say that one set of children is by and large stupider than the other. Since we are discussing a problem that manifests itself chiefly in racial terms, such an explanation has inflammatory suggestions of a theory of inherent racial inferiority. There is no persuasive evidence to suggest that we should take it seriously.

A second explanation would be quite contrary. This would be that the schools that turn out children with lesser academic attainments are indeed inferior schools. Perhaps the curriculum is less suitable, the teachers less skilled, the equipment inferior, and so on. As we have seen, these features are almost inevitably factors of the amount of money being spent on the schools. The two explanations clearly lead us to dramatically different conclusions. Under the first possibility, there are no recommendations to be made. If some people are naturally less talented than others in an academic direction, we can only accept the dispensation. But if the second explanation is more accurate, that an inequitable distribution of resources is the cause, then we have a situation of blame and responsibility and an obligation to rectify.

Again, modern research in the sociology of education puts some hard questions to this second thesis, though it certainly does not demolish it. We do now know that it is by no means always the case that central-city schools are shortchanged.[3] Often they are quite well placed financially when compared with rural schools and even with small-town schools and some suburban schools. Certainly there are schools in very affluent suburbs where much more money is spent per pupil than in central-city schools, but critical examination shows that the contrast between the rich, white suburban school and the poor, predominantly black city school does not stand up on a national basis.

If ghetto schools or inner-city schools are, in a comparative sense, not very successful in turning out young people with good academic achievement, the explanation seems to be much more complex than their lack of a fair share of the money being spent on education. It may be of course that the money is being spent on the wrong things, that more imaginative approaches to education could return better results, even for less money. If that is so, it is not a factor of state discrimination in the allocation of funds, and there is no evidence that more imaginative effort is going into educational techniques in white suburban schools than in poor, predominantly black inner-city schools.

There is a third possible explanation for inequality in educational output. (The explanations of course are not mutually exclusive.) This would be that children who come to school in poor neighborhoods are often considerably handicapped in their capacity to become well educated, not because of any innate lack of potentiality but rather because of a complex host of social and environmental factors. Some children may not be properly fed, or may be sick and not receiving medical attention. Children who are hungry or sick are not likely to absorb very much of even the best teaching. Then, children from poor or disrupted homes often lack the kind of stimulation and motivation to learn that children from middle-class homes receive and possess. This may have to do both with the atmosphere of the home and with the environment in the immediate community that surrounds the child. Indeed, recent studies in England appear to show that the most crucial years with respect to a child's capacity to become well educated are from birth to the age of seven.[4] Now, by the age of seven, the child has only been in school a year or two. The depressing lesson may be that a child may already have been so damaged by environment of home and community that he is virtually uneducable by the time formal education begins. When large numbers of such children are brought together in the same schools and the same classes, disciplinary problems of such gravity arise that most of a teacher's energy may be expended in keeping minimum order.

One conclusion would be that no matter how much money we might expend on inner-city or ghetto schools, the results would not be likely to be encouraging, simply because schools are by their nature unable to prevail over handicaps imposed on the child by accidents of environment. At least this may be so while the schools themselves fail to break down those very factors that may be having a stultifying impact on those children who otherwise might be able to progress. Some mix or mingling of children from different backgrounds in the same school might help, and this is a subject to which we shall have to return. But for the moment, the most important lesson is that we should not expect schools to undo all the evils that we inflict on children through other more pervasive inequalities in the social system. If we are really interested in equal education, we must think about what happens to children long before they get into school at all. We have to think about the homes and families they are born into, and the environments and communities in which they spend their earliest years. This drives us back to a general critique of social arrangements and the distribution of rewards and the relief of need in our society. In this way the most important of the keys to equal educational opportunity may not be in the hands of the educational apparatus at all.

But none of these doubts or cautions in the least warrants giving up the fight for equal education, as best we can define it. Suppose, for example, that equal education were achieved and this turned out not to improve very substantially the economic position of black people in America. Still, as John E. Coons observes, blacks have at least an equal right to be disappointed with white people.[5] The rich are constantly assuring us that money doesn't buy happiness, but most of us would like the opportunity to find out for ourselves. So it should be with education. Then, again, as we saw earlier, access to equal economic affluence is not the only defense of equal educational opportunity, though no doubt it would be the prime one for most people. The unleashing of intellectual and creative potential is another important goal. Yet a third one, and perhaps the most important of all, at least insofar as equal education means integrated schools, might be the promotion of racial harmony. There is some evidence that the simple juxtaposition of children of different races in the same schools helps them to get to know each other better and to live with each other more easily later in life. One of the strongest reasons for the almost total separation of the Catholic and Protestant communities in Ulster is the rigid segregation of their children in different school systems. Certainly there is no guarantee that fully integrated schools would bring about racial harmony; the sociological studies are mixed, and some are skeptical of the efficacy of integration in this direction. But on balance, the evidence does seem to show that some positive contribution to racial understanding is made by school integration.

Racially integrated schools might still of course differ in quality, so that problems of inequality of education might remain. Integration and equality in education could indeed be seen as aims and ideals that have no necessary connection with each other. But if it is true that the pursuit of equality in educational opportunity does in practice involve commitment to some degree of integration, then an improvement in relations between the races could be an important side benefit of the quest for equality.

Equality and the Courts

In 1896 a majority decision of the Supreme Court in *Plessy* v. *Ferguson*[6] held that a Louisiana statute that enforced segregation of the races in public transport did not offend the Constitution as long as equal facilities were supplied for all races. This "separate but equal" doctrine was held in many cases, though not in the

Supreme Court, to be controlling in the field of public education, and for fifty years the thrust of black plaintiffs was to prove that the particular facilities afforded by school authorities were not in fact equal to those enjoyed by whites.

The proceedings known as *Brown* v. *Board of Education*[7] that came before the Supreme Court in 1954 were a consolidation of cases from Kansas, South Carolina, Virginia, and Delaware. In the courts below there had been findings that the black and white schools involved had been equalized, or were being equalized, so that the facts presented the Court with a plain opportunity to examine the validity of the "separate but equal" doctrine. The Court itself posed the question up for answer. "Does segregation of children in public schools solely on the basis of race, even though the physical facilities and other 'tangible' factors may be equal, deprive the children of the minority group of equal educational opportunities?" They answered, "We believe that it does,"[8] and so struck down the laws requiring or permitting school segregation as offending against the Fourteenth Amendment's requirement of equal protection.

But the apparent simplicity of the *Brown* decision may be deceptive. The Supreme Court quoted from the opinion of the court below in the Kansas case.

> Segregation of white and colored children in public schools has a detrimental effect upon the colored children. The impact is greater when it has the sanction of the law: for the policy of separating the races is usually interpreted as denoting the inferiority of the negro group. A sense of inferiority affects the motivation of a child to learn. Segregation with the sanction of law, therefore, has a tendency to retard the educational and mental development of negro children and to deprive them of some of the benefits they would receive in a racially integrated school system.[9]

This and other statements in *Brown* can be given a broad interpretation and be taken to mean that distinctions based on race are simply impermissible, quite apart from the nature of the sociological testimony as to their effects. More narrowly, the decision may mean that racial segregation cannot be defended in the education context by an assertion of a "separate but equal" response, since racial segregation in this setting inherently leads, on the basis of the sociological evidence, to unequal education. Curiously, in the education area, it is the narrower understanding of the Court's statement that may point to more radical developments, for it is the narrow interpretation that speaks most directly to the recent concern with the problems of school segregation in northern cities.

DE JURE AND DE FACTO

Situations of school segregation are commonly divided into *de jure* and *de facto*. *De jure* segregation is that which is produced by state law or at least by some authoritative state action. In its pre-*Brown* form this often meant state statutes or local laws that expressly prohibited a racial mix in schools and made provision for separate schools for the races. After *Brown* such statutes have disappeared, but *de jure* segregation may still occur in other forms. School boards may redraw the boundaries of attendance zones, old schools may be closed and new schools built, and these actions may have the purpose of perpetuating or creating segregation. If that is so, the segregation is still *de jure*. *De facto* segregation, on the other hand, is that which arises not from state action but as a natural manifestation of the neighborhood school concept. It is a phenomenon as much or more of the North, East and West as of the South. Blacks and other minority groups have concentrated in inner cities or particular city districts, while many suburban areas are very largely white. The result of these residential patterns has been schools with a vastly predominant representation of one race among the pupils. Only affirmative steps, such as the busing of pupils, could break down this separation. But it is generally only in the area of *de jure* segregation that the courts have so far ordered affirmative action to desegregate.

In an attempt to ameliorate the poor achievements of inner-city schools, many educational authorities have mounted special programs, involving extra expenditures and efforts at "enrichment." These programs have often not been significantly successful. Studies in this area suggest that the most potent depressant in ghetto and slum schools is the exclusive concentration of children from the same social low-income group, and that the most potent stimulant is a placing of these children in schools where there is a majority or a substantial number of children from a more advantaged social background.[10] In the absence of such a commingling, remedial programs in the ghetto and slum schools may not have much impact.

Put in these terms, the problem is not so much one of race as one of poverty and social disadvantage. In the large cities, where the great majority of the inner-city poor are members of minority groups, the problem nevertheless presents itself as a racial one. Some states and cities have endeavored to meet the dilemma by modifying the neighborhood school concept and providing for the redrawing of school districts or even the transportation of children to schools some distance away from their homes, in order to achieve a greater racial and social mix in the student bodies. One example is a 1963 revision of the Illinois School Code that provides:

> As soon as practicable, and from time to time thereafter, the board shall change or revise existing attendance units or create new units in a manner which will take into consideration the prevention of segregation and the elimination of separation of children in public schools because of color, race or nationality.[11]

This Illinois provision was itself challenged in the courts as offending against the principle established in *Brown* that racial discrimination in public education is unconstitutional. The challenge rested on the position that *Brown* must be understood as prohibiting the taking of race into account for any purpose whatsoever in educational classification. Such an argument may seem to have a tinge of perversity, at least in this context of racial mingling in school populations, since it is difficult to see how therapeutic steps could be taken to combat *de facto* segregation without explicit adversion to race. In *Tometz* v. *Board of Education,*[12] the Supreme Court of Illinois rejected the challenge and upheld the code revision, holding that *Brown* did not prohibit and, indeed, might be understood to authorize the taking of affirmative steps to end racial imbalance, even if this arose through *de facto* rather than *de jure* segregation.

In the school cases it is of the utmost importance to distinguish between a court's decision as to what a school board *must* do and a decision as to what it *may* do if it wishes. *Tometz* decided only that if a board wants to take affirmative steps to redress *de facto* segregation, it may do so. There is no suggestion that such steps are mandatory, as may be the case where the segregation is *de jure*. This is the key to the crucial distinction between *de jure* and *de facto* segregation.

Where segregation can be viewed as *de jure*, the U. S. Supreme Court in the years since *Brown* has been gradually tightening and sharpening the duty laid upon the state and local authorities. *Brown* provided no particular timetable for action and required only that steps be taken to achieve racial mingling, "with all deliberate speed." By 1968, when the case of *Green* v. *County School Board*[13] came to be decided, the Court was beginning to lose patience with the slow progress of desegregation in many areas. It ruled that, where segregation remained as a legacy from a previous *de jure* situation, a full remedy must be devised and applied immediately. The task of shaping or approving such remedies in particular cases is primarily one for the lowest federal courts, the district courts. Anglo-American law has always recognized a general equitable jurisdiction in the courts to fashion flexible remedies to respond to complex wrongs. District courts in segregation cases usually proceed by ordering the local board to present a plan for desegregating. If the plan is unsatisfactory, or if the board is recalcitrant, the court may appoint experts to draw up a plan for the court's consideration. The order of the court may be appealed to a federal court of appeals, and perhaps ultimately to the U. S. Supreme Court, but, in the first instance, the burden of deciding whether *de jure* segregation exists and of fashioning a remedy falls on the district courts.

The remedial order made or approved by the district court may or may not involve the much-disputed device of busing. In 1971 the U. S. Supreme Court, in a *de jure* case, *Swann* v. *Board of Education*,[14] held that busing might be an appropriate remedy in some cases. This does not of course mean that it is always a mandatory remedy. The whole concept of an equitable jurisdiction confers discretion to fashion the response most suitable to meet the detailed configurations of a particular problem. Busing may often be inappropriate or unnecessary. Changes in attendance zones, or enlarging schools, or closing a school may often provide a sufficient answer. In *Swann* the Supreme Court in effect held that they would not disturb the order of a district judge that included mandatory busing if, on the facts, it was not realistic to envisage an adequate remedy without busing. They did add that busing would not be appropriate where the time or the distance involved in the busing is very great so that it might affect the students' health or disrupt the educational process.[15]

THE NORTH AND WEST

In 1973 the Supreme Court decided its first school segregation case from a large city outside the South. *Keyes* v. *School District No. 1*[16] came to the Court from Denver, where there had never been any express statutory scheme of racial separation for the schools. But the plaintiffs, who were parents of Denver schoolchildren, alleged that the school board, by manipulating attendance zones, selecting the sites of schools, and applying a neighborhood school policy, had created or maintained racially or ethnically segregated schools. The findings of fact by the district court judge in the proceedings below accepted the parents' contentions with respect to the schools in one district of the city. The district court accordingly made an order requiring a desegregation plan with respect to schools in that district. But the court was not willing to apply the same order to other schools in the city under the jurisdiction of the same board. Rather, it held that the plaintiffs would have to make separate proof of fostered segregation for each particular area of the city.

The Supreme Court's resolution of the appeal in the *Keyes* case contains important determinations but leaves much still to be settled. In the first place, the Court held that in determining whether schools are segregated, it is not proper to count separately the numbers of blacks and Hispanos in each school. Both these groups were historically discriminated against in education, and for these purposes should be counted as one entity. This will make it easier in some parts of the country for plaintiffs to show a condition of segregation. Second, the Court held that once the plaintiffs had succeeded in showing a condition of *de jure* segregation in a "substantial portion" of the schools under the jurisdiction of the board, then a presumption arises that any other segregated schooling that can be pointed to within the system is also malevolently fostered *de jure*. This applies whether or not the school district was segregated *de jure* at the time of the *Brown* decision in 1954. Once such a presumption arises, the burden of proof shifts to the school authorities to prove the contrary.

> In discharging that burden, it is not enough, of course, that the school authorities rely upon some allegedly logical, racially neutral explanation for their actions. Their burden is to adduce proof sufficient to support a finding that segregative intent was not among the factors that motivated their actions.[17]

Merely to point to a neighborhood school policy is not enough to rebut the presumption and discharge the burden of showing that there was no segregative intent.

Keyes again underlines the fundamental importance of being able to show some practice of *de jure* segregation. Once that threshold is crossed, the courts are willing to assist the plaintiff with valuable presumptions and to fashion affirmative remedial orders. On the other hand, *de facto* segregation has been traditionally seen as constitutionally inoffensive and, consequently, as not requiring any mandatory judicial intervention. The Supreme Court made that point in *Swann:*

> Absent a constitutional violation there would be no basis for judicially ordering assignments of students on a racial basis. All things being equal, with no history of discrimination, it might well be desirable to assign pupils to schools nearest their homes.[18]

A good example of judicial abstention from intervention in *de facto* segregation is *Deal* v. *Cincinnati Board of Education* (1966),[19] where the plaintiff tried to press for judicial relief in a situation where *de jure* segregation was difficult to prove. The plaintiff argued that the equal protection clause of the Fourteenth Amendment required the defendants to balance the races in the public schools, even if the imbalance was not caused by any acts of officially encouraged discrimination. The Sixth Circuit Court of Appeals decisively rejected the argument. Having conceded that a residential pattern existed which, coupled with the neighborhood school concept, combined to create some schools that were predominantly of one race, the Court went on:

> We hold that there is no constitutional duty on the part of the Board to bus Negro or white children out of their neighborhoods or to transfer classes for the sole purpose of alleviating racial imbalance that it did not cause, nor is there a like duty to select new school sites solely in furtherance of such a purpose. . . . It would be a mistake for the courts to read *Brown* in such a way as to impose one particular concept of educational administration as the only permissible method of ensuring equality consistent with sound educational practice.[20]

But, well fitted as it was for attacking the crudest forms of pre-*Brown* segregation, there is growing doubt whether the distinction between *de jure* and *de facto* segregation can withstand the more sophisticated analysis of segregative patterns of schooling that have developed since *Brown*. Attention has shifted from rural and small-town southern school segregation to the separation of the races in big-city schools in all parts of the country. Here in the cities the picture is not very different in the North, East, and West from the South. School segregation today appears roughly the same in cities that once had *de jure* practices as well as in those that never had laws mandating separation of the races. The reason evidently is that racial representation in schools is a product of the "white flight" from the inner cities, zoning policies in the suburbs that make it very difficult for people of low income to live there, and a consequent clustering of blacks, Hispanos, and other minorities either in inner cities or in particular city districts. This may have a great deal to do with generally unjust social arrangements regulating the distribution of wealth and housing, but the connection with early practices of *de jure* school segregation becomes more and more tenuous. Consequently, to impose peculiar legal duties to desegregate on cities that have an earlier history of *de jure* segregation, while abstaining from action with respect to cities that have no such history, becomes more and more indefensible a posture. As Senator Abraham Ribicoff of Connecticut remarked:

> Somehow residential segregation in the North was accidental or *de facto*, and that made it better than the legally supported *de jure* segregation of the South. It was a hard distinction for black children in totally segregated schools in the North to understand, but it allowed us to avoid the problem.[21]

One way of loosening the bonds of the dichotomy is to take a generous view of the meaning of *de jure* segregation. We could, for example, argue that wherever housing patterns that separate poor minority group members from more affluent whites have received any state support, this is sufficient state action to amount to *de jure* segregation in the schools. This appears to have been the view of Mr. Justice Douglas in his brief concurring opinion in *Keyes:*

> I think it is time to state that there is no constitutional difference between *de jure* and *de facto* segregation, for each is the product of state actions or policies. If a "neighborhood" or "geographical" unit has been created along racial lines by reason of the play of restrictive convenants that restrict certain areas to "the elite," leaving the "undesirables" to move elsewhere, there is state action in the constitutional sense because the force of law is placed behind those covenants. There is state action in the constitutional sense when public funds are dispersed by urban development agencies to build racial ghettoes.[22]

Mr. Justice Douglas' view thus still depends on finding *de jure* segregation through state action, but he enlarges the concept of relevant state action to apply to all situations where a "state forces, aids, or abets, or helps create a racial neighborhood." In *Keyes,* Mr. Justice Powell also wrote a separate concurring opinion, stressing the inequity of applying different standards to cities according to whether they once had *de jure* segregation or not:

> [T]he familiar root cause of segregated schools in *all* the biracial metropolitan areas of our country is essentially the same: one of segregated residential and migratory patterns the impact of which on the racial composition of the schools was often perpetuated and rarely ameliorated by action of public school authorities. This is a national, not a southern phenomenon. And it is largely unrelated to whether a particular state had or did not have segregative school laws.[23]

Mr. Justice Powell's solution would be to take the simple existence of a substantial degree of segregation within a school system as raising a *prima facie* presumption that the relevant school authority is responsible.

> The burden then shifts to the school authorities to demonstrate that they have in fact operated an integrated system. If there is a failure successfully to rebut the *prima facie* case, the question then becomes what reasonable affirmative desegregative steps district courts may require to place the school system in compliance with the constitutional standard.[24]

XIII

Elusive Educational Equality

In reflecting on the *de jure-de facto* dichotomy, it is helpful to remember that the distinction is nothing more than a particular way of phrasing the general requirement that inequalities are only unconstitutional when they are the product of state action. *Keyes* has left us with three views of what constitutes state action in this context. The majority position in the Supreme Court retains the emphasis on a strict *de jure* approach. Under this view, state action is present only when the state has taken malevolent steps in its educational administration with a segregative intent. The plaintiff has the initial burden of proving such conduct by the state, at least with respect to a significant portion of the schools in the district under scrutiny. In contrast, under Mr. Justice Douglas' approach, state action may be found whenever the state has given legal sanction to practices that effectively bring about economic (and thus indirectly racial) separation in residential concentrations. This enlarges the concept dramatically, but it still leaves the courts with the difficult and irksome task of finding a state fostering of segregation, however indirectly. Mr. Justice Douglas' opinion is so brief that it is not easy to say what kind of proof a plaintiff would have to make to satisfy this burden.

There appears to be much to commend the more radical cutting of the knot proposed by Mr. Justice Powell in an approach that he himself asserted was studiously aimed at fashioning a national rather than a regional standard. In Mr. Justice Powell's view, state action exists when the state has failed to take reasonable affirmative steps to remedy a condition of segregation in the schools, no matter how that condition came about. The plaintiff thus would have no initial burden of showing that segregation had a *de jure* aspect. He need only show significant *de facto* segregation, and the burden of proof would shift to the state to show that it was in fact operating an integrated school system. This does not mean that all schools must actually be integrated. It means rather that the state has taken and is taking all reasonable steps, within the bounds of practicality and with proper attention to other educational values, to see that the schools are as integrated as those limitations permit. The boundaries of reasonableness and the balancing of interests here can clearly be matters of keen dispute.

Implications of Different Theories

Any expansion of the concept of state action in this area expresses an identically expanded understanding of the right to equal educational opportunity. Until recently that has been understood as no more than a right that the state should not actively create or perpetuate a situation of segregation. The larger view would assert an affirmative state duty to take positive steps to bring about a situation of racial balance. What would be the constitutional ligatures of such a right? *Brown* itself can certainly be given the weaker interpretation that segregated education is inherently unequal only when the imprimatur of the state is affixed to it, thus producing a tacit stigma that clouds the educational process. But there is a body of sociological evidence to the effect that segregated education is inherently inferior, whether or not it is fostered by the state. A report published in 1966 by the Office of Education (known after its author as the Coleman Report) suggests that one of the most potent contributors to a low quality of educational product is the predominance in schools of children from a low socioeconomic background.[1] In the United States this of course has an extensive overlap with segregation by race. When minority group children are placed in integrated schools with large numbers of children from higher socioeconomic backgrounds, there is often a significant improvement in their performance. If these observations are borne out, then it may be that racial commingling in the schools is the *only* way in which significant improvements in the quality of education offered to minority group children can be brought about. Failure to take steps in this direction would then amount at the least to a passive perpetuation by the state of unequal education. It does not place an intolerable strain on the language of the Fourteenth Amendment to view this as a denial of equal protection.

But to rest this approach on the premise that integration contributes vitally to the quality of the educational product leaves it dependent on conclusions of the sociology of education that may be tentative and subject to revision as more information accumulates. There is considerable danger in dressing up what may be ephemeral propositions of social science in the armor of constitutional doctrine. Looking for more enduring foundations we could argue that, irrespective of the quality of the educational product, the right to equal educational opportunity inherently involves reasonable racial commingling in the schools. Racial separation has a bitter history of connection with servitude and discrimination. Even if official acts of discrimintion have ceased, a *de facto* separation of the races cannot but be associated with the American tradition of ascribing inferiority to the minority group. This has a tendency to poison the educational process and impose a sense of exclusion on minority group children. It is a kind of devaluation of their worth that in itself mandates corrective action, quite apart from any considerations of the impact on conventional measurements of academic success.

This road has its dangers too. If we follow it, could we stop with education? Would not the same arguments apply to *de facto* residential segregation, where the consequences of imposing affirmative duties on states and local authorities might be colossally disruptive, if not impossible of fulfillment? Dangers of such an escalation cannot be dismissed, but it is not difficult to trace legal principles that countenance the restriction of this approach to the public schools. Though its boundaries are not well defined, the courts have now for a long time recognized a right to equal educational opportunity. No such constitutionally grounded right to equal housing has emerged. (We are not speaking here of the prohibition on discrimination in the granting of public housing, which is a narrower question.) In view of the history and associations of educational segregation in the United States, it could be asserted that the fundamental right to equal educational opportunity entails a subsidiary affirmative right to integrated education, when there are no compelling reasons why the state cannot or should not provide it.

On the other hand, if the right to a properly mixed school

population stems chiefly from the danger of an inferior educational product rather than from arguments having to do with racial separation alone, then it is difficult to see how its thrust can be penned within the concept of race, for studies like the Coleman Report suggest that the main factor that disposes to a poor educational product is the predominant presence in a school of children from a low socioeconomic background. This is supported by some British studies.[2] Though there is a substantial overlap in the United States between belonging to a minority group and being poor, the circles are evidently not coterminous. Indeed, if there were a more natural and proportionate distribution of affluence between whites and blacks, the question of color might soon appear to have no connection whatever with educational product, but the link with socioeconomic background would surely remain. In this way, a journey down the road to equal educational opportunity may require a vigorous effort by school boards and other relevant authorities to build school populations that reflect a nice balance of different socioeconomic levels in the community at large. Such a proposition pushes us to the cliff edge of the question, which we shall examine in a later chapter, whether it is prudent and proper for courts to pursue such aims through the interpretation of the Constitution or whether they are not more appropriately matters for legislatures.

Remedial Action

To argue that a situation of *de facto* segregation imposes an affirmative duty on school authorities to take corrective action solves few problems, for there remains the vexing question of what steps school authorities can reasonably be expected to take. Some have suggested that the condition is often incurable, at least by anything that school authorities might do. Alexander Bickel has commented in this connection: "In most of the larger urban areas, demographic conditions are such that no policy a court can order, and a school board, a city or even a state has the capability to put into effect, will in fact result in the foreseeable future in racially balanced public schools. Only a reordering of the environment involving economic and social policy on the broadest conceivable front might have an appreciable impact."[3]

It is the proposed or actual busing of children to schools outside their own neighborhoods that inflames this discussion. Essentially the same question may present itself at two stages of the inquiry. First, what must a school board show to satisfy a court that it has been diligently striving to operate an integrated school system? Must it, in some cases, show that it has tried busing? Second, if a court is not satisfied with the showing of the board and decides to order further desegregative measures, when is it proper for this order to mandate busing? Many steps short of busing may be taken, such as the redrawing of attendance zones, control of size and location of new schools, and voluntary transfer programs with the provision of free transportation. But in metropolitan areas these steps alone without extensive busing are unlikely to bring about a satisfactory degree of integration.

If integration in a school board's jurisdiction can only be achieved through a high degree of medium-distance busing, experience teaches us that vehement protests will greet the proposal of such a solution. The opposition is by no means entirely racist, though it may be so in part. It also stems from a natural fear in parents for the welfare of their children, who, they feel, may be threatened in health, tranquility, and educational achievement by the shuttling around. Black parents sometimes share in these fears and join the opposition to busing schemes. This opposition arguably also has some constitutional tendrils. Some early cases in the Supreme Court have indicated that the right of parents to educate a child in the manner of their choice is, in some aspects, a "fundamental right," which cannot be displaced except by a compelling state interest. The courts have not yet recognized the extension of such a fundamental right to embrace the choice of a neighborhood school, but the human interests of parents and children in this area are not located far outside the circle of constitutional protection.

DISTRICT LINES

The situation is further complicated by the traditional carving up of school government within a state among a number of largely autonomous school districts, each one controlled by its own school board. Most desegregation lawsuits have been aimed solely at the activities of a single school board in operating the schools within its district, seeking remedial orders within those confines. But it may be the case that a school district, taken as a whole, contains a massive predominance of children of one color. No action addressed to that district alone could have any relevance to the problem of integration. To give the simplest example, if District X, containing 95 per cent white children and 5 per cent black, is contiguous to District Y, where the percentages are exactly reversed, it is apparent that no progress at all can be made while the courts are limited to making orders that operate only within the boundaries of District X or District Y. But once a court took upon itself the power to order Districts X and Y to co-operate and mingle their pupils to some extent, then great progress might be made toward integration. This problem has come to the fore with the concentration of interest on metropolitan school districts, which often border on suburban districts where whites predominate.

If a state has originally drawn up or later tampered with school district lines for the perceptible purpose of fostering or preserving segregation, then a court has a clear warrant to intervene and make a remedial order that vaults these malevolent hurdles. Where no such segregative intent can be shown in the arrangement of the boundaries, it has generally been thought that the lines were impermeable to interference, because of the absence of significant state action. But at least three arguments, depending on the facts, can be made to urge the propriety of an interdistrict remedy.

First, it may be possible to find other malevolent state action having a direct impact on the schools, such as the fostering of residential segregation. If, in this way, the state has helped to create a white enclave in the suburbs, then we have a warrant for ignoring the school district lines, since they are no more than an auxiliary to the state-fostered racial separation. Second, the duty of the federal court is to find a remedy for an existing situation of *de jure* segregation. Now, suppose the situation is like our earlier example, where the city schools are 95 per cent black, while the suburban schools are 95 per cent white. As we saw earlier, no remedy at all is possible within the confines of the city district. Even if the white pupils were shared out with precise equality among the schools, all the schools would still be 95 per cent black, and that does not look like integration. In following its duty to bring an end to segregation, the court, therefore, must order an interdistrict remedy.

A third argument, of the most dynamic potential, would be that the very failure by the state to redraw school district boundaries, when such a redrawing could alleviate segregation, is in itself sufficient state action, or, more appropriately, a constitutionally culpable omission. Why, it could be asked, should a state shelter behind the frozen lines of administrative subdivisions, unless it can be shown that there is a compelling state interest in leaving them unaltered? Clearly some state interests are present. The state can point to the administrative unmanageability of forcing districts to merge, and to the impact this would have on patterns of government. While these are legitimate state interests, it is at the least disputable whether they are "compelling" when viewed against the constitutional offense of segregated schools. At least, if an enlarged concept of equal educational opportunity has the status of a fundamental right, it would be proper to demand that the state make such a showing before it may escape a remedial order that crosses district lines.

By 1974 an important strategy of plaintiffs in metropolitan school litigation was to press for such interdistrict remedies. Necessarily this would involve some busing between city and suburbs. This appeared a frightening specter to many, although in fact the amount of busing involved could well be less than if remedies were pursued within a city alone, for the obvious reason that some parts of some suburbs are much closer to some districts of the city than are other districts of the city. After some signs of success in lower courts, the matter came squarely before the Supreme Court for determination in 1974 in *Milliken* v. *Bradley*.[4]

That case concerned school segregation in the city of Detroit. The record showed that this segregation was the product of a dismal history of malevolent action both by the school board and by the state of Michigan. The district court had held that, in view of the racial composition of the school population, the *de jure* segregation in Detroit could not be meaningfully overcome by any remedies that stopped at the city boundaries. Accordingly, the court ordered a corrective plan to be prepared that would have involved joining fifty-three suburban school districts with the city and treating them as one metropolitan unit. The circuit court of appeals substantially affirmed this decision.

The Supreme Court, by a five to four majority, reversed, and held that any remedy involving interdistrict orders was inappropriate. The opinion of the majority, written by Chief Justice Burger, is surprisingly brief in view of the complexity of the issues involved. It is also wooden and simplistic in its handling of the subtle skein of arguments that weaves around this problem. In essence the opinion declares that interdistrict remedies are suitable only when "racially discriminatory acts of the state or local school districts or of a single school district have been a substantial cause of interdistrict segregation."[5] Otherwise the remedy is inappropriate (a) because of the value we attach to local control of schools and (b) because of the upheaval that would result in some aspects of the structure of state government. The energetic and sometimes bitter dissents characterize the majority opinion as conferring a sanctity on administrative subdivisions that overrides constitutional violations.

There is certainly a narrowness about the Court's opinion in *Milliken* that signals, for the time being, the end of judicial vigor in the pursuit of educational equality. The great ideal of equal educational opportunity turns out to mean no more than the prohibition of racial segregation within a particular school district. In a later chapter, we will suggest that it is often a difficult question whether the Supreme Court should be bold and creative rather than cautious and circumspect. There can be no doubt that by its decision in *Milliken* the Court both reduced the level of its intrusion on the operations of other branches of government and placated a mounting wave of sharp opposition from a section of the public. At the same time, the decision reduces the constitutional right to integrated education to the point where it will be difficult to achieve any meaningful integration at all in many metropolitan regions.

For it is important to remember that if school segregation

is the product of residential separation, then residential separation is just as much, if not more, the product of school segregation. We have a truly vicious circle here, where white flight is accelerated by predominantly minority group schools, which in turn become more and more segregated as white flight continues and whites become uninterested in moving into a neighborhood that has segregated schools. If residential desegregation is the answer to the problem of racial imbalance in the schools, then it may well be true that a good racial mix in the schools is a prime answer to residential segregation. Many agencies of the states (and the federal government) would have to co-operate to bring about such solutions, for the remedies would include not only steps addressed solely and directly to school integration, but also the building of middle-income and low-income housing in all communities and the offering of inducements to whites to move into formerly ghetto neighborhoods. Such a broad social attack may not be a likely prospect in the near future, but while this work remains undone then school segregation still appears as the product of a complex of positive acts and failures to act by a number of state agencies. If that is so, it seems unreasonable to allow the state to deny the significant presence of state action or culpable inaction merely by pointing to boundary lines of school districts that were originally drawn with innocent intent. Courts have been willing to ride over state subdivisions in the reapportionment cases where the fundamental right to have one's vote count equally was at stake. The right to equal educational opportunity may be at least as strong a reason for such action.

More Obstacles

Even recognition of judicial power to make orders that mandate state action across school district lines would still leave unmanageable problems of achieving integration when faced with massive residential blocks of one color in metropolitan and sprawling suburban zones. The Constitution cannot require the impossible, and the notion of equitable remedies demands attention to the extent of disruption involved and the nature of the burdens to be imposed on children and parents. School integration is an ideal of importance and a constitutionally mandated goal, but it is not an ideal that should always triumph over all other values, nor a goal to be pursued at any price. The best courts can do and the most they ought to do is to push persistently to achieve reasonably possible integration with due attention to other compelling interests involved. As the decisions show, this certainly permits a degree of busing and may mandate it when other measures fail. At the same time, it does not require a doctrinaire commitment to busing on a large scale. In the last resort, the orders to be fashioned depend on the good sense and prudential evaluations of the federal district judges. Their orders are susceptible to review and correction when they misconceive the law or exceed the bounds of any reasonable exercise of discretion. But if integration is to be given a paramount value, then it can only seriously be pursued by political action and legislation that seek to eradicate the basic underpinnings of segregation, which are residential patterns heavily dependent on economic considerations.

The goal of school integration has a disturbing tendency to recede elusively, the nearer it seems to being grasped. The whole effort in the school segregation cases has been to get a reasonable mix of children of different races in the same schools. But how much has been achieved if they are then split up within the schools themselves in "tracks" or "streams" that professedly reflect their capacities for learning at a slow or accelerated speed and their suitability for highly academic as opposed to more vocational programs? Where a degree of integration has been achieved in some city schools, the situation has often reverted in this way to an interior pattern of segregation within the school itself. The explanation is usually said to be that economic, social, and cultural deprivation in very early years often leaves minority group children unable to compete effectively in learning skills and speeds with more advantaged white children.

One solution is what has come to be known as "heterogeneous grouping," a system by which children are offered the same curriculum and mixed together in classes in spite of their varying learning capacities. This may have the advantage of stimulating the slower children by some process of emulation or osmosis and so sharpening their skills and speeding up their progress. The clear disadvantage is that such a system may dilute the curriculum offered to the brighter children and slow their progress by tying them to the movement made by the slower children. By contrast, "homogeneous grouping," by which children are tracked in different groups according to ability, maximizes progress for the brighter children but tends to produce a situation of internal segregation within the school. It is possible that such internal segregation is as wounding and traumatic, if not more so, for the slower children than segregation in different schools.

This issue again brings us to a most excruciating intersection of educational policy and constitutional rights. It may be a reasonable assumption that educational policy makers are most of the time sensitively pursuing the best solution to a conflict of this complexity. Can we safely leave such decisions to these experts, or should courts intrude within the very schoolroom itself and assert a power to make orders with respect to curriculum and tracking on the ground that some policies and procedures in this area may amount to unconstitutional discrimination? To deny courts this power altogether may be unnecessarily sweeping. To assert that it must be exercised with the greatest caution would seem to be common sense. In a later chapter we shall return to this question when we consider more generally the wisdom of constitutional judicial intervention into areas of the detailed administration of social institutions.

School Financing

The concept of equality depends on the possibility of comparison. If I were living alone on a desert island, it would not be possible to say that I was treating myself unequally. I might force myself to get up at five o'clock every morning, and one might conclude that I was behaving neurotically and imposing an unnecessarily harsh discipline upon myself, but the concept of equality would not be relevant. But once someone else joins me on the island and one of us has power over the other, complaints about inequality may be made.

Not any comparison is appropriate for any concept of equality. The standard of living is generally much lower in many countries than in the United States. This may be a situation of significant inequality in terms of a global social morality, and arguably this places moral duties on the governments and people of wealthy nations to give aid to impoverished peoples in other countries; but the contrast is clearly irrelevant to the adjudications of the Supreme Court of the United States. The Court has a jurisdiction within which its powers and orders are confined. Moreover, even in taking notice of inequalities on the American scene, the Court is naturally limited to the task of giving force to the precepts of the Constitution. Among many other complexities this raises the question of the relevant standards of comparison when the Court has to apply the equal-protection doctrine.

Sometimes the practical result of a ruling in this area by the Supreme Court is to establish a national standard. For example, all states have systems of appeal after a criminal conviction. Decisions by the Court in recent years make it clear that no state may make the exercise of the right to take a first appeal from a criminal conviction depend on the financial position of the appellant. So an indigent appellant must be given free access to the appellate courts, which may involve the waiving of filing fees, provision of a free transcript of the proceedings in the trial court, and provision of counsel at the expense of the state or local authority. The national standard, though, is only in terms of eliminating a barrier to access or providing minimal facilities for access. When it is rather a question of the quality of services provided to citizens, the Constitution offers no concept that permits us to argue for equality among the states. That Maine and Mississippi, Oregon and Louisiana should each spend about the same amount of money per pupil on education is a proposition that would shatter our notions of a federal union and move us rapidly toward a unitary state. It is not a decision that the Supreme Court has any power to make, whether or not the states in question have approximately equal resources.

The Fourteenth Amendment requires that a state shall not deny to citizens the equal protection of the laws. We have already seen that the application of this guarantee to situations where governmental subdivisions of a state present different social and residential patterns has caused considerable difficulty in the school integration cases. The same problem has arisen with respect to the financing of schools. If courts cannot make orders that cross state lines, can they not, at least, scrutinize the internal actions of a state to ensure that no irrational inequalities exist with respect to the expenditure on education from district to district?

The great majority of states have traditionally funded expenditures on education at the precollege level by authorizing local school districts to levy a tax on real property, whether residential, commercial, or industrial. There will be the widest disparity among different school districts with respect to the strength of this "tax base." Some will have large clusters of expensive homes or factory buildings that permit considerable sums of money to be raised for education by a comparatively low tax rate. Other districts will lack both expensive homes and industrial property and will be able to raise only a modest sum for education even with the imposition of a heavy rate of taxation. Left in this posture, the situation would be intolerable, since some districts, even with the heaviest level of taxation, would not be able to afford a minimally acceptable education system, while others could provide lavishly with little effort.

To avoid such an inequity, states have generally devised equalization schemes by which the poorest districts are given subsidies from some centrally administered fund to bring their level of expenditure on education up to what is regarded as an acceptable minimum. Such schemes do rebut the charge that the state is failing to provide some of its children with any education worthy of the name, but they clearly do not cure all aspects of inequality. The residents of poorer districts will still pay more to get less, a practice likely to arouse the keenest sense of injustice. It is true that this inequitable distribution of burdens and dividends does not always harm poor people. We have to distinguish here between poor people and poor districts, for some poor people may live in rich districts, while some districts may be comparatively poor even though not many poor people live there. A district with a heavy concentration of very valuable industrial and commercial property may very likely have poor residents. Educationally, though, the district will be prosperous. Conversely, a district may be inhabited largely by lower-middle-class residents and have no industrial and little commercial property. Such a district may be educationally poor. But while there is no nice equivalence between educationally poor districts and the homes of poor people, there is often a substantial overlap.

While such arrangements may strike many as undesirable, it is not immediately obvious what kind of remedial action we might expect courts to take under the aegis of the Constitution. The demand clearly should not be for a crude equivalence of per capita expenditure for each child across a state, for there may be many rational and just reasons why more money should be spent in some districts than in others. One district may have a larger proportion of high school students than another, and it may be that high school education is inherently more expensive than junior high school education. Or one district may have a large number of retarded or physically handicapped children who need special and expensive services and training. Indeed, it could be argued that districts that are heavily populated by poor people have a just claim for a higher per capita expenditure per pupil than other areas, precisely because extra efforts may be necessary to overcome early environmental handicaps.

But if courts are not suitable organs for drafting the details of a perfectly just plan for educational expenditures, they can at least strike down features of existing arrangements that are so discriminatory as to be constitutionally offensive. By the late 1960s, litigants in a number of states were pressing the view that the local property tax base for educational expenditures could not survive a constitutional challenge. After some unsuccessful litigation, an important breakthrough occurred when the Supreme Court of California endorsed this argument in the case of *Serrano* v. *Priest*[6] in 1971.

The California court approached the problem in classic terms of the equal protection guarantee of the Fourteenth Amendment. Modern cases have held that where a right is fundamental, then discrimination among different classes of people in extending or protecting the right can only be justified if the state shows a compelling interest. A mere showing of some legitimate interest will not suffice. (As we saw earlier, a similar test is now used with the concept of "liberty" under the due process clause to protect rights to privacy or autonomy.) Also, if the basis of the distinction created by the state is inherently suspect (as with a person's color), again the compelling-interest hurdle must be crossed to sustain the state action. With respect to educational financing, the California Supreme Court took the view that the compelling-interest test was doubly required, both because equal access to education was a fundamental right and also because any distinction based on wealth was inherently suspect. The local district property tax base for educational financing might certainly serve some rational interests of the state, but these interests could not be characterized as compelling, in the court's view, when compared with the discrimination imposed on children. If the allegations about the nature of the California system could be proved, that system must be changed, the court held.

Serrano did not mandate the precise nature of the change. It did not even outlaw the property tax as the basis of raising funds for education. It simply forbade in California the disbursement of these funds by a formula that relates to the assessed value of the real estate in a particular district. Funds may still be collected on a statewide basis by means of the property tax, as long as they are not distributed in a discriminatory way. Many principles might still be acceptable for allocating more money per capita to some districts than others. All that *Serrano* demands is that these principles serve a compelling state interest or that they do not offend against the primary demands of equal protection. Giving extra money to districts that have an unusually large number of retarded children could be justified, either by arguing that it is not in itself a suspect classification, or alternatively by contending that it serves a compelling state interest.

Serrano was decided under the authority of the Fourteenth Amendment to the United States Constitution and the parallel provisions of the California Constitution. The principle could only acquire national status if the Supreme Court of the United States were also to embrace it. But in 1973, in the case of *San Antonio School District* v. *Rodriguez*,[7] the Supreme Court, by a majority of five to four, rejected the reasoning of *Serrano* and thus abruptly halted the gathering judicial pressure on states to change their methods of school financing.

In the first place, the Supreme Court did not regard the wealth-type distinction made in educational financing as a suspect one. In other areas where distinctions based on wealth had been struck down, the Court observed, they were of a kind that quite shut off a citizen from access to a privilege or facility offered to others, as where a convict was denied the right to appeal because he could not buy a transcript or pay filing fees. Those who live in poorer districts are not so denied, for they are still ensured an adequate education. Concededly there may be a difference in the quality of education if money can bring about such a result, but "the equal protection clause does not require absolute equality or precisely equal advantages."[8]

The Court had trouble too in seeing exactly who was being discriminated against. Clearly it is not poor people or their children who suffer as a class, since the wealth of school districts corresponds only imperfectly to the wealth of the residents. It is, though, apparent that unequal education is being inflicted on children who reside in districts that have a poor tax base, but the Court held that this did not amount to a suspect classification, since "the disadvantaged class is not susceptible of identification in traditional terms."[9] This refers to the contrast with the mainstream of earlier decisions that had to do with denying privileges to poor people on the basis of their being poor. But it is not a very persuasive distinction, for while it is true that educational finance systems in most states do not expressly discriminate against people on the basis of their being poor, they do discriminate against children for the accident of their parents residing in one part of the state rather than another. This points to a quite precisely identifiable class of people, and it is not easy to see why it is constitutionally proper to discriminate against the residents of one area but not against poor people. Would it be constitutionally defensible to discriminate in the provision of education, even against the rich? Difficult as it may be for them to enter the kingdom of Heaven, they should surely capture the ear of the courts if they happen to live in a district with a poor tax base. In fact, the rich who live in such areas can often escape the dilemma by sending their children to private schools, a remedy that is impossible for the poor and the lower middle classes.

Unwilling to view the case as one involving a suspect classification, the Court was no more ready to consider it as raising a fundamental right. While *Brown* and its progeny may have encouraged us to think of a right to equal education as "fundamental," *Rodriguez* makes it clear that, constitutionally speaking, it is not. Perhaps, the Court said, it may be that "some identifiable quantum of education is a constitutionally protected prerequisite."[10] to freedom of speech and the right to vote, but this does not rise to fundamental claims with respect to equality. What then have the courts been talking about for twenty years when they referred to "the right to equal educational opportunity"? After *Rodriguez* it must now be taken as a reference only to the impermissibility of racial separation in the schools, so that, in the end, the Constitution is invoked only because of racial classification and not because there is any general right to equality in education. In *Rodriguez,* since there was no question of classification by race nor even of classification according to income, the Court could not perceive anything suspect. And since at the same time the Court denied the fundamental nature of the right advanced by the plaintiffs, there was no ground at all for imposing a burden on the state to show a compelling interest. All the state had to do to vindicate its legislation was to meet the old weak equal protection test of showing some legitimate interest rationally aimed at in its legislation. This of course was not a difficult burden to discharge; references to the importance of local control sufficed.

PRESENT POSITION

The combined impact of the *Rodriguez* and *Milliken* decisions is of the greatest importance. They signal a throttling back if not an abrupt halt in the thrust of arguments to extend the judicial push toward equality. In *Milliken,* Mr. Justice Douglas suggested that the effect of the two decisions was to put the clock back to the barbarous state of affairs that existed before the "separate but equal" decision of *Plessy* v. *Ferguson* in 1896. For now, he argued, minority groups can be penned in inner cities where the schools will have very few white pupils and where the supporting tax base may be very low. In this way they can be perpetually consigned to separate and unequal education, which, in turn, may condemn them to many other kinds of separation and inequality during their lives.

Rodriguez has strong implications, if negative ones, for other areas too. One demon that has for some time frightened certain observers of the judicial scene has been the possible extension of equality-based constitutional arguments into areas other than education. This has been mockingly referred to as the "equal sewer" problem; if equalization of expenditure on education is mandated by the Constitution, how long can the administrative sharing out of other social services be immune from judicial scrutiny? And the problem might assume dimensions even more potent than a fair spreading of money over different districts of a state. If there is a fundamental right to education, then why not to health care or housing? And if these rights are fundamental, would there not be a constitutional duty on the states to ensure at least a decent minimum provision to everyone?

The pursuit of perfect equality in education is certainly distressingly frustrating if we believe that for most people it is the only key that can unlock important doors. The British system, although not plagued like the American scene with allegations of unequal expenditure among districts, has still lamentably failed in its efforts to provide equal educational opportunities. This is not only because of the devastating effects of environment in early years for children of low socioeconomic background, but also because of the deeply ingrained practice of upper-middle-class parents of sending their children to private schools, curiously known as "public" schools. Labour Party theorists in Britain have at times flirted with the idea of abolishing the public schools by legislation. This would no doubt result only in their transplantation to Belgium or Switzerland. Conceivably, we might insist that all children actually attend homogenized state schools. But such a measure savors of tyranny and, even then, how could one conceivably prevent wealthy parents from supplementing the school fare with extracurricular private tuition? Equal educational opportunity probably only comes after a thoroughgoing social revolution.

But the Supreme Court ought not to abstain from intervention simply because perfect equality is unattainable, nor was this the reason the court gave in *Rodriguez* for abstaining. The question in *Rodriguez* was the comparatively narrow one, whether it is constitutionally defensible for a state to permit the amount of money spent per capita on education to vary according to the comparative wealth or poverty of the real estate tax base from district to district. While we know that equal expenditure of money will not necessarily produce an equal educational product, there is certainly no reason to believe that it has no relevance. Spending more money, if it is wisely spent, can have a positive impact. Education is a unique early social experience, the quality of which will affect for many people the rewards and enjoyment that they will derive from life. It is strange that the Constitution of the United States permits a state to diminish that experience for some as compared with others whose only virtue is to live elsewhere.

In *Rodriguez,* in an equal protection context, the Supreme Court was chary of usurping a legislative role in creating new fundamental rights not precisely defined in the Constitution. Yet in the same year, in a liberty and due process context, they had found such a right with respect to a woman's claim to have an abortion. It seems that a state deprives a woman of her liberty in defiance of due process of law if it prohibits her from having an abortion; but a state does not deny its citizens the equal protection of the laws when it permits less money to be spent on their education than on the education of other children in state schools. This is one of the constitutional conundrums of the 1970s.

XIV

Preferential Treatment

The field of civil liberties and civil rights can never escape legal complexities. But its broad moral setting has traditionally been a comforting one in which we wage battles against malevolence and struggle to overturn the practices of those who believe others to be inferior or unworthy of equal treatment. Recently both the legal and the moral pictures have clouded over. Practices are called into question that are evidently not the expression of malevolence but that are justified as redressing past inequalities and imbalances or otherwise promoting desirable aims and applauded ideals. At the same time, they may appear in other aspects to threaten some traditional expressions of constitutionally protected values. Such very delicate and complicated moral dilemmas have emerged with any clarity only in the past few years, and they have so far produced only tentative and uncertain responses. Decisions of the courts offer only the most meager illumination in this troubled area.

Examples will help to make the dilemma more concrete. A public educational institution, perhaps the graduate school of a state university, may awaken to the fact that it has a lamentably small proportion of blacks among its students. Strenuous efforts to improve this position by attracting to the school black students who meet usual admission requirements fail, probably because there is only a small pool of black students nationally available with such qualifications, and they are competed for energetically by some of the most prestigious schools in the country. Accordingly, our school decides to abandon its traditional "color blind" policy and to accept black students whose qualifications are somewhat below those generally required for admission. This new policy may be announced publicly, or, more probably, it may simply be applied without fanfare. In either event, we assume that there is sufficient evidence of the general admission requirements and of the practice of lowering these in the case of black applicants. What would be the result if a white student, rejected by the school, should bring a suit in which he alleged that black students with qualifications less than his had been accepted and that this constituted a denial to him of the equal protection of the law?

Somewhat similarly, suppose that a public or private employer, in an apparently laudable desire to increase the number of blacks in its employment and in positions of executive responsibility, establishes a hiring practice of giving preference to black applicants when their qualifications are identical with those of white applicants, or even somewhat below, and acts similarly in its internal promotion practices. Could a white applicant, alleging superior qualifications to a preferred black appointee, bring a successful suit under one of the federal or state statutes that prescribe fair employment practices?

In a different context, we may suppose that a public housing authority, building a new development, is anxious to make it integrated and to keep it so. Perhaps a statistical projection is made that if available places in the development were filled from those people in the territorial jurisdiction of the authority who are most qualified or deserving of places according to criteria of income, nature of present housing, size of family, etc., then the new development would be filled with approximately 80 per cent blacks and 20 per cent whites. However, current sociological studies in the public housing field assert that after black occupancy of buildings passes a certain percentage, known as the "tipping point," whites tend to leave the dwellings and the buildings become all black. We may assume that in the area in question the tipping point has been set at 50 per cent black. Accordingly, the housing authority establishes a "benign quota" by which black occupancy is not to rise above 50 per cent. After this point is reached, a black applicant is refused and the place allotted to a white applicant who, on generally accepted criteria, leaving out the racial and integration questions, would have been less eligible. Does the rejected black have a remedy against the housing authority?

For a final example, let us suppose that black students at a state university persuade the university authorities to set up a black studies program that shall not be open to white students and to provide separate university housing for black students. If the university accedes to these requests, may a white student, denied admission to the black studies program or to the black housing facility, bring a successful suit against the university?

The examples above are not meant to suggest that there is at present in the United States a massive program of preferential treatment in favor of blacks that is posing grave threats to the civil rights of whites. But such practices are clearly in force in some institutions, and the moral and legal dilemmas they pose have to be confronted. As is so often the case in the United States, most of the moral arguments that can be made on either side will be found to be closely mirrored in the legal arguments as to constitutionality.

Ethics and Social Policy

A declaration that our master ideal is equality and equal treatment is by no means sufficient to dissolve the problems, for it could be immediately asserted that a society that is sensitively concerned with serving this ideal must be attentive to the past as well as the present and the future. Is a university properly serving the ideal of equality by adopting a color-blind admissions policy when pervasive social injustices have ensured that many young black people are so educationally ill-equipped that they cannot present the qualifications normally required for admission? Does not fidelity to the ideal of equality require that a compensatory allowance be made for this? Indeed, in this educational field a justification could be presented so as to avoid any allegations of unequal treatment. The university might assert that its duty in selecting students for acceptance is to identify those who are most likely to perform well in the context of higher education. In the past, certain standard indicators have been used for this purpose that did *de facto,* exclude a great number of black applicants. But, it could be argued, these traditional criteria, such as high school grades and performance on standard aptitude tests, can now be shown to be weighted in favor of white middle-class students. If provided with a proper motivation and proper teaching, certain black students are just as likely to do well in the university as certain white students who scored higher on the conventional tests. The university claims to be able to identify these black students by interviews and other procedures. If such an argument is uncontested, the university has now rebutted the charge of unequal treatment (assuming that the interviews were afforded to white students also) and has simply replaced its earlier selection procedures by ones that it claims can more sensitively and accurately identify those students most likely to do well in higher education.

But this is clearly to some extent a factual dispute. In response it could be said that standard tests used by universities for admission purposes do fairly accurately predict those who are most likely to succeed in an academic setting. There is some evidence with respect to aptitude tests used for tracking at the precollege school level that this is so.[1] To assert this is not of course to deny that these tests may be culturally biased or class-biased or (concomitantly) racially biased. Black and poor children may indeed be disposed by environmental factors and family cultural backgrounds to do poorly in these tests. But this does not mean that the tests are likely to be inaccurate as predictors. (Whether it entitles us to call the tests "unfair" is then clearly a more complicated question.) And once the tests are shown to be reasonably accurate (and the most accurate) predictors of academic success, a school or university that wishes to go beyond them to give preference to a black student who has performed less well than a rejected white student will have to move to another justification.

This might be that in the selection of students for places in a university, factors other than anticipation of the optimum academic performance are properly relevant. Certainly, many colleges have long been in the habit of according preference to children of alumni or to applicants with a particular regional connection. It would not seem a departure from such a tradition to recognize other reasons as establishing relevant criteria in selection procedures. One such reason might be a public obligation to make reparations to people who had earlier been subjected to disadvantage. On a different footing, it might be justified by pointing to the social need to have more black people in positions of responsibility and settings of relative affluence that can generally be reached only through higher education. Such a goal could be thought of both as correcting social injustice and, in a more utilitarian vein, as damping down the fires of discontent and leading to a more harmonious and productive society.

Are these proper objectives for a university in its selection of students? Even if they are proper, may they be pursued at the expense of individuals who might be better qualified by criteria relating to the prospect of optimum academic performance? Moving from the moral to the legal question, we are now asking whether a racial classification is ever permissible when it involves giving preference to members of one racial group at the expense of another. Even if the university's practice were changed somewhat and amounted to giving preference not just to blacks but to all who were classified as disadvantaged, moral and legal problems would remain, though they would lose the traditional cloud of intense suspicion that surrounds racial classifications.

Before pursuing these general considerations further, we should note that the arguments aired above in connection with preferential (or compensatory, or reparative) treatment for one group are not appropriate to the "benign quota" example in the housing field. The benign quota is not designed to confer any supererogatory benefit on black people, but rather to curtail their otherwise legitimate claims in furtherance of another social ideal which, presumably, is considered to be in the interest of society generally and so to benefit both blacks and whites. The benign quota is indeed not designed to benefit any particular group as such, nor is it designed with the purpose of inflicting a deprivation on anyone, though the result of its imposition may be to deny someone a benefit that he could otherwise claim. Here the complainant will not be a white person who claims that a black person has been unjustifiably preferred to him in pursuit of an ideal of reparation, but rather a black person who claims that a white person has been unjustifiably preferred to him in pursuit of an ideal of integration. Now, it is true that when we have spoken traditionally of the evils of *de jure* or *de facto* segregation, we have been most mindful of the alleged harm to blacks, but our black complainant might reasonably urge that he is less interested in the general ideal of integration than in securing for himself and his family decent housing to which he has an otherwise proper claim.

This position might be strengthened by the sociological argument that, while there is a body of evidence to the effect that segregated educational facilities do acute harm to black children, there is no evidence that segregated housing does comparable harm to black people. Indeed, the strongest arguments for integrated housing are in terms of its educational impact in breaking down prejudice both in whites and blacks, and it is not easy to see why blacks should have to pay a special price to secure this benefit for everybody. A subtle response here might be that segregated housing breeds *de facto* segregation in schools, but there may be other ways of achieving integrated schools than through integrated housing, and this is perhaps too remote an argument to justify the denial of housing to an individual black. Apart from the generally suspect history of quotas, which always at best tread a narrow line between beneficence and malevolence, there are strong moral arguments against any quota that is expressed in terms of a ceiling or maximum of any racial group. Quotas in terms of a minimum of a minority group will be discussed later.

The occasional demands by minority groups for special facilities that are to be closed to the majority present different questions again. In the case of such demands made in educational institutions, with respect to either housing or black studies programs, the justifications may be diverse. They may consist of a general assertion that black people have been so maltreated by the white majority that, before we can expect a harmonious integration, we must allow them to retreat into isolation for a period during which they can search for self-sufficiency. In the educational field we hear arguments that the value of black studies programs would be diminished if whites were permitted to be present, since this would inhibit black students from speaking freely. Such arguments might seem more appropriate in a therapeutic setting that is dedicated to healing a bruised psyche than in an academic context. Again, we are sometimes told that white students are unqualified by their background to participate in black studies programs. If the programs contemplate scholarly activity, it is difficult to see how this could be so, though it may indeed make sense if the programs are primarily conceived as therapeutic. It could be argued that the emotional health of students is a proper concern of universities and that classification by race may be necessary for therapeutic purposes in a medical program, but those who advocate black studies programs would presumably not want to rest on this ground, since they rightly present such programs as a suitable scholarly activity in an academic curriculum.

Housing facilities on campus explicitly reserved for a minority group seem equally difficult to defend. Arguments of a therapeutic nature might be repeated here, supported perhaps by the assertion that familiar objections to segregation are less appropriate where a minority, traditionally discriminated against, wishes to withdraw into its own enclave. A black request for separate accommodation, it could be urged, does not rest on an explicit or implicit assertion of superiority and, in view of the small minority of black people in the community at large and their generally depressed socioeconomic position, does not have any disadvantageous implications for the white majority. But such a justification would be enormously difficult to translate into any general principle of permission. Should it only apply in communities (municipal or educational) where blacks are in a minority, and should similar privileges be extended to whites where they are in a minority? Would it depend on an investigation of the motives of the separatists so that their request would have to be denied if it should be found that it has any basis in feelings of superiority? If blacks in any community, though in a minority, should ever reach a superior socioeconomic position to whites, should such a request then be denied? Rather than trade in such flimsy and shifting criteria, so pervasively open to abuse, it is almost certainly wiser to stick to a flat prohibition of segregation even if in the short run this should lead to hostile responses from black separatists.

The State of the Law

EDUCATION

The questions briefly considered in the preceding discussion touch on such burning debates in American life that we might expect to find full and ready answers in the law. Such an expectation would perhaps be naïve, for the questions are both novel and complex, and the courts will be wise to abstain from quick generalizations.

At several places in our discussion of earlier topics we have seen that, put in the broadest terms, state classifications through legislation or other forms of state action must seek to serve a legitimate state purpose in a rational manner. They must therefore be based on a discernible difference that is reasonably relevant to pursuit of the permissible state purpose. But when the classification is inherently suspect, as the racial ones we now consider pre-eminently are, then the courts will subject it to strict scrutiny and uphold it only if it serves an overriding or compelling state interest. Cases in which racial classifications have been so upheld are extremely rare. It is often said that the only clear and convincing examples are the Japanese-American relocation cases of *Hirabayashi* v. *United States*[2] and *Korematsu* v. *United States*[3] in 1943 and 1944, which held that in time of war against Japan it was permissible for government to enforce evacuation and detention orders against American citizens of Japanese descent living in western parts of the United States. The Supreme Court conceded in those cases that racial classification was especially suspect when it imposed such onerous burdens, but concluded that "pressing public necessity" justified the government action.

The most important Supreme Court review of racial classifications in the recent past has been in the miscegenation case of *McLaughlin* v. *Florida*[4] in 1964. In one sense a miscegenation statute does not appear to infringe on principles of equal protection, since it applies equally to white or black defendants who marry or cohabit with members of the other race. Historically such laws have been objectionable, since they seemed in fact to reflect the views of the white majority that their purity of race must be preserved from a commingling with blacks. Ought we to view such laws differently if both blacks and whites shared a strong wish to avoid commingling with each other in marriage or sexual acts? Such moral deliberation was avoided by the Court, which was able in *McLaughlin* to strike down the Florida cohabitation statute by holding that such a racial classification was not necessary for the accomplishment of a permissible state policy, even assuming for argument's sake that a ban on racially mixed marriages was a permissible policy to pursue. The language employed by the Court in *McLaughlin* will clearly be of importance in all future general discussion of this topic, for it reiterates that all racial classifications are constitutionally suspect and holds that, at any rate where criminal penalties are involved, the classification must not only be reasonably relevant to the purpose of the statute but also must be *necessary* to effect some overriding statutory purpose.

The concurring opinion of Mr. Justice Stewart went so far as to doubt whether any valid legislative purpose could ever be conceivable that would make "the color of a person's skin the test of whether his conduct is a criminal offense."[5] It may be doubted whether such a valid purpose is inconceivable. One writer has posed a hypothetical situation in which a new and virulently infectious disease may have appeared that afflicts only members of one racial group.[6] We may imagine that medical researchers can advance convincing scientific evidence why members of other racial groups are immune from this disease and are not carriers of it. If the legislature then enacts a law that requires members of the afflicted racial group to be vaccinated against this disease under penalty for noncompliance, it is by no means obvious that such a statute would be unconstitutional. Indeed, common sense and principles of social morality combine in leading to the conclusion that our Constitution cannot be so perverse as to demand such a holding. At any rate, even after *McLaughlin* the field is clearly open for plausible arguments to the effect that racial classifications are sometimes constitutionally permissible because they are necessary to serve a compelling interest.

Racial designations in record-keeping contexts have explicitly been held to be permissible by the Supreme Court where they serve a permissible function and do not have a discriminatory tendency, though the drawing of a line between situations where such designations are discriminatory and where they are not is a difficult and delicate matter. Furthermore, some of the cases discussed earlier, decided in state courts and the lower federal courts in the past decade or so on the questions of permissible or required steps to combat *de facto* segregation in schools, contain language that can be taken to approve and even to require racial classifications where these are necessary to combat actual patterns of segregation. But there is nothing in these cases that can be taken clearly to validate a preferential treatment of one racial group even as an interim compensatory technique.

The validation of such preferential treatment may, however, be detected in a federal decision of the District Court of New Jersey in 1969 in *Porcelli* v. *Titus*.[7] In the events leading to that case the school board had abolished the examination system for selection of suitable candidates for the post of school principal, allegedly in order to appoint to such positions a number of blacks who would not be qualified under the examination system. The plaintiffs were white teachers, who alleged that this action had discriminated against them and who sued under the Civil Rights Act of 1964. The court found on the record that "'Race,' in its broadest connotation, played a part in the Board's decision to suspend the promotion lists and abandon the examination system," but went on to find that on a fair reading of the record the new system was designed "not simply to appoint Negroes to promotional positions but to obtain for these positions qualified persons, white or black, whose qualifications were based on an awareness of, and sensitivity to, the problems of educating the Newark school population." On this basis the court found that "there was no intention on the part of the Board to discriminate against white persons."[8]

The *Porcelli* case does appear to hold that the color of a person's skin can explicitly be made a qualification for a public teaching position without a necessary inference of discrimination. The justifications in the opinion rely to a considerable extent on testimony in the record to the effect that the education of Newark's largely black student body was suffering from the absence in the administration of the schools of black authority figures with whom the pupils could identify. Put in this way, blackness becomes a qualification for the position of principal, so that express adversion to color in the evaluation of candidates can be presented as only one way of searching for the best appointee.

But this is a dangerous path to tread. Can a private employer expressly make race a factor in his appointments on the ground that his customers identify more with one race than with another?

Could such procedures ultimately involve us in degrading litigation, with Nazi and South African associations, on whether a person is properly to be classified as white or black? Is whiteness a special qualification for appointment to a principal's post in a predominantly white school? Would this depend on whether white students could identify with a black principal and on whether or not their education would suffer from lack of identification? How reliable are such sociological and psychological arguments, and even if they are reliable, are there not convincing and outweighing moral arguments on the other side?

Porcelli was affirmed on appeal by the Third Circuit Court of Appeals, in a brief opinion that perhaps dilutes the implications of the district court's decision by laying more stress on the propriety of the procedures as part of a general scheme to overcome segregation in the schools by working toward a more integrated faculty.[9] The Supreme Court let the decision stand by refusing to entertain a further appeal.

Much light was expected to be shed on the constitutional problems of preferential treatment when the case of *DeFunis* v. *Odegaard*[10] worked itself up to a decision in the Supreme Court in 1974. The white plaintiff in that case had applied for admission to the law school of the University of Washington, a public institution. He was eventually rejected and was able to show that, on the basis of a computation of previous grades and aptitude test scores employed as criteria for admission by the law school, several minority group students had been accepted whose qualifications were less than his. He sued in the state courts of Washington on the ground that he had been discriminated against on account of his race in violation of the equal protection clause of the Fourteenth Amendment. DeFunis prevailed in the trial court, which granted an injunction ordering the university to admit him into its law school. The university complied, and DeFunis accordingly became a student at the law school.

On appeal, the Washington Supreme Court reversed the decision and held that there had been no unconstitutional discrimination against DeFunis, who, by this time, was a second-year student at the law school. The Supreme Court of the United States agreed to hear the case, and DeFunis was allowed to remain in the law school until the case came up for a decision in the Supreme Court, by which time he was a third-year student. To the surprise and disappointment of much of the legal and educational communities, who had been expecting fresh wisdom, the majority of the Supreme Court disposed of the case on the technical ground that it had become moot. By this was meant that there was no longer a real controversy between the parties, since the university had agreed that in any event DeFunis would now be allowed to complete his legal studies. The Court, therefore, declined to discuss the merits of the case.

Four of the nine Justices dissented on the ground that the case had not become moot, but of these four only Mr. Justice Douglas addressed himself to the substantive issues. Mr. Justice Douglas made it clear that there can be no constitutional mandate that educational institutions make use only of certain standard tests in selecting well-qualified students. They may certainly supplement such tests by a variety of methods that seek to assess the potential of an individual for doing well in a course of study or a subsequent professional career. What the Constitution requires "is the consideration of each application in a racially neutral way."[11] The University of Washington law school scheme, in Mr. Justice Douglas' view, was suspect on its face, since it involved the "reservation of a proportion of the law school class for members of selected minority groups,"[12] rather than an attempt to sharpen the accuracy of the standard tests that predict academic success.

> There is currently no test available to the Admissions Committee that can predict such possibilities with assurance, but the Committee may nevertheless seek to gauge it as best it can, and weigh this factor in its decisions. Such a policy would not be limited to Blacks or Chicanos or Filipinos or American Indians, although undoubtedly groups such as these may in practice be the principal beneficiaries of it. But a poor Appalachian white, or a second-generation Chinese in San Francisco, or some other American whose lineage is so diverse as to defy ethnic labels, may demonstrate similar potential and thus be accorded favorable consideration by the Committee.[13]

Several elements combine in Mr. Justice Douglas' opinion: (1) that searching out of potential as opposed to preparation is perfectly proper, even if in practice this should lead to a favorable treatment for members of minority groups in the light of their past deprivations; (2) but such a search must not be expressly limited to those who belong to particular racial groups; (3) express quotas for racial occupancy are inherently suspect. With the first two propositions, warm agreement is possible. Many in our society are so handicapped by early environment and inadequate training that they are unable to exhibit the same degree of preparation for certain advancements as others who have been more fortunate. To condemn them to exclusion from avenues to success without a subtle inquiry into their potential, without a readiness to discount present inadequate preparation where that can be remedied, would be an offense against social justice. But since such disadvantage is not coterminous with racial minorities, a threshold racial test for the application of such sensitive evaluations would itself be offensively unjust. The fetters that shackle some of the runners in the race are not always colored.

The quota question is more complex. Where a racial group complains of exclusion from a field of, say, employment that requires no qualifications of special skill or education, and where there is evidence of past exclusionary practices, then the setting of a temporary minimum quota may be the only way to secure visible proof of compliance with constitutional duties to offer equal access to jobs. Where the job requires very special skills or qualifications, then quotas may be inordinately dangerous in threatening the quality of those who seek positions on which whole sectors of vital social service may depend. The field of admission to educational institutions may lie somewhere between these extremes. Certainly only a disservice is rendered by the admission of those who show no real potential for successful completion of a course of studies. But there may be many members of disadvantaged groups who, while they are unable to demonstrate as glittering a prospect of academic and professional excellence as some nondisadvantaged persons, may nevertheless be very well able to complete a course of studies successfully and lead a competent and useful professional life. If we add to this the circumstances that disadvantage is perpetuated for groups by excluding their members from avenues of advancement, and that the number of available places in certain spheres of higher education is strictly limited, then a case of some cogency develops for minimal admission quotas for such groups.

The DeFunis case involved a law school. Law schools are very obviously one of the training grounds for people who will be authoritative decision makers and who will hold positions of influence and power in society. The exclusion of minority group persons from such positions has historically been a very particular cause and result of their disadvantage. Reversal of this trend requires an affirmative effort to increase the number of minority group lawyers. If the only way to do this is to prefer some such applicants to "better qualified" whites, there is an impressive array of social arguments to support such a course of action. A university is not being irresponsible when it expresses such a position in the form of minimum quota. Neither is it as obvious, as Mr. Justice Douglas appears to think that this practice is unconstitutional—for, if the quota is suspect, it might well be thought of as furthering a compelling state interest.

EMPLOYMENT

In the area of employment, decisions of the courts offer even less guidance. Here attention for the most part is rightly still focused on practices that discriminate against minorities, particularly in so-called referral unions that operate hiring halls or supply quotas of workers for an employer. In an effort to open up more jobs for minority members, the federal administration, under the authority of an executive order forbidding discrimination in federal contract work, promulgated in 1969 the so-called Philadelphia Plan.[14] This requires good-faith efforts to be made to hire a gradually ascending percentage of minority group workers on designated federal projects over a number of years. It is thus an instance of a minimum quota, as opposed to the "benign quota" concept in housing discussed earlier, which is that of a maximum quota. In spite of this, the plan has come under attack from critics who argued that it offends against Title VII of the Civil Rights Act of 1964, which broadly prohibits discriminatory practices in private employment. Such an attack was turned aside by the Third Circuit Court of Appeals in *Contractors' Association of Eastern Pennsylvania* v. *Secretary of Labor* (1971),[15] the court finding the plan in all respects legal and constitutional.

While the university admission scheme that came before the courts in the DeFunis case was more or less frankly preferential, at least with respect to what had traditionally been accepted as relevant credentials, the Philadelphia Plan approach is much less so. It demands only a visible end to a previous situation of discrimination and sets a percentage of minority group employees as an evidentiary yardstick of such a reform. It is doubtful whether this can reasonably be thought of as a quota scheme at all in the traditional sense of that term. If it is viewed as setting up a quota, it is surely the least objectionable and the most defensible of them.

But there are two situations where efforts to fulfill mandatory percentages of minority group employees do raise grave issues of justice or social policy. The first would be where someone presently employed is removed to make room for a minority group person for no other reason than quota fulfillment. When a group consists only of applicants who are not yet jobholders, it may be tolerable to say that for a time, minority group applicants may be regarded with some favor to compensate for their past exclusion. For, in this situation, what the white applicant who is passed over has lost is a chance of getting something; this is bad enough, but it may be an inevitable price to exact if redress is ever to be given to minority groups. But where displacement occurs, the white jobholder has an existing interest wrenched away. This destruction of existing interests solely for racial reasons is too onerous a burden to ask anyone to bear, and the courts almost certainly would condemn such a procedure by regarding it as a violation of constitutional protections or fair employment statutes.

The second situation in which dangers are apparent is where government demands an escalation of minority employment in positions that require very specialized skills and talents. Universities have protested loudly at the "affirmative action" program by which the federal government, through the Department of Health, Education, and Welfare, requires universities with federal contracts to increase the numbers of racial minorities and women on their faculties. A report published in 1974 under the sponsorship of the Carnegie Commission on Higher Education suggests that efforts to comply with these demands may have resulted in the appointment of some professors without proper qualifications or at least with less impressive talents and accomplishments than white males who were not engaged.

Much of the dispute here is about facts. If allegations can be substantiated that persons of less than the highest available accomplishments are engaged for positions demanding great abilities, only on the basis of their race or sex, no defense is possible. Such practices threaten the quality of professional and intellectual life, the quality of education, and so, eventually, the material and cultural state of a nation. But it is also true that the hiring practices of universities deserve the strictest scrutiny with respect to charges of unfairness to minority groups and women. One of the vital questions here is the nature of the group to which we should look in order to make valid comparisons. Clearly blacks and women are underrepresented on university faculties in proportion to their quotient of the population. But this is an absurd standard of comparison. More rational is a test that looks to the number of university faculty relative to the number of doctoral degrees held by members of various groups. In a rough and ready way this may provide some coarse measure of whether universities have discriminated. The probability is that many have done so, at least with respect to women, both in hiring and in salary payments. Government pressure on universities is therefore justified as long as it is sensitively and delicately directed and does not amount to crude quota demands unrelated to the supply of persons endowed with the necessary excellence of qualification.

HOUSING

In the field of housing there are some decisions that on a superficial reading would appear to deny the legitimacy of any quotas based on race. In 1953, in *Banks* v. *Housing Authority*,[16] the Supreme Court of California struck down a San Francisco Housing Authority plan under which housing was to be allotted to all races in the same proportions as they bore to each other in existing residence patterns. The court said, "It is the individual . . . who is entitled to the equal protection of the laws—not merely a group of individuals, or a body of persons according to their numbers."[17] The U. S. Supreme Court denied certiorari in this case. But before too much significance is attached to this decision, it must be pointed out that the individual public housing units contemplated by the housing authority would have been segregated, so that the court's opinion can be viewed as a rejection of segregation, even when it wears an ameliorative garb.

More recent cases have employed language that at the least seems to view classification by race as proper for some purposes in connection with urban housing projects. In the case of *Norwalk CORE* v. *Norwalk Redevelopment Agency* (1968)[18] in the Second Circuit Court of Appeals, a number of black and Puerto Rican plaintiffs brought an action against the redevelopment agency, alleging that in planning and implementing the project the defendants did not assure or attempt to assure relocation for black and Puerto Rican displacees to the same extent as for whites, and arguing that this constituted a denial of the equal protection of the law. Taking the allegations of fact to be true, the court reversed the denial of a remedy in the court below and remanded the case for further proceedings. The court acknowledged that any remedy afforded the plaintiffs might involve classification by race, and went on, "That is something which the Constitution usually forbids, not because it is inevitably an impermissible classification, but because it is one which usually, to our national shame, has been drawn for the purpose of maintaining racial inequality. Where it is drawn for the purpose of achieving equality it will be allowed, and to the extent it is necessary to avoid unequal treatment by race, it will be required."[19] This statement by the court must be read in the light of the nature of the plaintiffs' claim to the effect that "the defendants acted, knowingly and deliberately, so as to compound the problem of racial discrimination in the Norwalk housing market, with the inevitable and intended result that some Negroes and Puerto Ricans would be forced to leave the city altogether."[20]

One of the most difficult questions courts may have to face in this area is the constitutionality of "benign quota" policies in new housing developments, where, as we noted earlier, the aim of integration clashes with the demands of the most deserving for housing. Such a problem came before the federal courts in New York in *Otero* v. *New York City Housing Authority* in 1973.[21] The plaintiffs in that case were for the most part blacks and Puerto Ricans who had been moved out of their original housing when it was demolished as part of a plan to build new public housing in the area. The plaintiffs claimed that they had been promised that they would be rehoused in the new buildings to be put up on the site. When these new buildings were completed, the plaintiffs were not offered apartments there, and one of the reasons advanced by the defendants to justify this refusal was that leasing to the plaintiffs would cause the "tipping point" to be reached and so make an integrated development impossible. The 1968 Civil Rights Act, the defendants argued, placed a duty on them to administer their public housing programs so as to secure residential integration. They were thus constrained by law to refuse housing to the plaintiffs, or at least justified in so doing.

The federal district court was ready to agree that the defendants had a general duty to create integrated housing patterns, but the court took the view that this should not be done at the expense of minority groups who, in the long run, were the intended beneficiaries of a policy of integration. The defendants wanted, as it were, to be cruel only to be kind, but the district court held that the cruelty was much more apparent than the kindness. The proposition that minority groups could be afforded better housing in the long run by depriving them of it in the short run was too casuistical to prevail over the plaintiff's contractual, statutory, and constitutional claims. But on this issue the Court of Appeals for the Second Circuit reversed,[22] holding that the pursuit of integration was an imperative duty for the defendants and that, if their contention about the "tipping" phenomenon were correct, they were justified in refusing housing to the plaintiffs.

This is one instance where the lower court seems to have been a good deal more sensible than the court of appeals. In recognizing the propriety of the benign quota, the Second Circuit Court of Appeals ignored a number of significant factual and moral aspects.

The plaintiffs here were former residents of buildings on the same site and had a special claim. They were not on the same footing as fresh applicants who had never resided in the neighborhood. Second, the tipping phenomenon is one still only imperfectly understood and analyzed. It is agreed that it varies greatly from locality to locality according to income levels, previous patterns of racial mixing, and a host of other factors. Most of the studies have centered around black movement into a neighborhood, whereas in *Otero* the plaintiffs not only came from the neighborhood but also were largely Puerto Rican. Third, once a racial classification was being employed to exclude the plaintiffs from public housing, as it undoubtedly was in this case, strict scrutiny should be applied and the procedure upheld only if it served an overriding or compelling state interest. Integration is certainly a state interest of importance, but it has reached that level only because of a recognition of the tendency of segregation in many areas of life to diminish opportunity and advancement for minority groups as well as to subject them to disrespect. Here integration is being viewed as a compelling interest when its pursuit involves the denial of good housing to the very people it aims to benefit. And that denial was accomplished in *Otero* by reneging on promises the faithful adherence to which are a prime justification for urban housing renewal.

Conclusion

These cases reiterate a growing theme to the effect that classification by race may be permissible if it is designed to combat segregation or to ensure proper recognition of minority rights. But it will be apparent that a number of issues are still left to be definitively resolved, though more or less tentative guesses as to their disposition can be hazarded. "Minimum quota" requirements, as in the Philadelphia Plan, will probably be approved by the courts; "maximum quotas," as in the benign quota housing possibility, are much more controversial. The patent distinction here is that the minimum quota may be presented as not having a direct exclusionary effect on anyone, whereas the maximum quota clearly does have such an effect. A minimum quota of, say, 20 per cent blacks to be employed on a certain job could of course be presented conversely as a maximum quota of 80 per cent whites, but an interpretation of the minimum quota can probably be reached to avoid such a bald conclusion. This would be to argue that the intention is to insist that employers must demonstrate a proper effort to attract black applicants and a readiness to hire them where they are minimally qualified to do the work, and that quotas are merely provisional demonstrations of a good-faith discharge of these obligations. Thus they need not be understood as a requirement to hire a less-qualified black over a more-qualified white. Interpreted this way, the quota requirement would not amount to preferential treatment, but rather to a remedial measure designed to eradicate previous unequal treatment by some visible and measurable yardstick. It does not seem possible to put up any defense of a maximum quota in these terms.

A further reasonable guess may be that the courts will not approve any scheme that is baldly stated to be a preferential one justified in compensatory or reparative terms tied to race. But as we have seen, this again should not be taken to mean that there is no way in which race might be overtly taken into account in selection procedures in a variety of contexts, for the justification of compensation or reparation may be abandoned, and in its place there may be advanced a justification in terms of fitness, suitability, or sensitivity for the post or place. As *Porcelli* v. *Titus* showed, there is at the least some possibility that in certain instances the courts may accept such justifications to overcome arguments of denial of equal protection or infringement of civil rights statutes. To do this is to play with fire, but perhaps a freezing man has to play such a dangerous game. The dangers can be somewhat avoided by adding to the fitness or sensitivity argument a further qualification that again it is only persuasive where the thrust of the process is to rectify existing racial imbalance that has adversely affected a particular group. This seems implicit in the *Porcelli* case.

One thing is abundantly evident. When American constitutional lawyers argue the propriety of some of the procedures discussed here, they are essentially engaging in philosophical debate about the demands of social justice. Lawyers' debate is not, of course, quite the same as philosophical discussion, because lawyers have to talk to each other and endeavor to persuade each other in the context of principles and decisions that have an authoritative aspect. The philosopher is unfettered by precedent and untrammeled by authority. But in this area, as this discussion has shown, the lawyer is dealing with questions that are not tightly controlled by precise statutory provisions or irrefutable precedents. The guiding constitutional principles allow almost unlimited room for argument and indicate a variety of alternative paths that might be followed.

The most radical arguments for express recognition of the validity of preferential, compensatory schemes are by no means impossible of plausible justification within the corners of constitutional debate. It is easy to understand why those who are impatient with the slow pace of social change might wish to urge such arguments. At the same time, we have seen that general declarations of the validity of theories of compensation and preference might lead to the entrenchment of doctrines that could offer great scope in the future for application to unworthy ends. Perhaps the most important question is whether such declarations are really necessary for any practical purpose. We have certainly not yet encountered a situation where a proposed project for redressing injustice to minorities has run into a serious constitutional roadblock. It might be said in response that this is because both government and private institutions are doing so little in this field, and that if massive efforts were made to restructure American society so as to eradicate the worst socioeconomic injustices then present interpretations of the Constitution could present substantial difficulties. This may or may not be so, and it is profitless for the courts to seek to anticipate such a remote eventuality.

A different question is whether or not the courts should again endeavor to take the lead in this area and to press upon the conscience of society the moral arguments for compensation and reparation by presenting them as legal duties to be fulfilled through preferential treatment. The next chapter takes up this question.

PART 5

Conclusion

XV

The Role of the Courts

While we have looked at a wide range of problems (victimless crimes in general, drug abuse in particular, civil disobedience and disruption, equal educational opportunity), they have all been linked by connecting bands of principle. In each case we have tried to canvass the field of moral argument relevant to the issues in dispute and then examine how the law reflects these moral judgments or disagreements. This has involved us in an analysis of how courts, and particularly the U. S. Supreme Court, work with the clauses of the Constitution, interpreting, developing, and shaping them to yield responses to the problems of the day that litigants bring to the bar.

But before offering any general comments on judicial intervention in these areas, we would first do well to remember the primary responsibility that rests with the legislature. Courts have a duty to cure the constitutional sins, whether of commission or omission, of other branches of government. So the better the legislature does its job, the less need there should be for judicial intervention. It is the state legislatures that are most relevant here. When it is a question of the criminalization of sexual conduct, the federal authorities have little reason or jurisdiction to intervene, except when interstate activities are involved. In drug offenses, federal participation is greater, but still the content and enforcement of the criminal law are primarily matters for the states. In educational administration, the structure is set by local districts operating under the aegis of state statutes; state legislatures always have the authority to revise the system so as to promote greater equality, whether it be through a different system of financing or redistricting or pupil movement.

But the state legislatures have diminished steadily in status and prestige as the federal government plays an increasingly critical role in the regulation of American life. As Washington assumes more and more the place of a centralist European capital, the state capitals have taken on the air of provincial backwaters, useful to politicians either as stepping-stones to national office or as handy vaulting poles in the practice of law. This is much to be regretted, for while Washington is the place where momentous decisions are taken that affect foreign relations and national economic affairs, the states still wield great authority in matters that profoundly affect our liberties and the quality and equality of the society in which we live. When state legislatures are primarily responsible for the criminal law and the provision of most social services, including education, then they are evidently dealing with the most basic stuff of personal freedom and social justice.

Too often they have failed to be forums for informed and rational debate about these great issues. Supinely perpetuating archaic criminal laws, interposing foolish and malevolent barriers in the way of implementing constitutional edicts of the U. S. Supreme Court, some state legislatures have often seemed to fulfill Yeats' prophecy of a society where,

The best lack all conviction while the worst
Are full of passionate intensity.

It is largely because of this shoddy performance by lawmakers that those interested in reform have come to look more and more to the courts.

Activism and Restraint

The image of the U. S. Supreme Court as a leader in social reform has become so bright over the past generation that we may need to be reminded that it is hardly more recent than that. In the 1950s and 1960s the Court was activist in what is usually accounted a liberal vein. It greatly expanded the ambit of constitutionally protected civil rights, notably in the area of criminal investigation and prosecution; it advanced the cause of racial equality; it even gave a constitutional push to demands for political equality through its legislative reapportionment decisions. But there are very few periods in American history in which the Court can be viewed in that light. The Court that so annoyed President Franklin Roosevelt by blocking New Deal legislation might fairly be characterized as an activist conservative Court—for conservatism, in its wide political connotation, is perfectly compatible with judicial activism. A court may actively interfere with legislative or executive acts to further either a liberal or conservative position.

The Supreme Court may at times be conservative in a different sense, in holding to a general posture of reluctance to interfere with legislative or executive actions, except in the strongest and clearest cases. This quietist position, which extols the passive virtues, was associated with the person of Mr. Justice Frankfurter in recent times and may now be reappearing. Just as in political styles, a period of activist reform is often succeeded by a period of conservative quiescence, so in the judicial sphere such a succession may be necessary for a healthy metabolism. At any rate, there is no natural or historical warrant for thinking of the Court as a constant force for reforming change.

When it is in the midst of an activist phase (whether conservative or liberal), the Court is likely to stir up a good deal of angry opposition. In its recent reforming period the Court was accused of playing a political rather than a judicial role, of legislating rather than applying the Constitution, of showing a sentimental and exaggerated tenderness for suspects and defendants, and many other sins. Much of this criticism, as we shall see, simply misconceives the nature of judicial responsibility in applying the Constitution. But, if not often justifiable, the irritation is at least sometimes understandable, for courts have certainly shown in the past few decades an intrusiveness into aspects of American life that were previously thought to be exempt from judicial edicts.

Nowhere more than in education has this been so evident. The past few chapters gave us many examples here. One more may be added to show the extent to which a commitment to a reformist line of constitutional interpretation may involve courts in reviewing and reordering the details of educational administration.

HOBSON V. HANSEN

In *Hobson* v. *Hansen* (1967),[1] suit was brought on behalf of black children and poor children in the District of Columbia, alleging that the District's Board of Education had unconstitutionally deprived them of their right to equal educational opportunity.

Among its findings of fact the United States District Court for the District of Columbia found that (a) "racially and socially homogeneous schools damage the minds and spirits of all children who attend them"; (b) "the scholastic achievement of the disadvantaged child . . . is strongly related to the racial and socio-economic composition of the student body of his school"; (c) "adherence to the neighborhood school policy by the School Board effectively segregates the Negro and poor children from the white and the more affluent children"; (d) "the teachers and principals in the public schools are assigned so that generally the race of the faculty is the same as the race of the children"; (e) "median annual per pupil expenditure . . . in the predominantly . . . Negro elementary schools . . . has been a flat $100 below the median annual per pupil expenditure for its predominantly white schools"; (f) "generally the 'white' schools are underpopulated while the 'Negro' schools generally are overcrowded"; (g) "as they proceed through the Washington school system, the reading scores primarily of the Negro and poor children, but not the white and middle class, fall increasingly behind the national norm"; (h) "the 'track' system as used in the District's public schools is a form of ability grouping in which students are divided in separate, self-contained curricula or tracks ranging from 'Basic' for the slow student to 'Honors' for the gifted. The aptitude tests used to assign children to the various tracks are standardized primarily on white middle-class children. Since these tests do not relate to the Negro and disadvantaged child, track assignment based on such tests relegates Negro and disadvantaged children to the lower tracks from which, because of the reduced curricula and the absence of adequate remedial and compensatory education, as well as continued inappropriate testing, the chance of escape is remote. Education in the lower tracks is geared to . . . the 'blue collar' student. Thus such children . . . are denied equal opportunity to obtain the white-collar education available to the white and more affluent children."[2]

The court went on to hold that *de facto* segregation and other features, such as the tracking system, amounted to a violation of equal educational opportunity, and that an order for the reform or abrogation of these practices was an appropriate exercise of equitable jurisdiction. Accordingly the court issued a decree which, among other things, ordered (a) an injunction against racial and economic discrimination in the school system, (b) abolition of the track system, (c) transportation for volunteering children from overcrowded schools to underpopulated schools, (d) substantial integration of the teaching staff of each school, and (e) that the defendants file a plan for approval by the court providing for pupil assignment to eliminate racial and economic discrimination and for teacher assignment to integrate the teaching staffs.

Hobson v. *Hansen* may be one of the strongest examples of the intrusiveness of the judiciary into American life. Being the decision of a district court, the case is not of great weight in the doctrine of precedent,[3] but it is of considerable interest in pointing to the complexities of any serious-minded enforcement of the right to equal educational opportunity. In the findings of fact as well as in the content of the decree, the court made it clear that racial separation alone was not the sum of the evils it was moving against. The separation of poor white children from children of more prosperous background was equally to the fore. Fashioning a remedy for such a disease involved such judicial determinations as the sweeping away of the track system and a general directive to the school authorities to bring about a more even socioeconomic mix in their schools.

PRINCIPLED ADJUDICATION

"It is regrettable, of course, that in deciding this case the court must act in an area so alien to its expertise. It would be far better indeed for these great social and political problems to be resolved in the political arena by other branches of government. But these are social and political problems which seem at times to defy such resolution."

These are the words of the court in *Hobson* v. *Hansen*. They reveal the judge's awareness of the kind of criticism that would be turned against such a display of judicial activism. Such judgments and orders, critics say, rely on shifting social science evidence, which may be properly cited for the day-to-day prudential judgments of administrators but ought not to be frozen into constitutional doctrine. They involve the courts in treating as matters of law, issues that are inherently nonjusticiable since they rest on the balancing of subtle and complex factors that can only properly be assessed by professional experts. Even worse, such procedures force the courts into a continuing scrutiny of the day-to-day administration of the educational system, a task for which they are quite unsuited and that they cannot hope to discharge properly. This was an important theme of the Supreme Court's opinion in refusing to sanction busing across district lines in *Milliken* v. *Bradley*, considered in an earlier chapter.

Those who approve of the holding in *Hobson* v. *Hansen* would no doubt agree that a court is a quite unsuitable and inadequate instrument for administering an educational system. But courts can, they would reply, at least curb obvious abuses, bring pressure to bear for change, and focus national attention on the shortcomings of institutions. The judge in *Hobson* v. *Hansen* was properly fulfilling those duties. Are these disputes over the rightness of decisions like *Hobson* v. *Hansen*, on the one hand, or *Milliken* v. *Bradley*, on the other, nothing more than expressions of preference for liberal or conservative social policies? Certainly the decisions themselves may evince such preferences, but if they embody nothing more, then no tenable distinctions could be made between the business of legislation and the business of adjudication under the law. This would challenge our customary perception of a difference. We are accustomed to thinking of decision making by judges as being controlled by rules, by duties to consult the law and observe precedents, unlike the freedom of a legislature to enact laws on the basis of considerations that are drawn only (if things are done right) from principles of justice and efficiency and prudence.

This conventional understanding is itself too sharp in its distinction, for, except in the narrowest and most obvious cases, all judging involves the exercise of creative discretion. Judges are not oracles, plucking prefabricated answers from the clouds. They have to work with materials in order to shape answers. And the materials are always more or less general, more or less abstract, and therefore almost inevitably admitting conflicting interpretations and room for argument in marginal cases. Cases before courts are usually marginal, for if something reasonable could not be said on both sides, the dispute would be unlikely to end in litigation.

If this is true of all courts, it is seen at its sharpest in that very peculiar court, the Supreme Court of the United States. The Supreme Court has a mandate to override legislative or executive acts that conflict with the Constitution, a power not found in many nations. With such a mission it would be foolish not to think of the Court as having one foot in the field of political decision making. Its interference with the political or executive process is not of course untrammeled. It is bounded by the rights guaranteed in the language of the Constitution. But these in turn are for the most part general assertions of principles of equality and fairness, leaving much room for reasonable disagreement about their elaboration.

It is true that there is a history of precedent that develops and expounds these principles, and the Court, like any other court, has a duty to be attentive to precedent. To be attentive, though, does not mean to be enslaved, and the Court, as do all good courts, will sometimes flatly overrule an earlier precedent as being ill-conceived or quite unsuitable to meet changed conditions. In any event, when a case gets to the Supreme Court for decision, it is usually because it is not precisely controlled by earlier decisions; it is a case where what lawyers call the principle of *stare decisis* (being bound by earlier decisions) simply is not plainly dispositive. What the Court has to work with thus is in effect a body of theory. This theory has grown in dimension through its repeated application to different fact patterns in the past. Each such application has generated a cluster of expository and critical essays, in which we include the opinions of the Court (and the opinions of dissenting Justices) and the writings of commentators.

RULES AND ORDERS

In such a creative process of interpretation and application, the will of the founding fathers becomes less and less relevant with the passage of time. If, for example, *de facto* school segregation is the problem at hand, it should not matter at all that the framers of the Fourteenth Amendment never had it in their minds. In evaluating the spreading ambit of a principle, it is not the contemplation of the suggested application by the framers of the rule that is important, as much as the reasonableness of the extension in the light of accumulated experience with the principle's operation in seeking to fulfill broad purposes. This is because a rule or principle in a legal system (and most especially in a constitution) is not like an order given in a more personal relationship. If there is uncertainty about the scope of a personal order, then it is often possible to go back to the person who is the source of the command and seek clarification. Statutes and constitutions do not ordinarily include the possibility of reference back to the makers for clarification.

Orders, too, are usually of narrower compass both in terms of duration (extension into the future) and in terms of application. Certainly, of course, orders may sometimes be ambiguous, and there may often be doubts about tacit or implied exceptions or qualifications that must be resolved by the recipient if he cannot contact the commander. A military superior may order an officer to storm a position and, having lost contact with his superior, the officer may indeed responsibly be undecided whether he should carry out the command when it now seems that its execution would involve taking 50 per cent casualties. But in such a situation, where obedience is the prime value, the task of the subordinate is simply to make the best-informed guess that he can about the commander's intent and wish with respect to the situation now confronting him.

We cannot so appropriately see ourselves as bound to carry out the commands of those who frame constitutions and statutes. The position would be better described by saying that we regard rules and principles that have been established in a certain way as being authoritative, and we acknowledge, therefore, an obligation to make decisions under them and in the light of them. The concerns that prompted the original framers of the Bill of Rights are of course of some relevance in making decisions and settling interpretations, for they give us a platform of history and tradition on which to stand. But the relevance is in the broad sense of contributing to the construction of principles for guidance, rather than in the narrower sense of being pregnant with correct answers for problems that could not have occurred to the minds of the draftsmen.

The Constitution is constant, except for those occasional and cumbersomely mounted formal amendments. This enduring and unchanging form of words must impress itself upon the flux of events and the surfacing of new interests and new perceptions of values and claims with which life confronts us. To reverse the metaphor, new claims and concerns, if they cannot get legislative recognition, must search for constitutional planks to which to cling. And this process cuts both ways, because, as we have seen in several instances, when a new claim does gain legislative recognition, those who oppose it may then look for constitutional grounds on which to mount a challenge in the courts. Caught between the claims and arguments of opposed litigants, where both sides have some reason and sense to urge, to what can the Supreme Court look for guidance in applying the Constitution to the areas that have been the subject of much of this book?

A set of supplementary principles does exist from which the Court draws sustenance in its great task of applying the Constitution to new situations. Because of the special role and task of the Supreme Court, these principles, standards, and guides are not of a distinctively legal character. They have a mixed provenance, with roots in ethics, political prudence, and history. Insofar as they have a legal character, it is only to the extent that they have themselves been stated and reiterated by the Court to the point where they begin to acquire some patina of precedential authority.

Nor should we be dismayed or even surprised if these principles sometimes seem to contradict each other. Narrow rules cannot logically contradict each other within the confines of the same system. We could not imagine one section of a statute telling us that a will must be signed at the end and another telling us that it can be verified by a signature at the beginning. But principles are different from rules. They may helpfully be compared with proverbs, those pithy expressions of folk wisdom where we can often face off opposites. "Many hands make light work" and "Too many cooks spoil the broth" appear to be giving contrary advice, but it would be a mistake to decide that we have to choose between them and strike one off the roster. The fact is that they both perform a valuable service by alerting us to different aspects of a situation to which we should be attentive in reaching a decision on the particular facts. So it is with those general guides to which courts should look in interpreting statutes or applying a constitution. Some are of a conservative or cautionary bent, while others counsel boldness.

Cautionary Principles

RELATIVE JUDICIAL INCAPACITY

For some social ills, the only effective remedy would necessarily entail a large remodeling of institutions carried out through a regulatory code and a substantial bureaucracy. Suppose we decided that the only effective response to scarifying inequities in the distribution of health care in the United States would be an elaborate national health service. It is theoretically possible to imagine the Supreme Court mandating legislatures and executives to set up such a scheme. But in practice the possibility quickly takes on an air of absurdity—for acting on such an order would require vastly complex legislation and implementation, the progress and supervision of which would no doubt at frequent points be brought back to the courts for review, once the matter had been given a constitutional mandate. There would be something disorienting about such a process, a feeling of gross usurpation of legislative and executive functions by a body not designed or fitted for such tasks.

A recognition of relative judicial incapacity is then to acknowledge that the roots of some wrongs can only be torn up by remedies that would be inappropriate for a court to order. Inappropriateness here is not entirely a question of the natural capacities of a judicial body, though it has a good deal to do with that. It is also in part a received notion in our political consciousness of a suitable division of function among different organs of government, something we have roughly summed up as the separation of powers. When a social inequity has dimensions that would lead a court into inappropriate action, if an effort to give a full remedy were made, then the question always arises of balancing the benefits that may flow from partial remedies against the dangers of running too close to the border of inappropriate judicial behavior. It is not easy to take only one step into a bog.

This principle is most relevant where claims of inequality are pressed under the equal protection clause of the Fourteenth Amendment. Our earlier discussion showed that the Supreme Court has already traveled a long way from *Brown* v. *Board of Education* in implementing equal educational opportunity. Of late it has drawn back, partly because of an expressed reluctance to enter into territory that would require increasingly detailed supervision of educational systems by the courts.

In part this reluctance is sensibly rooted, for, as we argued earlier, educational inequality in the United States has more to do with general social arrangements of an inequitable kind outside the educational system than with racial separation in the schools, though that is of course both a product and a cause in the circular process. But any serious attack on educational inequality would be predestined to failure if it were made only in terms of desegregation, whether *de jure* or *de facto.* If there is a right to equal educational opportunity, it would be sad to discover that it meant no more than that blacks and whites must be educated together, important as that is. Without other social reforms, the inevitable outcome would be that most blacks and some whites would be educated together and poorly, while many whites and some blacks would be educated together and reasonably well.

Perceptions of the inadequacy of struggling for equal educational opportunity in terms of race alone explain the wider condemnation of socioeconomic segregation that we find in the court's opinion in *Hobson* v. *Hansen.* This is surely an accurate perception, but just as surely it identifies a social evil that courts cannot fully eradicate. Even judicial orders to bus across school district lines to achieve socioeconomic as well as racial integration, coupled with supervision over curriculum and so forth, would probably not take us very far along the road. But it would take us some part of the journey. Should courts pay the substantial price of considerable embroilment with the supervision of education, even though their capacity to achieve equality is inherently very limited? This is at least a question that prudence dictates should be asked, though the caution contained in it, like all the others listed here, should not be dispositive without a careful appraisal of other principles that urge intervention.

EPHEMERAL FINDINGS OF FACT

While policy makers, legislators, and administrators must pay the closest attention to the current state of expert opinion, there are considerable dangers in the Supreme Court's rushing to embrace any particular professional theory and dressing it in constitutional attire. Suppose majority expert opinion among educationalists tomorrow will agree that one kind of curriculum is less well suited than another to prepare a student for entrance to college. Does that curriculum become an offense to the Constitution if used in some schools, while other schools use the "better" one? There is a temptation here to hand over to experts the notion of what constitutes equal educational opportunity, and simply to translate their edicts of the day into constitutional law. One commentator has expressly issued such an invitation:

"Equal education has to be given concreteness, specificity, and refinement as educational policy. The contours of equal education as a constitutional requirement and its design as educational policy, practice, or methodology should be virtually the same. Where educational policy concludes that equal education requires certain specific practices, the courts should make these practices a part of the constitutional dimensions of the equal protection guarantee. Educators have simply failed to tell us what equal education connotes as educational policy, and the courts have been forced to rely on their own judgment concerning what the equal education guarantee requires or prohibits."[3]

This passage shows a touching faith in the wisdom of experts and great expectations that they could provide the right answers if only they weren't lazy or stubborn or whatever. Which questions experts are more competent to answer than the rest of us is itself a complicated issue, but in constitutional decision making courts should surely listen to them with a mixture of respect and skepticism. This is particularly the case with regard to education. The social sciences are in their infancy and are far from exact. Not very much is in fact known about how best to educate children which, indeed, in turn depends on what we think we are educating them for. If the impact of a constitutional decision is going to be to enforce uniformity in the educational process, then it should be reached with great deliberation and reluctance, for the uniformity is quite likely to be that of mediocrity and the stifling of experiment.

NONREPRESENTATIVE ORGANS

The theory of Western democracy traditionally invests courts with a comparatively narrow role, because, among other reasons, judges are generally not elected and are not thought of as representing constituents. More than most countries, the United States has experimented with electing judges. Other important values in the administration of law may be eroded by such an electoral process and, in any case, it is not very relevant here, since we are for the most part concerned with federal judges, who are appointed by the executive.

The nonrepresentative nature of the Supreme Court, joined with the peculiarly fixed authority of a judicial decision, counsel caution and deliberateness in extending the boundaries of constitutionally imposed duties. Legislation of course is also authoritative, but it may be reversed simply by a recognition on the part of the legislature that a mistake was made in setting goals or in selecting the most efficient techniques to pursue them. Courts can correct their mistakes too, but here we use the concept of mistake somewhat differently. The doctrine of precedent makes valuable objects out of decided cases. When they are decisions of the Supreme Court, they are of special worth and can only be overturned by that Court itself, which will do so only rarely and for very persuasive reasons. To treat Supreme Court decisions more lightly would be to devalue them and so upset the settled, authoritative nature of the system.

To concede a legislative mistake may be nothing more than

to confess that things can be done somewhat better. But for the Supreme Court to overturn an earlier decision requires it to argue persuasively that that decision is wrong in terms of the present understanding of constitutional principles. The logic of an adjudicative system, given continuity and consistency by a practice of following precedent, makes this overruling a serious matter. Since decisions, once made, are not easy to overturn, the Supreme Court ought to have a strong warrant before making significant innovations in constitutional interpretation.

SHOCK TO THE BODY POLITIC

The legislature or the executive may regard a decision of the Court as an encroachment on its own sphere of jurisdiction, and this may cause strains and tensions or even precipitate a constitutional crisis. This is not of course always a decisive reason for abstention. If it were, the Court could be hamstrung by any premonitions of sharp legislative or executive disapproval. This would be a craven posture, which the Court has often rejected. But when the Court has moved against the executive or legislature, as in cases to do with reapportionment, or steel nationalization, or in Watergate-connected matters, one can always perceive that at least one powerful organ of government or a considerable body of public opinion was in sympathy with the Court's action. Situations can be imagined where the logic of the Constitution is so compelling that the Court should have the moral courage to fly in the teeth of united hostility from other branches of government and the popular majority, but such a move would clearly carry considerable damage for the institutional future of the Court itself.

The prospect of hostility to a decision among the general public is much less of a cautionary signal. The hostility may stem from irrational prejudice or bigotry, which deserve no respect. Only in two circumstances, both of which are likely to be exceedingly rare, ought the Court to pause at all for this reason. The first would be where attempts to enforce the decision would arouse such outrage that substantial civil disorder would result. Even this must be risked if failure to decide the case in the unpopular way would plainly involve acceding to the invasion of people's constitutional rights. The second case would be where the decision by its nature can be of little or no efficacy without the voluntary co-operation of large numbers of those who resolutely oppose it. If their co-operation is not to be expected, the decision will stand on the books in an empty way and may injure the reputation of the Court and the efficacy of its future decisions. But this danger too has to be balanced against the persuasive impact in the passage of time of the Court's pronouncement.

DOCTRINAL LEAPS

Starting with the general precept that no state shall deny any person the equal protection of the laws, the Supreme Court has already made something of a journey in the field of equal education. The destination has not yet been reached and may constantly recede. Nor should we expect that any particular step along the path will be immediately connected with the starting point. But in this area, as in all, the development of the law should not be a series of leaps across chasms. A continuing line of exposition and debate within the four corners of rules and principles is at the heart of the idea of the rule of law. In constitutional decision making we are entitled to expect that a retracing of the path back from any particular decision will uncover the flight of steps that led the Court carefully and persuasively to its present position. Where a sufficient foundation has not been laid in professional discussion and argument, it is often unwisely premature to make a great move forward.

Principles of Expansion

The principles we have just noticed are all ones that offer cautionary advice, tending toward abstention and judicial passivity. Arrayed against them are principles that encourage action and justify intervention.

SPECIAL DUTY TO MINORITIES

The equal protection clause of the Fourteenth Amendment was born out of a desire to throw a mantle of protection around racial minorities who had never before been accorded even the most rudimentary legal shelter. Through the Fourteenth Amendment and others, such as the First Amendment's guarantee of freedom of speech, the Court has been historically cast in the role of special protector of minorities, whether racial, religious, or political, and has a particular obligation to defend their rights even, and perhaps especially, against the legislature and executive.

DANGER OF ATROPHY

If the Court decided cases only in terms of the concerns of the eighteenth and nineteenth centuries, both the Court and the Constitution would soon fall into disrepute. The Constitution and its place in our society retain importance only if it yields morally acceptable answers to new claims of inequality and injustice arising out of new conditions and new perceptions. This does not mean that the answers must always be the same as those that might be given by a moral philosopher, for, as we have seen, there are other principles to do with the separation of powers, the development of precedent, and so on, that come into play in constitutional adjudication. But the answer must be justifiable within that compendium of principles, and this sometimes requires vigilant and even innovative adaptation of doctrine to new circumstances or new awareness.

DUTY TO SUPPORT

Sometimes when executive officials wish to put into force a policy that they believe to be just and proper, they run into severe popular hostility. Such has often been the case when educational authorities have proposed measures to promote integration in the schools. It is a strength of the American system that in such cases the executive can often secure the backing of the courts by engineering or participating in litigation in which the proposed plan is declared to be constitutionally required. This may not quiet opposition, but it may moderate its intensity and reinforce the desire and purpose of the executive.

SPECIAL PLACE OF PERSONAL LIBERTY

There are a number of reasons why the Court may properly be more innovative in its decisions that have to do with personal liberty than in other areas. In the first place, this is a peculiarly cherished value in our traditions, embodied in the Constitution not only in the Fourteenth Amendment but also in others, such as the First Amendment, the Fourth Amendment, and so on. Then, ideas about the proper scope of personal autonomy have expanded with particular vigor in the past century. As we saw in Part 1 of this book, the Court has to a considerable extent marched along with this enlarged vision. A third reason is perhaps especially important in terms of principles of judicial prudence. When a law or practice is challenged because it infringes on personal autonomy, intervention by the Court will usually take the form of annulling a statute, or part of one, or some executive practice. The remedy will not involve any affirmative directives to government to embark on some large new scheme of activity. Government will simply be ordered to desist from interfering with the lives of certain people in certain ways.

Now, this judicial intervention may still be unpopular with the majority. But there is a difference between the reaction of X (who believes that homosexuality is immoral) when he is told that Y, a homosexual, will not be prosecuted for his activities, and the hostility of X (a parent of white children in the suburbs) when he is told that his children will be bused to school in a black district of the inner city. This is of course because the first case is only a matter of something not being done to someone else, while the second is a case of something actively being done to X or his family. It is thus much easier for the Court to confront the first kind of opposition, and this has clearly been a factor in the decisions of the Supreme Court of the 1970s, which has been moderately venturesome in extending personal autonomy but quite conservative in the equal protection field.

Conclusion

At the beginning of this book we suggested that the Supreme Court always writes for two audiences: the public at large and the legal profession. Its judgments also look to the past and to the future. Though the judges of the past cannot criticize the work the Court does now, the profession, both academic and in practice, undertakes that task by scrutinizing the Court's opinions in the light of earlier precedents. To escape overwhelming criticism, the Court must at the least convince a respectable body of professional opinion that it is not doing violence to the past, that change is fulfilling and not destroying the Constitution. And the Court must hand on to its successors judgments and opinions that are fitted for future use. This cannot include foreseeing the problems of the future, but it does demand an illuminating exposition of principles and a careful avoidance of commitment to the ephemeral.

None of this means that the personalities of individual judges do not count. Certainly their individual liberal, radical, or conservative dispositions in a general political sense may be decisive and, as a comparison of the 1970s with the 1960s shows us, a change in the composition of the Court may bring a significant shift in the trend of decisions in some areas. But the judge, whether liberal or conservative, if he is to retain our respect, must convince us through his opinions that he has given serious attention to the language of the Constitution and the accumulation of reasoning found in precedent, to the broad ethical considerations that the Constitution embodies and to that mixed collection of historical, political, and prudential principles some of which we have reviewed in this chapter. We may not agree with the outcome of the judgment, but we can respect it if we find the marks of care and craft upon it.

In protecting personal liberties we have seen that courts, within the framework of our Constitution, can do a great deal. Where the goal is promoting social equality, their role is more delicate and limited. As the education cases show, the difficulty is not in stating the doctrinal generalizations that have grown out of the application of the Fourteenth Amendment. We could sum up the relevant theory by saying that differences in the quality of services offered to the public by the state are unconstitutional if the following conditions are satisfied: (a) either the basis on which the difference rests involves an inherently suspect classification, or the enjoyment of the service is a fundamental right, and (b) the state cannot show a compelling interest to justify the difference.

In applying that theory to new cases on the frontiers of equal education law, the Supreme Court has had to blend a weighing of analogies and distinctions derived from precedent with considerations of the political and prudential principles discussed in this chapter. In the two cases we looked at that have decisively braked the forward movement, *Milliken* (denying an interdistrict remedy) and *Rodriguez* (refusing to order financial equalization), the Court surely was overly deferential to principles of caution. *Milliken* takes a very narrow view of what amounts to state action and thus allows the perpetuation of a separation of the races in the schools, which all our history condemns as a mark of enduring social inequality. *Rodriguez* is quite unpersuasive in arguing that the classification involved (the accident of place of residence within the state) should not be regarded as inherently suspect when it is vital to the amount of money spent on education. Common sense suffices to tell us that, if it is spent wisely, more money can improve education. In both cases the state's inertia in allowing public arrangements to continue that lead to serious inequality in the provision of a public service amply justifies intervention. These are two decisions that we shall come to regret and that we may hope will not endure for too long.

Hobson v. *Hansen*, not of course a decision of the Supreme Court, is perhaps, by contrast, an example of hyperactive intervention that does seriously violate principles of caution. It rests on fragile allegations of educational sociologists, unsupported by history or common sense, and now challenged by other workers in the field. It involves detailed judicial supervision of internal curricular matters. Parts of the opinion and order do not rest on a solid development of earlier cases. In this way the decision pays too high a price for dubious gains.

Within these confines we should not expect too much of courts in the way of reforming society. America is consumed by anxieties about grave domestic problems centering around economic inequality, poverty, race, and urban degeneration. Faced with legislative and executive inertia and moved by deep moral feelings about the intensity of social injustice, many people in the 1960s got into the habit of looking to the courts as the most hopeful institution for achieving social progress. And it is true that grosser examples of official discrimination can be purged by the judges.

In that way courts do have an important part to play in civilizing society. But it is much less clear that they can be seen as proper agents to secure radical reforms. Short of revolution, political action and political change are the only ways to make the social arrangements of American life humane and equitable.

Notes

CHAPTER I

1. Alexander Bickel, *The Least Dangerous Branch* (1962), p. 184.
2. Ronald Dworkin, "Lord Devlin and the Enforcement of Morals," 75 *Yale Law Journal* 986 (1966).
3. The most relevant work by Bentham is *Principles of Morals and Legislation* (1789). Mill's essay "On Liberty" (1859) is central. James Stephen's riposte is found in his book *Liberty, Equality, Fraternity* (1873).
4. Lord Devlin's position was advanced in a lecture, "The Enforcement of Morals," published under that title in 1959. The lecture was reprinted in 1965 under the title, "Morals and the Criminal Law," in a book by Lord Devlin entitled *The Enforcement of Morals.*
5. 408 *U.S.* 238.
6. This point is well made by Ronald Dworkin, "The Jurisprudence of Richard Nixon," New York *Review of Books* (May 4, 1972), p. 27.

CHAPTER II

1. Mary Melendy, *The Perfect Woman* (1901), pp. 38–39.
2. St. John Ervine, *Oscar Wilde* (1951), p. 35.
3. Westermarck, *History of Human Marriage,* Vol. 2 (5th ed., 1921), p. 192.
4. White, "Definition and Prohibition of Incest," 50 *American Anthropologist* 416 (1948).
5. Tylor, "On A Method of Investigating the Development of Institutions," 18 *Journal Anthropological Institute* 245, 267 (1888).
6. Jeremy Bentham, *Theory of Legislation,* ed. Hildreth (1876), p. 5.
7. Ibid., pp. 3–4.
8. 475 *F. 2d* 829.
9. 381 *U.S.* 479. This case and some others will be mentioned frequently in the text. The citation will not be repeated on each occasion.
10. 381 *U.S.* 484–86.
11. 381 *U.S.* 498–99.
12. 405 *U.S.* 438.

13. 410 U.S. 113.
14. 394 *F. 2d* 873.
15. *Schaefers* v. *Wilson,* 11 *Criminal Law Reporter* 2252.
16. 12 *Criminal Law Reporter* 2531.
17. 417 *F. 2d* 1161.
18. 326 *F. Supp.* 924.

CHAPTER III

1. See Joel Feinberg, "'Harmless Immoralities' and Offensive Nuisances," in *Issues in Law and Morality* (ed. Norman S. Care and Thomas K. Trelogan, 1973), pp. 85–86.
2. Ibid., pp. 100–1.
3. See *Loving* v. *Virginia,* 388 *U.S.* 1 (1967).
4. See *Chaplinsky* v. *New Hampshire,* 315 *U.S.* 568 (1942).
5. The California court's opinion is reported as *People* v. *Cohen,* 81 *California Reporter* 503 (1969). The U. S. Supreme Court's disposition is found at 403 *U.S.* 15 (1971).
6. 394 *U.S.* 557.
7. New York *Times* (Oct. 25, 1970), p. 71.
8. H. L. A. Hart, "Social Solidarity and the Enforcement of Morality," 35 *University of Chicago Law Review* 1 (1967).
9. Quoted in a letter from Samuel Williston to Karl Llewellyn. See Twining, *Karl Llewellyn and the Realist Movement* (1973), p. 290.
10. Devlin, *The Enforcement of Morals* (1959), p. 15.
11. Bickel, 22 *The Public Interest* 25 (Winter 1971).
12. Hart, op. cit., p. 2, n. 8.
13. 354 *U.S.* 476.
14. 383 *U.S.* 413.
15. 402 *U.S.* 351.
16. 413 *U.S.* 15.
17. 413 *U.S.* 49.
18. 413 *U.S.* 57.
19. *Miller* v. *California,* 413 *U.S.* 24.
20. Ibid., p. 25.
21. 413 *U.S.* 32.
22. 418 *U.S.* 153 (1974).

CHAPTER IV

1. Schwartz, "Morals Offenses and the Model Penal Code," 63 *Columbia Law Review* 669, 675–76 (1963).
2. This point is also independently made, with use of the same example, by Feinberg, "'Harmless Immoralities' and Offensive Nuisances," in *Issues in Law and Morality* (ed. Norman S. Care and Thomas K. Trelogan, 1973), p. 97.

3. Bentham, *Principles of Morals and Legislation* (ed. Wilfrid Harrison, 1948), p. 412, n. 1.
4. 410 *U.S.* 113.
5. Roger Wertheimer, "Understanding the Abortion Argument," 1 *Philosophy and Public Affairs* 67, 91 (Fall 1971).
6. See Judith Jarvis Thompson, "A Defense of Abortion," 1 *Philosophy and Public Affairs* 47, 57 (Fall 1971).
7. 31 *N.Y. 2d* 194.
8. 410 *U.S.* 179.
9. 198 *U.S.* 45.
10. 410 *U.S.* 163.
11. 410 *U.S.* 181.

CHAPTER V

1. Mill, "On Liberty" (1859), pp. 13 and 109 (1955 ed.).
2. Gerald Dworkin, "Paternalism," in *Morality and the Law* (ed. Richard A. Wasserstrom, 1971), p. 107.
3. 13 *Criminal Law Reporter* 2376.
4. 411 *U.S.* 677.
5. 15 *Criminal Law Reporter* 2001.

CHAPTER VI

1. See Edward M. Brecher, *Licit and Illicit Drugs* (1972), pp. 101–15. This book, a publication of Consumers Union, is an invaluable survey of the field.
2. Alfred R. Lindesmith, *The Addict and the Law* (1965), p. x.
3. See Horace Judson, "The British and Heroin," *The New Yorker* (Sept. 24, 1973), p. 76 (Oct. 1, 1973), p. 70.
4. See generally Troy Duster, *The Legislation of Morality* (1970).
5. No longer relevant to criminal liability.
6. 21 *U.S.C.* Chap. 13.
7. See task force report *Narcotics and Drug Abuse*, President's Commission on Law Enforcement (1967), pp. 18–19.
8. 370 *U.S.* 660.
9. 392 *U.S.* 514.
10. 21 *U.S.C.* Sec. 802 (1).
11. 486 *F. 2d* 1139.
12. 49 *Ill. 2d* 338.
13. 387 *Mich.* 167.
14. 387 *Mich.* 91.
15. 53 *Hawaii* 327.
16. Ibid., p. 334.
17. 477 *F. 2d* 349.
18. Ibid., p. 352.

CHAPTER VII

1. See James Markham, "Heroin Hunger May Not a Mugger Make," New York *Times* Sunday magazine (Mar. 18, 1973), p. 39.
2. See Edward Preble and John J. Casey, "Taking Care of Business—The Heroin User's Life on the Street," 4 *International Journal of Addictions* 1 (1969).
3. *New York Mental Hygiene Law*, Secs. 200–12.
4. For an excellent discussion of this issue, to which I am indebted, see Note, "Civil Commitment of Narcotic Addicts," 76 *Yale Law Journal* 1160 (1967).
5. See the discussion of the British situation in Horace Judson, "The British and Heroin," *The New Yorker* (Sept. 24, 1973), p. 76 (Oct. 1, 1973), p. 70.
6. See, e.g., *Sas* v. *State of Maryland*, 334 *F. 2d* 506 (Fourth Circuit Court of Appeals, 1964).
7. *New York Penal Law*, Art. 220.
8. 477 *F. 2d* 353.
9. Ibid.
10. J. W. Fairbairn quoted by Eric Clark, "The Problems of 'Pot' Reform," *New Statesman* (Feb. 2, 1973), p. 155.

CHAPTER VIII

1. Frances Gearing, "Methadone Maintenance—Six Years Later," *Contemporary Drug Problems* (Spring 1972), p. 191.
2. See n. 5, Chap. VII.
3. See generally Dorothy Nelkin, *Methadone Maintenance: A Technological Fix* (1973).
4. See n. 5, Chap. VII.
5. Edward M. Brecher, *Licit and Illicit Drugs* (1972), pp. 115–17.

CHAPTER IX

1. In this discussion I am indebted to the important article by Richard Wasserstrom "The Obligation to Obey the Law," 10 *U.C.L.A. Law Review* 780 (1963).
2. For a very valuable discussion, see John Rawls, *A Theory of Justice* (1971), Chap. VI.
3. Archibald Cox, "Direct Action, Civil Disobedience, and the Constitution," in *Civil Rights, The Constitution, and the Courts* (1967), pp. 22–23.
4. 355 *U.S.* 255.
5. See Ronald Dworkin, "A Theory of Civil Disobedience," in *Ethics and Social Justice* (ed. Kiefer and Munitz, 1968), p. 225.

CHAPTER X

1. The Supreme Court decided in *Illinois* v. *Allen,* 397 *U.S.* 337 (1970), that the confrontation clause of the Sixth Amendment does not preclude the removal from the courtroom of an unruly defendant.
2. Haywood Burns, "Can a Black Man Get a Fair Trial in This Country?," New York *Times* Sunday magazine (Jul. 12, 1970), p. 46.
3. Ibid., p. 5.
4. Hall, Kamisar, LaFave, and Israel, *Modern Criminal Procedure* (3d ed., 1969), pp. 8–9.
5. Kenneth Culp Davis, *Discretionary Justice* (1969), pp. 80–96.
6. *Snowden* v. *Hughes,* 321 *U.S.* 1, 8 (1943).
7. 254 *Cal. App. 2d* 256.
8. 14 *N.Y.* 901.
9. Hall et al., op. cit., pp. 773–74, n. 4.
10. Comment, 61 *Columbia Law Review* 1007 (1961).
11. 64 *N.Y. Misc. 2d* 63.
12. Bruce R. Jacob and K. M. Sharma, "Justice After Trial: Prisoners' Need for Legal Services," 18 *Kansas Law Review* 493 (1970).
13. *Morris* v. *Master of the Crown Office* (1970), 2 W.L.R. 792, 801.

CHAPTER XI

1. See F. Mosteller and D. Moynihan, *On Equality of Educational Opportunity* (1972). The most important and stimulating general recent study with reference to education is Christopher Jencks et al., *Inequality* (1972).
2. See Joel Feinberg, *Doing and Deserving* (1970), Chap. 9.
3. John Rawls, *A Theory of Justice* (1971).
4. Ibid., pp. 60, 83.
5. W. G. Runciman, *Relative Deprivation and Social Justice* (1966), pp. 265–66.
6. Ibid., pp. 275–76.
7. 25 *U.S.C.* Chap. 2A.
8. See Boris Bittker, *The Case for Black Reparations* (1973), a very valuable survey of the legal and practical problems.

CHAPTER XII

1. See Christopher Jencks, *Inequality* (1972), Chap. VI.
2. See F. Mosteller and D. Moynihan, *On Equality of Educational Opportunity* (1972).

3. See the important study by J. Coons, W. Clune, and S. Sugarman, *Private Wealth and Public Education* (1970), for a general background to this topic.
4. See R. Davie, N. Butler, and H. Goldstein, *From Birth to Seven*, a report of the British National Child Development Study (1972).
5. Coons et al., op. cit., p. 30, n. 3.
6. 163 *U.S.* 537.
7. 347 *U.S.* 483.
8. Ibid., p. 493.
9. Ibid., p. 494.
10. See *Equality of Educational Opportunity* (1966), published by the United States Office of Education and known after its author as the Coleman Report.
11. Ill. *Rev. Stat.* 1967, Chap. 122, pars. 10–21.3.
12. 39 *Ill. 2d* 593 (1968).
13. 391 *U.S.* 430.
14. 402 *U.S.* 1.
15. Ibid., pp. 30–31.
16. 413 *U.S.* 189.
17. Ibid., p. 210.
18. 402 *U.S.* 28.
19. 369 *F. 2d* 55.
20. Ibid., p. 61.
21. 118 *Congressional Record* S2542 (Feb. 24, 1972).
22. 413 *U.S.* 216.
23. Ibid, pp. 222–23.
24. Ibid., pp. 236–37.

CHAPTER XIII

1. See the Coleman Report, n. 10, Chap. XII.
2. See *From Birth to Seven*, n. 4, Chap. XII.
3. Alexander Bickel, *The Supreme Court and the Idea of Progress* (1970), p. 132.
4. 418 *U.S.* 717 (1974).
5. 41 *L.Ed. 2d* at 1091 (1974).
6. 96 *California Reporter* 601.
7. 411 *U.S.* 1.
8. Ibid., p. 24.
9. Ibid., p. 25.
10. Ibid., p. 36.

CHAPTER XIV

1. See Comment, "Ability Grouping in Public Schools," 1 *Connecticut Law Review* 150 (1968).
2. 320 *U.S.* 81.
3. 323 *U.S.* 214.
4. 379 *U.S.* 184.
5. Ibid., p. 198.
6. John Kaplan, "Equal Justice in an Unequal World," 61 *Northwestern University Law Review* 363, 383, (1966).
7. 302 *F. Supp.* 726.
8. Ibid., pp. 723–33.
9. 431 *F. 2d* 1254.
10. 416 *U.S.* 312 (1974).
11. Ibid. at 334.
12. Ibid. at 338.
13. Ibid. at 331–32.
14. Issued in pursuance of Executive Order No. 11246 (1965).
15. 442 *F. 2d* 159.
16. 120 *Cal. App. 2d* 1.
17. Ibid., p. 6.
18. 395 *F. 2d* 920.
19. Ibid., p. 926.
20. Ibid., pp. 931–32.
21. 354 *F. Supp.* 941.
22. 484 *F. 2d* 1122. For a valuable discussion, see William R. Sneed III, "Racial and Ethnic Quotas: The Tipping Phenomenon," 4 *New York University Review of Law and Social Change* 1 (1974).

CHAPTER XV

1. 269 *F. Supp.* 401.
2. Ibid., pp. 406–7.
3. Robert Carter, "The Right to Equal Educational Opportunity," in *The Rights of Americans* (ed. Norman Dorsen, 1970), pp. 11–12.

Index

Abortion, 12, 60–76
contraception and, 64
freedom and, 66
Great Britain, 62
the law on, 68–76
morality and, 61–62, 64–66
murder and, 61–62
New York, 68–69, 70
privacy and, 71
rights and, 67–68, 70–75
society and, 65
substantive due process, 71–73
Texas, 69, 74
U. S. Supreme Court, 12, 33–34, 61, 64, 68–76, 89
Addiction to drugs, 99, 100, 101, 102–3 104, 106–10, 116–29, 135–60
Advertising
gambling, 92
offensiveness, 47–48
pornography, 92
Alaska, prostitution, 90
Alcohol, 91, 96, 97, 98, 100, 102–3, 129, 131–33, 151, 152, 159
barbiturates and, 101
hallucinations from, 98
health and, 156, 157
heroin and, 143
marihuana and, 156
U. S. Supreme Court, 107–8
violence and, 97, 157
American Indians as disadvantaged, 209, 212, 218, 219, 220
American Law Institute, 31
American Psychiatric Association, 24
Amphetamines, 95, 101–2, 110, 133
Animals, cruelty to, 58–60
Anti-Semitism, 42–43
Antony and Cleopatra (Shakespeare), 97
Assassination, 183–84
Australian aborigines, 18

Banks v. Housing Authority, 275–76
Barbiturates, 95, 100–1, 102, 104, 115, 116, 133, 159
alcohol and, 101
Bentham, Jeremy, 6, 60, 62–63
Bickel, Alexander, 47–49, 244
Bisexuality, 22
Blackmail, homosexuality and, 25
Blacks
civil disobedience, 173
as disadvantaged, 209, 211, 212, 216, 218, 219–23
disruption, 189–91, 194–95
education, 221, 227–29, 231, 233, 236, 238, 245, 247–49, 260–73, 285–87
preferential treatment, 260–80
Blockaders, 144–45
Brewster, Kingman, 189
Brouwer, Adriaen, 158
Brown v. Board of Education, 232–35, 237, 238, 242, 257, 293
Bugging, drugs and, 119
Burger, Chief Justice Warren, 248
Burns, Haywood, 189–91
Busing, 226, 238, 245
Byrn v. New York City Health & Hospitals Corp., 68–69, 70

Caffeine, 117, 131–33
California
disruption, 193–95
drugs, 106–7, 108, 109, 122
education, 254–55
preferential treatment, 275–76
Canada
drugs, 129–30
racial minorities, 43

Cannabis, 95, 99–100, 129–30, 156
Carnal Knowledge (movie), 54–55
Carnegie Commission on Higher Education, 275
Cigarettes, 99, 123, 131–33
Civil disobedience, 3, 163–81
  blacks, 173
  collateral, 174
  conscientious, 170–74, 176, 179, 180, 182–83
  core of the concept, 169
  disruption and, 182–84, 189, 198
  freedom and, 163
  Germany, 164, 175
  Great Britain, 164
  India, 164
  the law and, 163–81
  morality and, 164, 165, 168, 173–77
  nature of, 167–70
  religion and, 163, 173
  revolution and, 163, 164
  rights and, 173
  Roman Catholic Church and, 163
  sacrifice and, 170, 182–83
  sexual conduct and, 168, 169–70
  social contract theory and, 163, 168–69
  society and, 166, 168–69, 176–77
  two kinds of, 170–73
  unconstitutional laws, 177–81
  violence and, 163, 165, 168
Civil Rights Act of 1964, 269, 273–74
Civil Rights Act of 1968, 277
Cocaine, 101–2, 105, 110, 115, 116
Coffee, 117, 131–33
Cohen v. California, 43–45
Coleman Report, 242, 244
Collateral civil disobedience, 174
Colorado, education, 236–37
Commission on Obscenity and Pornography, 40, 46
Comprehensive Drug Abuse Prevention and Control Act, 105
Conception, sexual intercourse and, 20
Connecticut, education, 239
Conscientious civil disobedience, 170–74, 176, 179, 180, 182–83
Conscientious objectors, 171, 179, 180
Contraception, 20, 21, 51
  abortion and, 64
  U. S. Supreme Court, 33, 55, 89, 113
Contractors' Association of Eastern Pennsylvania v. Secretary of Labor, 274
Coons, John E., 231
Cotner v. Henry, 34
Cox, Archibald, 175
Crime
  drugs and, 104–5, 107, 117–21, 124–25, 152
  gambling and, 77–78
  pornography and, 40
Crisis centers, 160
Cruelty to animals, 58–60
Culture
  incest and, 27
  offensiveness and, 46–50
Cyclazocine, 144

Davis, Kenneth Culp, 192
Deal v. Cincinnati Board of Education, 237–38
Death penalty, 8–10
De facto segregation, 262, 264, 265, 268, 286–87, 290, 293
DeFunis v. Odegaard, 270–73, 274
De jure segregation, 233–40, 241, 246, 248, 264, 293
Delaware, education, 232
Denmark, pornography, 40, 48–49
Depressants, 98, 100–1
Desmond, Chief Judge Charles S., 194
Detoxification, 135–36, 146
Devlin, Lord, 7, 47
Disadvantaged, 3–4, 203–80
  American Indians, 209, 212, 218, 219, 220
  blacks, 209, 211, 212, 216, 218, 219–23
  collective responsibility, 205–24
  compensation, 205–7
  discrimination, 3–4
  economic inequalities, 214, 215–16
  education, 225–59
  Germany, 218

guilt and, 210–13
justice claims, 213–17
Kansas, 218
the law and, 205–6
liberty and, 214
meaning of, 208–10
morality and, 205–6, 222
preferential treatment, 260–80
racial minorities, 209, 210–12, 216, 218, 219–24
reform, 222–24
reparations, 217–22
respect and, 216–17
society and, 207, 213–15
Disruption, 3, 182–201
blacks, 189–91, 194–95, 198
California, 193–95
civil disobedience and, 182–84, 189, 198
in the courts, 186–201
discriminatory enforcement, 188–91
drugs, 195–96
freedom and, 184
Great Britain, 199–200
morality and, 184
New York, 194
New York City, 195–96, 198
police discretionary powers, 192–93
public duties and, 197–201
racial minorities, 189–91, 194–95, 198
revolution and, 183, 184–86, 188, 189, 190
rights and, 196–97
society and, 185–86, 191
South Africa, 188
violence and, 182, 183–84
District of Columbia
drugs, 108
education, 285–87
homosexuality, 35
prostitution, 90–91
Doe v. Bolton, 69
Dole, Dr. Vincent, 136
Douglas, Associate Justice William O., 239, 241, 257, 271–72
Drugs, 2, 19, 93–160
addiction to, 99, 100, 101, 102–3, 104, 106–10, 116–29, 135–60
barbiturates, 95, 100–1, 102, 104, 115, 116, 133, 159
blockaders, 144–45
bugging and, 119
California, 106–7, 108, 109, 122
Canada, 129–30
classification of, 98–103
contagion of, 125–26
cost of, 116, 118, 121, 149
crime and, 104–5, 107, 117–21, 124–25, 152
the criminal law and, 95–114
death from, 101, 102, 149
depressants, 98, 100–1
detoxification, 135–36, 146
disruption and, 195–96
distributors of, 119–20, 154
District of Columbia, 108
future recommendations, 154–55
gang warfare and, 119
Great Britain, 129–30, 137, 141–42, 149
hallucinogenics, 19, 98–100
happiness and, 95–96
hard, 106–10
Hawaii, 112–13
health and, 102–3, 130, 131, 148, 153
Illinois, 111, 112
importers of, 119–20, 154
maintenance, 136–43, 149
mental illness and, 123–24
Michigan, 111, 112
morality and, 107, 116, 120, 121, 129
muggings and, 118
narotic, 19
new, 131
New York, 122–23, 124, 126, 127, 129, 142–43
opiates, 102–3, 104, 105, 117, 135–36, 144–45, 150, 152–54
pharmacological intervention, 135–45
pleasure ethic and, 97
prostitution and, 118
psychedelic, 96, 99–100
psychoactive, 95, 98
psychotomimetic, 99
racial minorities and, 119
regulations on, 115–34

sedative-hypnotic, 159
for sleep, 101
society and, 95–99, 151
soft, 110–14
stimulants, 101–2
tensions and, 96, 102, 151
Texas, 107–8
theft and, 118, 121
therapeutic communities, 145–48, 149
tolerance factor, 99–100, 101, 103, 122, 152–53
tranquilizers, 98, 135
U. S. Supreme Court, 106–10, 122, 155
violence and, 118–19, 121
wiretapping and, 119
withdrawal, 101, 127, 135, 149
work ethic and, 97
See also names of drugs
Dworkin, Gerald, 86–87
Dworkin, Ronald, 5–6, 179

Eccentricity, offensiveness and, 42
Economy
incest and, 27
prostitution and, 82
Education, 225–59
blacks, 221, 227–29, 231, 233, 236, 238, 245, 247–49 260–73, 285–87
busing, 226, 238, 245
California, 254–55
Colorado, 236–37
Connecticut, 239
Delaware, 232
the disadvantaged, 225–59
District of Columbia, 285–87
elusive equality, 241–59
environment and, 229–30
equal opportunity, 225–59
Great Britain, 244, 258
heterogeneous grouping, 250–51
homogeneous grouping, 251
Illinois, 234–35
inequality and, 227–31
inferior schools, 228–29
Kansas, 232
Louisiana, 231–32, 252
Maine, 252
Michigan, 247–48
Missisippi, 252
Ohio, 237–38
Oregon, 252
preferential treatment, 260–73
process inequality, 227–28
product inequality, 227, 228
racial minorities, 221, 227–40, 242, 243, 245, 247–49, 260–73, 285–87
religion and, 231
school districts, 245–49
school financing, 226, 251–59
segregation, 221, 226, 231–59, 264, 265, 268, 286–87, 290, 293
society and, 229–30
South Carolina, 232
success and, 225–26
taxes and, 253–59
Texas, 255–59
U. S. Supreme Court, 231–42, 245, 247–48, 252, 254–59, 285–87, 293–95, 297, 301
Virginia, 232
Eisenstadt v. Baird, 33, 55, 71
Emotions, homosexuality and, 24
Employment, preferential treatment, 272, 273–75, 278–79
Enterprise liability, 206–7
Entertainment
homosexuality and, 24
offensiveness, 48, 49
prostitution, 83
Entrapment, homosexuality and, 25
Environment
education and, 229–30
incest and, 27
offensiveness and, 48–49
Ervine, St. John, 20
Eugenic risk, incest, 27–28

Family, the
homosexuality and, 22–23
incest and, 27, 28
Feinberg, Joel, 38
Fellatio, 168
Fetishists, 27
Florida
miscegenation, 267–68
preferential treatment, 267–68
France, prostitution, 83

Frank, Judge Jerome, 200
Frankfurter, Associate Justice Felix, 285
Freedom, 86–87
  abortion and, 66
  civil disobedience and, 163
  disruption and, 184
  prostitution and, 87–88
Freedom of speech, offensiveness and, 39, 43, 50
Free will, 85–88
Freud, Sigmund, 17
  on incest, 26
Frontiero v. Richardson, 90
Furman v. Georgia, 8–10

Gamblers
  compulsive, 88
  gambling and, 80–81
Gambling, 3, 77–81, 87–92
  advertising, 92
  crime and, 77–78
  gamblers and, 80–81
  Great Britain, 92
  New York City, 77
  obsession with, 88
  rewards and, 79–80
  society and, 78–79
  violence and, 78
Gandhi, Mahatma, 164
Gang warfare, drugs and, 119
Gearing, Dr. Frances, 136–38
Germany
  civil disobedience, 164, 175
  disadvantaged, 218
Goldberg, Associate Justice Arthur, 33
Great Britain, 8, 9, 12
  abortion, 62
  absence of an overt act, 106
  civil disobedience, 164
  disruption, 199–200
  drugs, 129–30, 137, 141–42, 149
  education, 244, 258
  gambling, 92
  homosexuality, 7, 19
  prostitution, 7, 81
  racial minorities, 43
  slavery, 219
Green v. County School Board, 235
Grinspoon, Dr. Lester, 130
Griswold v. Connecticut, 33, 34, 35, 45, 51, 55, 56, 57, 71, 89, 113

Hallek, Judge, 35
Hallucinations from alcohol, 98
Hallucinogenic drugs, 19, 98–100
Hard drugs, 106–10
Harrison Act of 1914, 105, 106, 142
Hart, H. L. A., 46, 49
Hashish, 98–99
Hawaii, drugs, 112–13
Health
  alcohol and, 156, 157
  drugs and, 102–3, 130, 131, 148, 153
  tobacco and, 156, 157
Heroin, 95, 97, 99, 101, 103–4, 110, 134, 135, 147–55, 159
  alcohol and, 143
  blockaders, 144–45
  cost of, 116, 118, 121
  future recommendations, 154–55
  general truths about, 148–50
  legal sale of, 153–54
  maintenance, 140–43
  marihuana and, 132, 155
  methadone and, 135–40
  regulations on, 115, 116–29
Heterosexuality
  consenting adults, 36
  homosexuality and, 20, 23, 31
Hirabayashi v. United States, 267
Hitler, Adolf, 164
Hobson v. Hansen, 285–88, 293, 301
Holmes, Associate Justice Oliver Wendell, 72
Homosexuality, 2, 7, 19–25, 29, 88, 299
  blackmail and, 25
  consenting adults, 19, 23, 31, 35
  District of Columbia, 35
  emotions and, 24
  entertainment and, 24
  entrapment and, 25
  the family and, 22–23
  Great Britain, 7, 19
  heterosexuality and, 20, 23, 31
  Illinois, 19
  as an illness, 24
  incest and, 26–27, 29

increase in, 23–24
invasion of privacy and, 22
law reform, 29–37
life-styles and, 24
morality and, 21–22, 25
New York, 36–37
offensiveness of, 22, 23, 24
procreation and, 21
public taste and, 24
religion and, 19–20
sexual intercourse, 21
as a sexual orientation disturbance, 24
society and, 19–20, 24–25
survival of the species, 20
underpopulation and, 20, 21
unhappiness and, 24–25
unnaturalness of, 19–20, 22
Housing, preferential treatment, 261, 264–65, 266, 275–78

Illinois
drugs, 111, 112
education, 234–35
homosexuality, 19
Illinois School Code, 234
Incest, 19, 25–37
age of consent, 28–29
biological aspects, 27–28
consenting adults, 36
culture and, 27
as a defense mechanism, 27
economy and, 27
environment and, 27
eugenic risk, 27–28
the family and, 27, 28
Freud on, 26
homosexuality and, 26–27, 29
instinct and, 26
law reform, 29–37
morality and, 29
offensiveness of, 26
as a taboo, 25–27
India, civil disobedience, 164
Indian Claims Commission, 218
In re Labady, 37
Instinct, incest and, 26
Iowa, sodomy, 32

Japanese-American relocation, 267
Jellum v. Cupp, 32
Jenkins v. Georgia, 54–55

Kansas
disadvantaged, 218
education, 232
Keyes v. School District No. 1, 236–37, 239–40
Kidnaping, 183–84
Korematsu v. United States, 267
Ku Klux Klan Act, 218–19, 220–21

Lambert v. California, 178
Levinson, Judge, 112–13
Lindesmith, Alfred R., 102–3
Lochner v. New York, 72
Lotteries, 77
Louisiana, education, 231–32, 252
LSD (lysergic acid diethylamide), 98, 99–100

McLaughlin v. Florida, 267–68
Maine, education, 252
Marihuana, 19, 98–99, 100, 102–3, 105, 110–14, 148, 155–59
alcohol and, 156
harm of, 130, 131
heroin and, 132, 155
legalizing, 132–34, 158–59
regulations on, 115, 129–34
Masturbation, 17–18
pornography and, 40
Memoirs v. Massachusetts, 51
Mental illness, drugs and, 123–24
Methadone, 102, 135–40, 147, 149
advantages of, 135–38
heroin and, 135–40
Methaqualone, 159
Michigan
drugs, 111, 112
education, 247–48
Mill, John Stuart, 6, 85–87
Miller v. California, 52–57, 75
Milliken v. Bradley, 247–48, 257, 288, 301
Miscegenation
Florida, 267–68
U. S. Supreme Court, 42, 267–68
Mississippi, education, 252
Model Penal Code, 31, 59
Modern Criminal Procedure, 194–95
Morality, 1, 2, 4–7
abortion and, 61–62, 64–66
civil disobedience and, 164, 165, 168, 173–77

disadvantaged and, 205–6, 222
disruption and, 184
drugs and, 107, 116, 120, 121, 129
homosexuality and, 21–22, 25
incest and, 29
offensiveness and, 42–43, 44, 46, 47
pornography and, 40
preferential treatment and, 260
Morphine, 103, 104–5, 116, 142, 151–52
Muggings, drugs and, 118
Murder, 168
abortion and, 61–62

Nalaxone, 144
Narcotic drugs, 19
National Conference of Commissioners on Uniform State Laws, 105
New Jersey, preferential treatment, 269–70
New York
abortion, 68–69, 70
disruption, 194
drugs, 122–23, 124, 126, 127, 129, 142–43
homosexuality, 36–37
New York City
disruption, 195–96, 198
gambling, 77
preferential treatment, 277–78
prostitution, 82
Nicotine, 99, 156
Nixon, Richard M., 46
Norton v. Macy, 36
Norwalk CORE v. Norwalk Redevelopment Agency, 276
Nyswander, Dr. Marie, 136

Obscenity, 38–39, 41, 43–45, 53, 57
U. S. Supreme Court, 44–45, 51
Oedipus complex, 26
Offensiveness, 38–57
advertising, 47–48
culture and, 46–50
eccentricity and, 42
entertainment, 48, 49
environment and, 48–49
freedom of speech and, 39, 43, 50
of homosexuality, 22, 23, 24
idiosyncracy and, 42
of incest, 26
minority rights and, 39
morality and, 42–43, 44, 46, 47
obscenity, 38–39, 41, 43–45, 53, 57
pornography, 38–41, 45–57
privacy and, 47, 50–51, 55, 56
racial minorities, 41–42
rights and, 39, 42, 51, 55, 56
Off-track betting, 77
Ohio, education, 237–38
"On Liberty" (Mill), 85
Opiates, 102–3, 104, 105, 117, 135–36, 150, 152–54
blockaders, 144–45
See also names of opiates
Opioids, 150
Opium, 102, 104, 105
Oregon, education, 252
Otero v. New York City Housing Authority, 277–78
Overpopulation, 20

Paris Adult Theatre I v. Slaton, 52–57, 75
Paternalism, 85–88
Pennsylvania, preferential treatment, 273–74
People v. Gray, 193–95
People v. Lorentzen, 111, 112
People v. McCabe, 111
People v. McMurty, 195–96
People v. Sinclair, 112
People v. Walker, 194
Phenobarbital, 100
Philadelphia Plan, 273–74, 278
Plessy v. Ferguson, 231–32, 257
Police discretionary powers, 192–93
Porcelli v. Titus, 269–70, 279
Pornography, 12, 38–41, 45–57, 75, 88, 91–92, 113
advertising, 92
crime and, 40
Denmark, 40, 48–49
the law on, 50–57
masturbation and, 40
morality and, 40
Nixon on, 46
U. S. Supreme Court, 45, 51–55

Powell, Associate Justice Lewis F., Jr., 239–40, 241
Powell v. Texas, 107–8
Preferential treatment, 260–80
  blacks, 260–80
  California, 275–76
  education, 260–73
  employment, 272, 273–75, 278–79
  ethics, 262–66
  Florida, 267–68
  housing, 261, 264–65, 266, 275–78
  minority groups, 260–80
  morality and, 260
  New Jersey, 269–70
  New York City, 277–78
  Pennsylvania, 273–74
  social policy, 262–66
  U. S. Supreme Court, 270–73, 276
  Washington, 270–73
Pregnancy, sexual intercourse and, 18, 20
Privacy, 32–33, 89
  abortion and, 71
  offensiveness and, 47, 50–51, 55, 56
Procedural due process, 73
Prostitution, 5, 81–85, 87–92
  Alaska, 90
  as degrading, 82–84
  as dehumanizing, 82–84
  District of Columbia, 90–91
  drugs and, 118
  economy and, 82
  as entertainment, 83
  France, 82
  freedom and, 87–88
  Great Britain, 7, 81
  men, 82, 90
  New York City, 82
  as a public nuisance, 81
  rights and, 89–90
  society and, 82–85, 88
  venereal disease and, 81–82
Psychedelic drugs, 96, 99–100
Psychoactive drugs, 95, 98
Psychoanalysis, 26
Psychotomimetic drugs, 99

Racial minorities, 297–98
  Canada, 43
  as disadvantaged, 209, 210–12, 216, 218, 219–24
  disruption, 189–91, 194–95, 198
  drugs and, 119
  education, 221, 227–40, 242, 243, 245, 247–49, 260–73, 285–87
  Great Britain, 43
  offensiveness and, 41–42
  preferential treatment, 260–80
Rape, 168
Rawls, John, 213–15, 222, 225
Religion
  civil disobedience and, 163, 173
  education and, 231
  homosexuality and, 19–20
Repression in sexual conduct, 17–19
Revolution
  civil disobedience and, 163, 164
  disruption and, 183, 184–86, 188, 189, 190
Ribicoff, Senator Abraham, 239
Rights
  abortion and, 67–68, 70–75
  civil disobedience and, 173
  disruption and, 196–97
  fundamental, 34
  offensiveness and, 39, 42, 51, 55, 56
  prostitution and, 89–90
Robinson v. California, 106–7, 108, 109, 122, 124, 127
Rockefeller, Nelson, 122, 124, 129
Roe v. Wade, 33–34, 61, 69–70, 71, 72–76, 89
Roman Catholic Church, civil disobedience and, 163
Roosevelt, Franklin D., 284
Roth v. United States, 51
Runciman, W. G., 215–16, 217

Sacrifice, civil disobedience and, 170, 182–83
Sadomasochists, 27
Salmon, Lord Justice, 199–200
San Antonio School District v. Rodriguez, 255–59, 301
San Francisco Housing Authority, 275–76
Schwartz, Louis, 59

Sedative-hypnotic drugs, 159
Segregation
  de facto, 233, 237–39, 241–43, 262, 264, 265, 268, 286–87, 290, 293
  de jure, 233–40, 241, 246, 248, 264, 293
  education, 221, 226, 231–59, 264, 265, 268, 286–87, 290, 293
  U. S. Supreme Court, 221, 231–32, 235–37, 241, 245, 247–48
Serrano v. Priest, 254–55
Sex
  pleasure in, 20–21
  relief in, 20–21
Sexual conduct, 2, 17–37
  civil disobedience and, 168, 169–70
  homosexuality, 2, 7, 19–27, 29–37, 88, 299
  incest, 19, 25–37
  masturbation, 17–18, 40
  prohibitions, 17–19
  prudery, 17–19
  repression, 17–19
  Victorian age, 2, 17–19
Sexual intercourse
  conception and, 20
  homosexuality, 21
  pregnancy and, 18, 20
Shakespeare, William, 97
Sit-ins, 171–72
Slavery, 87, 219
  Great Britain, 219
Social contract theory
  civil disobedience and, 163, 168–69
  the law and, 163–64
Social insurance, 206–7
Social Security, 85
Society
  abortion and, 65
  civil disobedience and, 166, 168–69, 176–77
  disadvantaged and, 207, 213–15
  disruption and, 185–86, 191
  drugs and, 95–98, 151
  education and, 229–30
  gambling and, 78–79
  homosexuality and, 19–20, 24–25
  prostitution and, 82–85, 88
Sodomy, 20, 31–35, 168
  Iowa, 32
Soft drugs, 110–14
South Africa, disruption, 188
South Carolina, education, 232
Stanley v. Georgia, 45, 51, 56, 57, 113
State v. Fields, 90
State v. Kantner, 112–13
Stephen, James, 6, 7
Stewart, Associate Justice Potter, 268
Stimulants, 101–2
Substantive due process, 71–73
Suicide, 85, 86
Survival of the species, 20
Swann v. Board of Education, 235–37

Task Force on Narcotics and Drug Abuse, 95
Taxes, education and, 253–59
Texas
  abortion, 69–74
  drugs, 107–8
  education, 255–59
Theft, drugs and, 118, 121
Theory of Justice, A (Rawls), 213–15
Therapeutic communities, 145–48, 149
Thurlow, Lord, 46–47
Title 42 of the United States Code, Section 1983, 218–19, 220–21
Tobacco, 99, 103, 117, 123, 131–33, 156
  health and, 156, 157
Tolerance factor, 99–100, 101, 103, 122, 152–53
Tometz v. Board of Education, 234–35
Totem and Taboo (Freud), 26
Tranquilizers, 98, 135
Tylor, Sir Edward Burnett, 27

Unconstitutional laws, 177–81
Underpopulation, 20, 21
Uniform Drug Act, 105
Union of Soviet Socialist Republics, 123
U. S. Bill of Rights, 7, 32, 33, 55, 71, 113
U. S. Constitution, 7, 10, 300

constancy of, 291
police discretionary powers, 193
First Amendment, 43, 44, 51, 53, 57, 298, 299
Fourth Amendment, 32, 299
Sixth Amendment, 197
Eighth Amendment, 9, 36, 106, 197
Ninth Amendment, 32–33
Fourteenth Amendment, 7, 9, 31, 33, 55, 68–69, 70, 71, 72, 73, 90, 91, 106, 111, 113, 232, 238, 242, 252, 254–55, 270, 290, 297–98, 299, 300
U. S. Department of Health, Education and Welfare, 274–75
U. S. Office of Education, 242
U. S. Supreme Court, 7–13, 283–302
abortions, 12, 33–34, 61, 64, 68–76, 89
activism, 284–92
alcohol, 107–8
the body politic and, 296–97
cautionary principles, 292–97
contraception, 33, 35, 89, 113
death penalty, 8–10
drugs, 106–10, 122, 155
education, 231–42, 245, 247–48, 252, 254–59, 285–87, 293–95, 297, 301
ephemeral findings of fact, 294–95
fundamental rights, 34
image of, 284
Japanese-American relocation, 267
miscegenation, 42, 267–68
nonrepresentative nature of, 295–96
obscenity, 44–45, 51
orders, 289–92
pornography, 45, 51–55
preferential treatment, 270–73, 276
principled adjudication, 287–89
relative judicial incapacity, 292–94
restraint, 284–92
rules, 289–92
school financing, 254–59
segregation, 221, 231–32, 235–37, 241, 245, 247–48
selective law enforcement, 193
unconstitutional laws, 177–81
See also names of cases
United States v Doe, 35
United States v. Kiffer, 113–14, 130
United States v. Moore, 108
United States v. Reidel, 51
United States v. Wilson, 90–91

Venereal disease, prostitution and, 81–82
Victorian age, sexual conduct, 2, 17–19
Vietnam War, 171, 179, 180
Violence, 12–13
alcohol and, 97, 157
assassination, 183–84
civil disobedience and, 163, 165, 168
disruption and, 182, 183–84
drugs and, 118–19, 121
gambling and, 78
Virginia, education, 232

Washington, preferential treatment, 270–73
Washington, University of, 270–73
Westermarck, Edward Alexander, 26
West Indies, 219
Wilde, Oscar, 20
Wiretapping, drugs and, 119
Withdrawal, 101, 127, 135, 149
Wolfenden Report, 7

Younger, Judge, 195–96